Learning to be

The world of education
today and tomorrow

Learning to be

The world of education

today and tomorrow

Edgar Faure
Felipe Herrera
Abdul-Razzak Kaddoura
Henri Lopes
Arthur V. Petrovsky
Majid Rahnema
Frederick Champion Ward

Unesco Paris   1972

First published in 1972 by the United Nations
Educational, Scientific and Cultural Organization,
Place de Fontenoy, 75700 Paris,
and George G. Harrap & Co. Ltd, 182–184 High Holborn, London WC1V 7AX

First edition, August 1972
Second impression, November 1972
Third impression, January 1973
Printed by Arts Graphiques Coop Suisse, Basle

Fourth impression, September 1973
Printed by offset-lithography

ISBN 92-3-101017-4

Presentation of the report

Letter from the Chairman, Edgar Faure, to
René Maheu, Director-General of the
United Nations Educational, Scientific and
Cultural Organization

18 May 1972

My dear Director-General,

I have the honour and the pleasant duty of submitting to you the report of the International Commission on the Development of Education, of which you appointed me chairman at the beginning of 1971 and which has now concluded its work.

This is not to imply that the content of the subject has been exhausted or that its scope would not have justified our spending many more months on further studies or longer reflection. Our task was an immense one, and the very considerable work my colleagues and I have put into the production of this modest-sized report could have been continued and deepened for a long time. However, you wanted not so much an exhaustively erudite study as a critical reflection by men of different origins and background, seeking, in complete independence and objectivity, for over-all solutions to the major problems involved in the development of education in a changing universe. If reflection aimed at action is to be fruitful, we must know when to call a halt to it: the Second Development Decade is under way already, and if this report was to be of use to the international community its publication could no longer be postponed.

It would be presumptuous of me to try to predict how far the report will come up to your expectations or how much it will contribute to the progress of education in the world, but I believe it is faithful in spirit to the terms of reference you set the commission.

We were entirely independent and free in formulating our ideas, and therefore did not feel obliged to be neutral.

Four basic assumptions underlay our work from the start. The first, which was indeed the justification for the task we undertook, is that of the existence of an international community which, amidst the variety of nations and cultures, of political options and degrees of development, is reflected in common aspirations, problems and trends, and in its movement towards one and the same destiny. The corollary to this is the fundamental solidarity of governments and of peoples, despite transitory differences and conflicts.

The second is belief in democracy, conceived of as implying each man's right to realize his own potential and to share in the building of his own future. The keystone of democracy, so conceived, is education—not only education that is accessible to all, but education whose aims and methods have been thought out afresh.

The third assumption is that the aim of development is the complete fulfilment of man, in all the richness of his personality, the complexity of his forms of expression and his various commitments—as individual, member of a family and of a community, citizen and producer, inventor of techniques and creative dreamer.

Our last assumption is that only an over-all, lifelong education can produce the kind of complete man the need for whom is increasing with the continually more stringent constraints tearing the individual asunder. We should no longer assiduously acquire knowledge once and for all, but learn how to build up a continually evolving body of knowledge all through life—'learn to be'.

As you wished, we decided to begin with a critical assessment of the educational situation in 1972, that is, looking at the world as a whole, to try to discern common features, many of which can only be accounted for in terms of the past, like the new trends which seem to be emerging in most countries and systems, and the factors which, for the first time in history, are now determining or accompanying educational development; this led us to the idea of 'dead ends', to which we have devoted part of this report. Traditional formulae and partial reforms cannot meet the unprecedented demand for education arising out of the new tasks and functions to be fulfilled. We accordingly rejected timid, half-measures which are, in fact, costly because of their very inefficiency and turned our attention to discoveries and other factors holding promise for the future: recently developed intellectual procedures, conceptual approaches and technological advances—to the extent, of course, that these were set in the context of over-all innovation, corresponding to that broad ultimate aim of education to which I referred earlier: that of educating the complete man. National policies must give detailed expression to this aim, which may be common to all educational systems, in terms of objectives adapted to each country; their strategies must indicate the suitable combination of ways and means for achieving these and, finally, be incorporated in a system of planning. We have tried to make a contribution to the methodological effort necessary to the development of national strategies by analysing these ideas and presenting them as an interlocking sequence. And since our task was being undertaken at the level of the international community, we concluded by examining the tangible expression of international solidarity, namely, co-operation and aid.

The report we are submitting to you shows that there is broad agreement among the members of the commission: Felipe Herrera, Abdul-Razzak Kaddoura, Henri Lopes, Arthur V. Petrovsky, Majid Rahnema, Frederick Champion Ward, and myself—although reservations on some points are indicated in certain parts of it.

But I should not like to give the impression that it contains nothing but our own contributions and a record of the frequently animated discussions that took place in the conference rooms you made available to us. This report is of a practical nature; it is meant to lead to action, and it owes a great deal to the missions we carried out in twenty-three countries, thanks to the facilities which you yourself and the governments concerned afforded us. Much of the realism which, I hope, this report contains is due to this direct contact with the realities of education and the people who deal with them day by day. Furthermore, we have drawn abundantly on the experience which Unesco has acquired in the course of twenty-five years of reflection and operational action; without that experience, a report of this kind could not have been prepared, and in this sense, too, it is timely. We also owe much to the large quantity of preparatory documentation assembled for us, which enabled us, especially at the beginning of our work, to benefit from the reflections of eminent thinkers and specialists in education, and from their original studies.

My colleagues on the commission have asked me to draft a preamble to serve as an introduction to the report as a whole, and I intend to send this to you in the immediate future.

It goes without saying that we would have been unable to carry out our task successfully had it not been for the high degree of competence and the indefatigable labours of the Secretariat, under the direction of Aser Deleon, which, despite the constraints of a rigorous timetable and the difficulty of the job itself, never failed us, either in the organization of our work or in the exact and scrupulous interpretation of our intentions. To them I extend my heartful thanks.

To you personally, I should like to express the gratitude that my colleagues and I feel for the complete intellectual independence you gave us. I regard this as a mark of your confidence, and I think it also secured the objectivity and even temper which, I may assure you, prevailed throughout our work.

With kindest regards,

Yours sincerely,

EDGAR FAURE

Reply by René Maheu,
Director-General of Unesco,
to the Chairman, Edgar Faure

29 May 1972

My dear Chairman,

I have pleasure in acknowledging your letter of 18 May by which you submitted to me the report of the International Commission on the Development of Education.

May I first express once again my deep gratitude for all the work which, under your chairmanship, the commission succeeded in completing so quickly, considering the magnitude of the undertaking.

The report, which I intend to study more closely, seems to me on a first reading both to answer its purpose and to meet the needs of the hour.

Under your leadership the eminent persons forming the commission, differing in cultural and professional background but united in a common concern for objectivity, have given an account of present-day education and defined a global conception of education for tomorrow that are without doubt more complete than any formulated hitherto.

Nor need I tell you how pleased I am that a survey of such high competence should have confirmed ideas already guiding the work of the Organization, namely that education should extend throughout life, should not only be available to all but be a part of every individual's life, and should have as its aim both the development of society and the realization of man's potentialities.

Your work, however, has not been confined to reflection upon education, however remarkable in quality. I am glad to see that, as I had hoped, it has led to practical recommendations which should provide guidelines for action by Unesco, governments and the international community.

Such results amply justify the decision taken by the General Conference, following my suggestion, to establish your commission.

I propose to submit the report, together with my comments, to the Executive Board at its 90th session and to the General Conference at its seventeenth session.

I also intend to have the report widely distributed for the information of the general public and of all people throughout the world who are concerned with and working for education.

Finally, I consider it essential that the report, stressing as it does the importance of the ties between education and social progress, should be made available to the institutions which in one way or another are concerned with development. I shall therefore bring it to the attention of the executive heads of the organizations and agencies of the United Nations System and of various financing institutions.

In conclusion, may I ask you to convey to the members of the commission my sincere gratitude, which I know will be shared by many institutions and persons in all countries.

Yours sincerely,

RENÉ MAHEU

Members of the commission

This work is the collective effort of the International Commission on the Development of Education, established by Unesco, whose membership is as follows:

Edgar Faure (France), Chairman, former Prime Minister and Minister of Education.

Professor Felipe Herrera (Chile), University of Chile, former President of the Inter-American Development Bank.

Professor Abdul-Razzak Kaddoura (Syria), Professor of Nuclear Physics at the University of Damascus.

Henri Lopes (People's Republic of the Congo), Minister of Foreign Affairs, former Minister of Education.

Professor Arthur V. Petrovsky (U.S.S.R.), Member of the Academy of Pedagogical Sciences of the U.S.S.R.

Majid Rahnema (Iran), former Minister of Higher Education and Sciences.

Frederick Champion Ward (United States of America), Adviser on International Education, The Ford Foundation.

Secretariat of the commission:

Aser Deleon (Executive Secretary), Paul Lengrand, Lê Thàn Khôi, John G. Massee, John G. Slater, Peter R. C. Williams, Louis Ziegle.

With the collaboration of Nicolas Bodart, Henri Dieuzeide, François Furet, Sylvain Lourié

Editorial co-ordination: Marc Gilliard

English translator: Patrick W. Bowles

The main purpose of the footnotes that appear throughout the report and the passages quoted in Epilogue II is to illustrate the many varied opinions and tendencies that exist in connexion with the subject under discussion. It is evident that these quotations do not necessarily reflect the views of the commission as a whole and even less those of each individual member.

The 'Illustrations' to be found throughout this report and especially in Chapter 8 have been chosen as examples expressing the commission's theses or suggestions in concrete form, but are not for all that intended to be in any way exclusive or even to be considered as 'recipes' to be followed. Equally interesting and significant examples could have been taken from other countries and other fields of educational activity. Experiments and innovations under way are already so numerous and varied that it is impossible to make a completely representative or satisfactory selection. However, those 'Illustrations' which have found a place in this report will have served their intended purpose if they stimulate research on other possible innovative solutions, or help spread information on successful innovative experiments.

Contents

Part Three: Towards a learning society

Preamble

by Edgar Faure

Education and man's destiny

Very many countries regard the education of modern man as an exceptionally difficult problem, and all countries regard it as one of the greatest importance. And for all those who want to make the world as it is today a better place, and to prepare for the future, education is a capital, universal subject. When Unesco set up the International Commission, it made a timely move, in keeping with the contemporary world's political calendar.

Wherever we find a traditional educational system which has stood the test of time and was generally thought to need no more than a few occasional minor improvements, a few more or less automatic adjustments, it is currently unleashing an avalanche of criticisms and suggestions which often go so far as to question it in its entirety. Some young people are now more or less openly protesting against the pedagogic models and types of institutions imposed on them, although it is not always easy to delimit the influence of this particular phenomenon, with its vague uneasiness and flashes of rebellion.

Serious anomalies appear where the educational system has been set up only recently, and is copied from foreign models—usually the case in developing countries. When they emerged from the colonial period, the Third World countries flung themselves whole-heartedly into the fight against ignorance, which they quite rightly viewed as the all-important condition for lasting liberation and real development. They believed it would be enough to snatch the instrument of technical supremacy, as it were, from the colonizers' hands. They have now become aware that these models (often obsolete, even for the people by and for whom they were devised) are adapted neither to their needs nor to their problems. Their investments in education have become incompatible with their financial possibilities. The production of graduates is greater than the capacity of their economies to absorb them, giving rise to unemployment among certain particular groups, the drawbacks of which are not confined to that of unprofitability; it also causes psychological and social damage which is so extensive that it is imperilling the balance of society. Since it is out of the question for those concerned to give up one of their fundamental aspirations for which they have sacrificed so much, suffered and fought, an 'agonizing reappraisal' becomes necessary. This is the kind of situation which calls for an effort by the better-endowed nations in favour of solidarity.

Finally, it should be noted that certain States consider that their own educational systems are satisfactory, broadly speaking at least, and no authority is empowered to tell them they are right or wrong. They may possibly be deluding themselves, unaware of some deep-lying deterioration. In that case, the awakening, when it comes, will be a rude one, as happened in France in May 1968. But equally possibly these countries may have succeeded, through particularly good management or some other concatenation of circumstance, in achieving this kind of adaptation to conditions which others seem to find so difficult.

None the less, those modern States which consider themselves in a fortunate position and accordingly safe from the risks of crises or pangs of conscience do not for all that deduce they have no problems and no worries. On the contrary, they generally pay great attention to modernizing and ceaselessly improving their institutions and methods, and are not frightened of innovative experiments. They appreciate that fresh progress is possible and desirable, by making the highest possible level of knowledge available to the greatest possible number of 'learners'. Nor can they be unaware of the fact that constant developments in scientific discovery and innovations will make this requirement more urgent as each day passes, while at the same time the prospects of reaching that goal grow increasingly distant.

Even if they take their own interest fully into account, it can hardly fail to occur to them that enhanced international co-operation and far freer, more systematic exchanges of documents and experiments would help them to make far cheaper and quicker progress in an undertaking of this kind. Yet achievements in this field remain weak and sporadic.

But above all, they cannot turn a blind eye to the rest of the world.

At a time when they are advancing towards the heights of knowledge and power, how can they fail to feel some anxiety and even anguish over those vast, sombre areas of the planet which constitute the geography of ignorance—like the continuing geography of hunger and of premature mortality? Not only is it desirable to prevent economic, intellectual and civic disparities from becoming more acute, in the radically changing modern world, and to see a certain level of welfare, education and democracy become accessible to all peoples; it is something which we can no longer regard merely as a matter of philanthropy, charity, benevolence or loftiness of spirit.

The great changes of our time are imperilling the unity and the future of the species, and man's own identity as well. What is to be feared is not only the painful prospect of grievous inequalities, privations and suffering, but also that we may be heading for a veritable dichotomy within the human race, which risks being split into superior and inferior groups, into masters and slaves, supermen and submen. Among the risks resulting from this situation would be not only those of conflict and other disasters (for present-day means of mass destruction might well fall into the hands of destitute and rebellious groups) but the fundamental risk of dehumanization, affecting privileged and oppressed alike. For the harm done to man's nature would harm all men.

The scientific and technological revolution: education and democracy

Some people think that these considerations are permanently valid, that they could have been formulated in other times and that there is consequently no reason to 'melodramatize' the present problem. This is an extremely mistaken view. The situation we are considering is entirely new and has no discoverable precedent. For it does not proceed, as all too often repeated, from a simple phenomenon of quantitative growth, but from a qualitative transformation affecting man's most profound characteristics and, in a manner of speaking, renewing his genius.

If we take an over-all look at the evolution of educational activity through time, we soon see that progress in education accompanies economic progress and, consequently, evolution in production techniques, although it is not always easy to discern the respective causes among the complex, interacting elements.

In stable, agrarian-type societies, education is concerned with the transmission of professional skills, of traditions and values. It gives rise to few special problems of its own in isolation from social, political and religious problems.

When economic progress assumes a certain pace, the educational system naturally tends to dispense an increasing amount of knowledge to an increasing number of people, since more elaborate processes of production require more highly skilled labour, while the labour force itself sparks new technical improvements, and people with inventive and innovative minds emerge from it.

In addition, over a long term, education stimulates, accompanies or sets a seal on social and political development, as well as on technical and economic development. More highly educated people tend to assert their claims as citizens, and when there are large numbers of them they tend to make demands for democracy. The view which consists in presenting educational institutions as purely conservative and even repressive is not accurate. Every institution probably exerts some stabilizing influence, by its very nature; and the very activity of teaching involves, furthermore, a tendency to repetition, to seek out and cultivate forms, formulae and formulations, like juridical activity. This dual trait becomes more striking in times of rapid change: education then seems at the same time to run counter to and stimulate social change.

This dual evolution has continued throughout history, whether long-drawn-out, and making hardly perceptible progress, or, at other times, in quicker and more important social changes, capturing attention and marking significant turning-points in history.

Until the present day, however, there has been nothing comparable in its consequences to what we now call the scientific-technological revolution.

For in fact, much technical progress was made in earlier days through scientific observation and the discovery of 'recipes' which involved no special intellectual grasp of the secret forces of nature. Only in relatively recent times have conquests through fundamental research penetrated to the core of the problems examined, while at the same time their ever-quicker practical application has led to their introduction into the daily lives of the masses.

In contrast to the eighteenth-century industrial revolution and the first machine age, which replaced and multiplied the physical and muscular aspects of the human faculties, the scientific-technological revolution has simultaneously conquered the mental world, with its immediate transmission of information over any distance and its invention of increasingly perfected, rationalized, calculating machines.

This is a phenomenon which necessarily affects all of humanity.

While the effects of economic expansion differ greatly in different regions and among different social groups, the revolution in mass media and cybernetics affects everyone everywhere. Hardly a single human being is now unable to clamp his ear to a transistor radio, transmit sounds through a microphone, or by merely pressing a button unleash an infinite series of mechanisms of the greatest complexity and trigger the most varied and most significant effects. The scientific-technological revolution therefore places problems of knowledge and training in an entirely new light, giving man entirely new possibilities of thought and action; and, for the first time, it is truly universal.

Its communicational nature—in the broad sense of the term—makes it unique in enabling us to apprehend the greatest dimensions of space, the most infinitesimal measures of time and the entire scale of numbers. In this way it may be differentiated from all the historical changes to which it is sometimes compared, such as the Renaissance or the industrial revolution, whose messages could only be distributed at a very uneven speed to different parts of the world and even to different sections of the population.

This fact inevitably comes to mind but it must be stressed that people do not always deduce its logical consequences.

Earlier periods of development, whether slow or sudden, set off (even at the cost of passing crises) semi-automatic mechanisms which kept the balance of supply and demand between the three fields of education, the economy and political rights. Heavy demands for education were not felt in the backward countries, nor was there any great demand for democracy among the uneducated peoples. These adaptation systems, reminiscent of a market economy, have become obsolete in a world characterized by spontaneity and the communication of models.

So far as the economy, welfare and standards of living are concerned, people no longer resign themselves so easily to inequality dividing class from class, or to frustration afflicting entire nations, as in the days when all was seen as an arrangement by the Almighty of the natural order of things. Nor do they resign themselves any more readily to educational underdevelopment, particularly since they have been led to believe that the universalization of education was to become their absolute weapon for the achievement of an economic 'take-off' and the recovery of lost ground. Finally, democracy itself has become a more impressive problem than ever. For, on the one hand, the peoples now aspire to democracy quite independently of their GNP and their rates of school enrolment; but at the same time, they aspire to a different kind of democracy from the one to which we have until now been accustomed.

This is a domain in which no nation feels really satisfied with its progress and development, and it is a domain in which personality-training has a decisive part to play.

For the development of mass-communication media has provided political and economic authorities with extraordinary instruments for conditioning the individual, in whatever capacity we consider him, and especially as a consumer and as a citizen. The latter must therefore be able to combat the risk of personality-alienation involved in the more obsessive forms of propaganda and publicity, and in the behavioural conformity which may be imposed on him from the outside, to the detriment of his genuine needs and his intellectual and emotional identity. Meanwhile, machines designed to carry out rational operations are ousting him from a certain number of areas in which he used to feel able, at least, to move freely and pursue his ends after his own fashion. However, this innovation should be to the individual citizen's advantage, shielding him from a great many mistakes and freeing him from a large number of chores and constraints. Awareness of necessity may lead to freedom from constraint, provided that it is consciously assimilated and interpreted; at this point, it becomes indispensable for the individual to be able to solve his own problems, make his own decisions and shoulder his own responsibilities, in his own particular, irreducible field of action.

What is known as formal democracy—which it would be wrong to deride, for it marked great progress—has become obsolete. The delegation of authority for a fixed period had and still has the advantage of protecting the citizen from the arbitrary exercise of power and of providing him with the minimum of juridical guarantees. But it is not capable of providing him with an adequate share of the benefits of expansion or with the possibility of influencing his own fate in a world of flux and change; nor does it allow him to develop his own potential to best advantage.

The technological era brings undeniable benefits and opens vast new prospects, but not without disadvantages of its own. Scientists are currently warning us against a variety of dangers, the somewhat picturesque presentation of which tends to camouflage their hallucinatory nature: the human race multiplying in profusion to the point where population density becomes absurd, the soil and land devastated, the towns suffocating, power and food resources exhausted, the melting of ice in the polar regions leading to another Deluge, the atmosphere polluted with intelligence-destroying chemicals, etc.

Some people go so far as to propose entirely halting the growth rate—'zero growth'—on the grounds that this would limit the damage, while others, without openly adopting such an extreme position, recommend a revival of Malthusianism in the form of an ecological policy. Solutions of this kind are likely to consolidate inequality among the peoples and even to accentuate present-day distortions still further. Growth must accordingly be continued, but to avoid its dangers and reduce its harmful effects communities must organize their requisite priorities and disciplines democratically. This presupposes that the people concerned will be sufficiently educated, informed and aware.

The new man must be capable of understanding the global consequences of individual behaviour, of conceiving of priorities and shouldering his share of the joint responsibility involved in the destiny of the human race. Growth oriented towards the quality of life and the search for balance in human affairs cannot be a task for governments alone, entangled in their problems of management and, often, in systems shot through with prejudice. Only public opinion, if it manages to become world opinion, will be able to impose such simple, obviously necessary yet continually elusive measures as the renunciation of nuclear weapons and the allocation of a portion of the credits, which now go to sterile investments in preparation for wars, to the enhancement of life. If the people are to use their own intelligence for such a purpose, and they are quite capable of doing so, then they must become conscious of themselves, of their aspirations and their strength; they must shed their fatalism and, if we may use the expression, 'de-resign' themselves, and they can only gain such psychological self-assurance through an education readily available to all.

Strong support must be given to democracy, as the only way for man to avoid becoming enslaved to machines, and the only condition compatible with the dignity which the intellectual achievements of the human race require; the concept of democracy itself must be developed, for it can no longer be limited to a minimum of juridical guarantees protecting citizens from the arbitrary exercise of power in a subsistence society; furthermore, and in conjunction with this, more support must also be given to educational requirements, for there cannot—or will not—be a democratic and egalitarian relationship between classes divided by excessive inequality in education; and the aim and content of education must be re-created, to allow both for the new features of society and the new features of democracy.

For these reasons the commission stressed the fact that education must be regarded as a domain where political action is of especially decisive importance.

Since these requirements, at least so far as their new-found force is concerned, are themselves among the results of the scientific and technological revolution, any educational action must lay stress on:

A common conception of what may be described as 'scientific humanism'. It is humanistic in that it is mainly concerned with man and his welfare as an end in itself; and it is scientific to the extent that its humanistic content remains defined—and thereby enriched—by the continuing new contributions of science to the field of knowledge about man and the world.

Technology, that is to say the systematic application of science and, in more general terms, of organized knowledge, to practical, concrete tasks, enabling man not only to gain a better understanding of the objective processes taking place in his environment, but, above all, to enhance the effectiveness of all his activities.

For these reasons the commission considered that it was essential for science and technology to become fundamental, ever-present elements in any educational enterprise; for them to become part of all educational activities designed for children, young people and adults, so as to help the individual to control not only natural and productive forces, but social forces too, and in so doing to acquire

*mastery over himself, his choices and actions; and, finally, for them
to help man to develop a scientific frame of mind in order to promote
the sciences without becoming enslaved by them.*

The qualitative change:
motivation and employment

We believe that laying stress on the universal nature of the basic
facts underlying the education problem provides further justification for the commission's decision not to approach the situation
in developing countries in isolation. These countries probably are
facing special difficulties and have more stringent obligations than
others, and we shall often have occasion to refer to them in this
report. However, apart from the fact that it is always risky to
adopt a classification based on necessarily rough-and-ready criteria,
it seemed to us that the broad distinctions between the categories
in question derived mainly from quantitative evaluations or from
practical application (which, besides, should be defined not in relation to huge groups of nations but to each particular nation,
without prejudice to regional similarities).

As far as the principles determining major options are concerned,
both the industrialized and the developing countries will have to
devise closely comparable strategies, while making use of different
means.

The industrialized nations' educational system retains—at least
in very many cases—its dual nature; the education dispensed is
pre-technological, while recruitment, socially speaking, is élitist
(we are of course referring to high-level studies). This selfsame
system, with the same characteristics, has, in general, been introduced into developing countries, where it has the additional disadvantages of being adapted neither to the cultural environment
nor to the social and human setting.

The problem in both cases is therefore, first, to move from the
pre-technological to the technological stage and second, to build up
an educational system catering to the broad mass of the people,
while beginning with one which remains restricted to the minority,
to which it more or less guarantees high-level economic and
administrative employment. Logically this dual change should be

part of a single process. But this has not always been the case. Certain industrialized nations which have attempted to institute mass education without at the same time setting up a modern, technological system have, to greater or lesser extent, met with failure. Their failure is evinced by the small proportion of working-class pupils managing to gain access to higher education; while all evidence, both from the experience of certain countries and from reliable scientific research, indicates that intellectual capacity is more or less evenly distributed among the various social classes and levels of wealth.

From the educational standpoint, this means that the so-called 'developed' countries are—surprisingly—facing an internally underdeveloped situation. In these countries, faulty adaptation and failure are, comparatively speaking at least, symptoms character-istic of pupils whose origins lie among the people, a state of affairs similar to the one found in formerly colonized countries whose pupils are products of a western-style education imported lock, stock and barrel.

Both cases highlight the related problems of motivation and employment which govern, respectively, entry and exit from the educational cycle, by determining inflow and outflow and con-ditioning success.

The study of motivation is the key to every modern educational policy. This depends—either cumulatively or alternately—on the search for employment (at a level and with benefits corresponding to the level achieved in studies) and on the desire for learning, the *libido sciendi*. It is, however, striking to note that the first aspect (the search for employment) generally outweighs the second, which, besides, is often regarded as of negligible importance.

And yet curiosity, the desire to understand, know or discover, remains one of the deepest drives in human nature. And 'the no-tations developed in science today enable the least-gifted people to assimilate concepts the discovery of which required the greatest genius'.

This would ordinarily be the strongest kind of motivation, if it were encouraged, which, precisely, it is not. Conversely, stimu-lation through ambition and the search for employment is not enough to guarantee higher education in a number of industrialized countries becoming democratic, nor is it enough to ensure that school-attendance in developing countries remains constant.

We accordingly find the paradoxical situation, in certain regions where only half of all children are able to enter school, that half again of that half fail to adapt to it, and become discouraged even during primary education.

Motivation deriving from employment, on the other hand, seems unable to ensure true democratization. It also has the great disadvantage of giving credit to the idea that every degree brings with it the right to correspondingly qualified employment. The consequence of this is that graduates unable to find work corresponding to their qualifications feel cheated, and prefer to settle into unemployment rather than demean themselves by practising a less-reputed skill which—furthermore—the system has omitted to teach them.

It is typical of the logic of the traditional system that a specific educational level should have its corresponding and guaranteed professional level and remuneration, since access to the system is limited and since, furthermore, education is regarded as hard, even boring work, the joy of which is not its own reward and which must accordingly be paid for once completed.

Modern democratic education requires a revival of man's natural drive towards knowledge. At the same time it should dismantle the diploma-employment mechanism which the economies of many countries (even the industrialized ones) will not always be able to satisfy.

It is not difficult to define the main obstacles to the free play of motivation or, correspondingly, the main lines of a reform designed to reduce the drop-outs, the repeating and the lack of direction which lead to so much failure on both the academic and the human levels.

Because today there is a science of education, and because this science has a technology, we know that from the very earliest age the child's experience plays an essential part in his training, and we can also promote pre-school education, which is all the more valuable as it can compensate, in the developing countries, for the handicap suffered by the mass of the people through lack of cultural support in the family environment.

It is well known that cultural and, above all, linguistic estrangement in the child constitutes an equally serious, if not more serious, handicap. It is essential that the language spoken in a child's family be used during the first stages of his education.

At a time when abstract knowledge is part of a continual process, acting on and reacting to daily life, it should be accepted that the common stream of education at elementary schools and, the case arising, at secondary schools, must combine theory, techniques and practice, intellectual and manual labour; that schools must not be separated from life; that the child's personality must not be split between two worlds, each out of contact with the other—one in which he learns, like a disembodied creature, and the other in which he fulfils himself through some anti-educational activity.

One implication of the scientific and technological era is that knowledge is being continually modified and innovations renewed. It is therefore widely agreed that education should devote less effort to distributing and storing knowledge (although we should be careful not to exaggerate this) and more to mastering methods of acquiring it (learning to learn). Since knowledge will have to be revised and completed all through life, we may accordingly suppose that studies may be shortened while the relationship between introductory theory and professional practice in higher education—which is sometimes inordinately protracted—may be revised. It would indeed seem an extraordinary anomaly that in an age when theory is, in essentials, combined with practice and human beings, biologically speaking, reach maturity earlier, students are left marking time until the age of 25 and more, in a kind of waiting-room, where they are held at a remove from real life, productive activity, independent decision-making and responsibility.

It is also generally agreed that the academic model which is still highly regarded in so many countries, and which, under certain social and temporal circumstances, has produced the results expected of it, is today out of date and obsolete, not only so far as the working classes are concerned, but even in its utility to young people from the bourgeois class for which it was originally devised. It implacably reproduces the quirks of preceding generations. It relies excessively on theory and memory. It gives a privileged role to conventional, written and repetitive expression, to the detriment of the spoken word, of spontaneity and creative research. It arbitrarily isolates the humanities (considered as non-scientific) from the sciences (considered as non-humanistic), and persistently fails to recognize the advent of the 'scientific humanities'. It divides so-called general education from so-called technical education, displaying a preference for abstraction which would appear to embody the social prejudices of the aristocracy against practical application, regarded as servile—just as Plato condemned the founders of mechanics. It remains extraordinarily allergic to all practical work.

Finally, it has the serious disadvantage of preparing people only for a limited number of professions, and of ruling out the possibility for its graduates, when jobs are scarce, of turning, even temporarily, to the technical and practical activities they have been taught to despise.

The democratization of education might be reconciled with rationalized economic procedures by stimulating motivation and organizing polyvalent education. But those who benefit from it—and their numbers are increasing—must appreciate the opportunity given them for learning and training themselves; they must not consider they owe the State an absolute debt of gratitude.

The fact that a graduate may fail to find the kind of employment corresponding to his own particular or optimal qualifications should not be regarded as scandalous. But the fact that such a person cannot or does not want to take over a socially useful function and personally accept that function is, however, a sign of the bankruptcy of the educational system.

Given an over-all conception of this kind, it becomes possible to reject the neo-Malthusians' view that instruction should be rationed and kept closely in line with employment prospects. A universal *numerus clausus* system, which in the richer countries would maintain existing social injustices in education, and perpetuate the under-equipped intellectual condition of the poorer countries, would nowadays be regarded as intolerable. Still more strikingly, the neo-Malthusian theory is untenable even when we accept its own purely utilitarian assumption. Drafting a graph of correlations between the levels of general education and professional activities would, indeed, be a thorny undertaking: in a changing economy, we have few means of forecasting, with any certainty, the number and nature of jobs likely to become available; few means of setting these against specific professional qualifications, and even fewer when we come to deal with economies on the point of being launched into development.

For these reasons the commission has suggested that any neo-Malthusian trend and any attempt to slow down educational development be excluded from educational policies and strategies, on cultural, political and economic grounds. The aim of education is to enable man to be himself, to 'become himself'. And the aim of education in relation to employment and economic progress should be not so much to prepare young people and adults for a specific, lifetime vocation, as to 'optimize' mobility among the professions and afford a permanent stimulus to the desire to learn and to train one-self. In brief, without abandoning the expansion of education, its objectives, methods and structures should be thoroughly reappraised.

Schools and the learning society

Yet we find certain educationists drawing far more radical conclusions than those we have broadly outlined above, although in many cases they set out from the same basic principles.

Some critics propose abolishing the educational system rather than reforming it, on the grounds that it is often antiquated and sclerotic. And since schools must be brought closer to life, others propose quite simply suppressing them. Views of this kind are usually presented as progressive and even revolutionary, but if they were put into practice on any scale, their effects would certainly be of a reactionary nature, like the economic ideas of the partisans of 'zero growth' to which they are often linked.

The scientific and technological revolution, the enormous flood of information available to man, the existence of gigantic communication-media networks, together with many other economic and social factors, have considerably modified traditional educational systems, brought out the weakness of certain forms of instruction and the strength of others, broadened the scope of self-learning activities and enhanced the value of active and conscious attitudes in the acquisition of knowledge. The prestige of teaching based on reflection is constantly increasing. The problems involved in instructing and educating pupils of all ages, adults included, require us to use a multiplicity of out-of-school forms of learning. Out-of-school education comprises a wide range of possibilities which all countries should use productively. Disdain for it is merely a relic of times past, and no progressive pedagogue can subscribe to this. Schools, that is to say establishments devised to dispense education systematically to the rising generations, are now and will remain in the future, however, the decisive factor in training men to contribute to the development of society, to play an active part in life, men properly prepared for work. Especially in modern society, processing a huge volume of information received through an ever-greater number of increasingly varied channels requires systematized knowledge, aptitudes and skills. Scientific knowledge, and ideas, regarded as a distillate of what is general and essential in things and phenomena, and more especially, systems of knowledge and methods enabling individuals to form their own personal interpretation of this mighty flow of information, and assimilate it in positive fashion, almost always require organized education, dispensed by properly designed educational institutions.

Admittedly, certain kinds of school and certain forms of teaching must be strongly criticized, if on different grounds for different countries, and many aspects of school education call for thorough-going reappraisal and reformation. None the less, abandoning the idea of school as an essential, if not exclusive, element in education would be tantamount to surrender in the struggle to introduce hundreds of millions of human beings to the kind of education which involves systematic assimilation of knowledge. And while human culture may not be limited to knowledge, knowledge remains today an integral and indispensable part of it.

The position adopted by the commission accordingly involves a dialectical approach comprising, on the one hand, improvements to be made to existing systems and, on the other, alternatives to these. It therefore marks itself apart from the limited approach of those who remain straitjacketed by existing structures, and also from those who dream of some radical structural upheaval, flinging themselves into the unknown without considering realities and possibilities.

For these reasons the commission laid stress above all on two fundamental ideas: lifelong education and the learning society. Since studies can no longer constitute a definitive 'whole', handed out to and received by a student before he embarks on adult life, whatever the level of his intellectual equipment and the age at which he does so, educational systems must be thought out afresh, in their entirety, as must our very conception of them. If all that has to be learned must be continually re-invented and renewed, then teaching becomes education and, more and more, learning. If learning involves all of one's life, in the sense of both time-span and diversity, and all of society, including its social and economic as well as its educational resources, then we must go even further than the necessary overhaul of 'educational systems' until we reach the stage of a learning society. For these are the true proportions of the challenge education will be facing in the future. It is by no means certain that conservatism of a cultural nature will be easier to overcome than economic or political resistance. But once in a position to measure the stakes against the price, how can we refuse to fight the fight?

And the weapons we need for that fight are available.

The instruments of change

The 'age of change' has provided us with the instruments needed to meet the quantitative and qualitative demand for education which it has stimulated. It remains for us to recognize them for what they are and to be able to use them for that purpose.

The two great innovative systems most characteristic of the technological era, the mass media (the transistor radio and television) and cybernetics, are both linked to information, transmitting it instantaneously, coding it, discovering and using it, and are in consequence adapted by their very nature to the activities of learning, education and training.

And yet today we find comparatively little development of programmed education, while radio and television are insufficiently used for educational purposes, and computers even less so. Apart from exceptional cases, radio and television are put to use outside and parallel to education strictly speaking.

There is a widespread belief that radio can only be used to advantage to excite interest and that it can play only a negligible part in properly educating and training people. And we find authorities merely inserting television into existing educational procedures, instead of thoroughly reorganizing these so that they benefit from this modern technological aid. Meanwhile programmed education is confused with the utilization of very modern and costly methods with which most educational systems are unable to equip themselves. The result is that applications of advanced pedagogic methods remain very limited. It is commonly felt that computerized data processing should be restricted to higher studies; yet, on the contrary, it is most important to plan to give very young children some introduction to the elementary language of machines. First, because algorithms correspond to a remarkable logical method. Second, because contact with this 'mysterious' power often greatly strengthens motivation towards knowledge.

It is necessary, even indispensable for all countries, whatever their level of development, to use educational technology and technological principles on a large scale, or in other words, to use post-machine-age intellectual technologies.

This is true of the developed countries, even of those which feel that their economies are flourishing and that they can afford to make every necessary contribution to achieve their educational objectives. Whatever their circumstances, recourse to these new methods would certainly enable them to obtain greater efficiency from the same investment. The essential problem for such countries is to combat routine, arouse public interest and, above all, to have their teachers co-operate in this undertaking. This latter condition is indispensable, not only in order to tranquillize susceptibilities among certain sections of the population, but in particular, because the use of new technologies in education requires them to be integrated into the educational system.

These technologies are therefore a very valuable asset for developed countries; but for the developing countries they would appear to be the basic pre-condition for dealing with the entire problem. So far as developing countries are concerned, or most of them, at least, the firm introduction of innovations in this area is the only way they can hope to advance towards a satisfactory solution within a reasonable period of time.

Current procedures can solve neither the illiteracy problem, when this affects a large proportion of the population (notwithstanding undeniable progress through functional literacy) nor, in many cases, can it guarantee universal school enrolment or the yield therefrom. Finally, these procedures are unsuitable for creating opportunities for training adults and gradually applying the concept of lifelong education. Generally speaking, a few additional allocations of credit or aid would not markedly improve this situation, for the countries in question would fairly quickly develop other bottlenecks (insufficient teacher-recruitment or supply of textbooks, etc.).

The field of possibilities takes on a very different aspect once we decide to make use of educational technologies on an appropriate scale, and, above all, of the dual method of programmed education (it may be recalled in passing that this procedure is not confined to computer-programmed education, which we emphasized earlier because of its extreme importance) and of educational radio and television. We would then find ourselves in a situation comparable to the transition from a subsistence-level economy to a rapidly expanding one.

So far as the choice of methods for modernizing education is concerned, it would appear to us that developing countries should make simultaneous use of advanced technologies, so far as possible, while paying greater attention to intermediate technologies and the application of technological principles likely to increase efficiency and generally contribute to education, without, for all that, introducing sophisticated and costly technological or mechanical aids.

The commission accordingly underlined the fact that despite doubts and differing orientations, and whatever the progress or saving which might be obtained from certain changes in the traditional educational system, the very heavy demand for education due on the one hand to the gradual prolongation of school-attendance to optimal age, and, on the other hand, to the institution of a genuine lifelong education, can only be met if instruments derived from modern technology, with its limitless possibilities, are put to use on an adequate scale and with appropriate means.

International co-operation

If we agree that the time has come to overhaul education, that education today is facing a critical challenge and that we must think it out afresh in its entirety, then international solidarity and world co-operation become more clearly necessary than ever before.

To begin with, we must maintain intellectual and operational co-operation among all countries: the industrialized countries must co-operate with each other, so must developing countries; so, too, must countries close to each other, for demographic, linguistic or social reasons; and each country must co-operate at various levels with educational, scientific and cultural institutions whose experience, attempts at innovation and reflections on the future of education must be regarded as part of the same world treasury. Exchanging shares in this jointly owned wealth is, today, both an urgent duty and the best way to international co-operation.

Another requirement is operational, technical and financial solidarity in relation to developing countries. The renewal of education calls for experiments, and since these involve the risk of failure, resources must be made available correspondingly. Public expenditure will in many cases, however, be found to have already reached (or exceeded) the ceiling acceptable to the economy and the budget. Furthermore, many educational systems are embroiled in contradictions of a nature more likely to discourage than stimulate potential suppliers of aid, who may be prompted to lend a sympathetic ear to the neo-Malthusians' unfortunate counselling, and to other pessimists, certain of whom have even made their constrictive theses and disenchanted warnings known to the commission.

These were the fundamental reasons which led certain members of the commission to envisage setting up an international Programme for Educational Innovations. Dealing with innovations in all fields, or more precisely, with over-all educational renewal, a programme of this kind could be particularly useful and effective in introducing educational technologies. Any productive investment requires an initial outlay of capital, but management at a later stage could become less costly and far more profitable.

The less-developed countries could not, alone, find the necessary capital; the developed countries would therefore have to help, in new but specific ways. They would intervene, for example, if the installation of a television network were to require communications-satellite relays, which usually cover several countries at the same time.

There are various reasons for believing that the more-favoured countries would agree to this renewal of solidarity; for they could then be sure that their help would be effective while their initial expenses would be amortized, management-assistance becoming less indispensable once the process of technological re-equipment began to yield its first positive results.

However, the duty of solidarity goes much further than this defence of it on the grounds of its utility to the recipient country: it also has a kind of feedback effect on the donor countries, and a beneficial influence on the entire international community.

The research organizations which would have to be founded or developed to work on the various forms of technological aids to education could be useful to all countries; for many developed countries are presently faced with the need to innovate. Essentially, and fundamentally, their problems are hardly different from those which they should be helping the less-advanced countries to solve. Nor is there any reason why we should not envisage one and the same organization working for some customers at a price and for others freely or cheaply. Work carried out in the framework of aid would enlighten the donors as to their own needs and inadequacies, and would probably move them to organize their own exchanges and relationships better, to avoid wastage and other inconveniences.

The enhancement of intellectual achievement among the peoples of the Third World benefits the industrialized nations in many ways (sometimes excessively, in the form of the brain drain).

More important still, nations which only acceded to independence recently have often remained closer than others to traditional modes of culture, and are all the more concerned to safeguard or regain their own particular 'authentic' qualities after experiencing fears that it might be obliterated beneath the alien veneer imposed in the days of colonialism. Thus, they may be able to contribute the richness of their many-sided culture to the world community, and help it to build a defence against the obsessively monotonous forms of life and patterns of thought which may so easily accompany an expanding economy if it becomes synonymous with a civilization based on the profit motive.

The commission noted that neither present forms of bilateral and multilateral aid, nor the resources available for it, nor, even, the conceptions on which it is based are capable of meeting the world community's present educational needs. And they will be particularly inadequate if renewing the educational enterprise becomes an over-riding consideration. Ways of broadening and strengthening solidarity must be found. Some of these emerge from our analyses and suggestions. Others must be developed later. But we remain convinced that this can be done, given initiative and expertise among the nations, the peoples, the educators and researchers and also with the help of international organizations, especially Unesco, which has a leading role to play in this field.

Knowledge is not all that a culture requires. The commission was not in a position to extend its field of study, in the breadth and depth which might have been desired, to all those functions which are extrinsically educational, and to bring in the whole range of family, vocational and urban relationships, and those of social groups and professional and spiritual communities. However, all our observations helped to confirm our certainty that all these different intrinsic and extrinsic functions together make up a

whole, and that the various sectors of human development and
social life are inseparable from each other. If we suppose that technological means—and more especially, machines reproducing
mental operations—represent the equivalent, for the human brain,
of what might otherwise have been obtained by some biogenetic
mutation, then we may say that it will be necessary for the new
man to be capable of achieving a balance between his increased
capacities for understanding, for power, and the potential counterpart of these in his emotional and moral personality-structure.
Uniting *Homo sapiens* and *Homo faber* is not enough; such a man
must also feel in harmony with himself and others: *Homo concors*.

This will be necessary if he is to overcome the dangers and other
harmful consequences of the exponential growth rate and the
material aspects of development. It will be necessary if he is to
shoulder his civic and social responsibilities and react to contradictions and injustice. Individuals must be able to use the power
inherent in consciousness through the agency of historical and
group consciousness, through research, through preserving their
authentic identity and, finally, through each individual's feeling
that he fully belongs to the entire species. In this way, the twin
poles of the singular, which is irreducible, and the universal,
comprising diversity within identity, will achieve expression.

This age, which has been called that of the finite world, can only
be the age of total man: that is to say, man entire and all of man.

PART ONE

Findings

CHAPTER 1

The question of education

As we begin this report, before turning to examine the present, we shall—like Telemachus, son of Ulysses, setting out on a new journey—glance back briefly to the past, over the centuries of man and his education, to its roots and its development. This perspective may later help us to perceive more clearly the dimensions of the present educational universe, where so many ages are mixed, where some monuments are majestic and others decayed, where there are new edifices and vast constructions under way, and where we may see the man of the future.

In so doing, we do not pretend to write history. But it so happens that one of the observations, if not one of the theses, in this report is that history exerts a powerful influence on education, in the sense that educational development is a function of societies' historical development, that education bears many traces of the past and, finally, that it is time for education to help make history by preparing for it.

Hence the following few pages in which we have attempted, in a brief review, to depict this movement and its influence in the light of the present day.

The heritage of the past

From the earliest times, man has consciously used his gift for speech to communicate from individual to individual, group to group and generation to generation a store of practical experience—codes for interpreting natural phenomena, rules, rites and taboos—thereby making the socialization of individual memories an essential means for survival of the species.

Education as biological necessity

Biologically and physiologically man was naked and not specifically suited to his environment, yet he gradually managed—despite inherent weakness in his instincts—to ensure his survival and then his development.

Locked in a permanent struggle against environmental conditions, he organized his existence and little by little created his society for group endeavour. Beginning with the family unit and the primitive tribe, concentrating on vital material tasks, he progressively acquired knowledge and experience, learned how to know and express his desires and aspirations and so defined and fashioned his intellectual faculties.

In pointing to man's biological, physiological and instinctive needs, scientific evidence shows the role which this evolution—necessarily implying forms of education—played in the survival of the species.

On the whole, the various human races have undergone only minimal evolutionary changes since prehistoric times in the process of adapting themselves to various ways of life and different environments. Yet modern man has never ceased conquering new environmental conditions, as if his biological ability to adapt were growing. This is mere illusion. In reality, man is able to survive today in a polluted environment (in which he could never remain physically and mentally healthy if he did not know how to protect himself against harmful elements) because of knowledge handed down and enriched from generation to generation, that is to say because education is more widespread and comprehensive.

Education as social necessity

As far back as we can go in the history of education—which admittedly is not very far—it emerges as a natural characteristic of human societies. It has contributed to the destiny of societies in all phases of their development. It has never itself ceased to develop. It has been the bearer of humanity's most noble ideals. It is inseparable from the greatest individual and collective exploits in human history, the course of which it reproduces, fairly faithfully, with its strong and weak periods, its times of striving and times of despair, its harmonies and discords.

Primitive society

In primitive society, education was complex and continual. It aimed at forming the character, aptitudes, skills and moral qualities of an individual who educated himself through a kind of symbiotic process, rather than being educated. Life in the family or

4

clan, work or play, rites and ceremonies were all day-to-day opportunities for learning, from motherly care to lessons from the hunter-father, from observing seasonal changes to watching familiar animals, or listening to tales told by the elders and chants of the tribal shaman. These natural, uninstitutionalized forms of learning have prevailed to the present day[1] in vast regions of the world where they still provide the only form of education for millions of people. Furthermore, things do not happen so differently as might seem at first sight in contemporary school-going societies, for it remains true that children—and adults—receive a large part of their education from the environment, their family and society, drawing directly, existentially, on experience. The knowledge so obtained is all the more important in that it conditions receptivity to school education, which in turn provides the learner with the framework enabling him to order and conceptualize knowledge drawn from the environment.

These ideas, long obscured by didactic, scholastic pedagogy, are the essential elements in the concept of a consciously learning society, which is our central theme.

African tradition

The African tradition, like many others elsewhere in the world, still bears witness to this ancestral condition of education. 'The fact that precolonial Africa did not have "schools"—except for short periods of initiation in some tribes—did not mean that the children were not educated. They learned by living and doing. . . . Education was thus "informal"; every adult was a teacher to a greater or lesser degree. But this lack of formality did not mean that there was no education, nor did it affect its importance to the society.' This quotation from Julius Nyerere hints at the reasons for regarding traditional African education as one of the very interesting experiences in non-formal education, however inadequate and limited it may have been in reality.[2]

1. 'But in all societies, both primitive and highly civilized, until quite recently most education of most children has occurred incidentally, not in schools set aside for the purpose. Adults did their economic work and other social tasks; children were not excluded, were paid attention to, and learned to be included. The children were not formally "taught". In many adult institutions, incidental education has always been taken for granted as an essential part of the functioning, e.g. in families and age peer groups, community labour, master–apprentice arrangements, games and plays, prostitution and other sexual initiation, and religious rites. In Greek *paideia*, the entire network of institutions, the *polis*, was thought of as an educator. As John Dewey beautifully put it, the essence of all philosophy is the philosophy of education, the study of how to have a world' (Paul Goodman, *Unusual Ideas about Education: Education of the Young*, p.2, Paris, Unesco, 1971, document of the International Commission on the Development of Education, Opinions Series, 37).
2. 'Very effective when it is simply a matter of handing down experience from generation

Findings

A review of education's roots, provided one avoids falling into the trap of retrospective idealization, may be fertile for pedagogic thought and enrich present-day education with unduly neglected values and experience.

Birth of the school

Evidence that the school as an institution was historically necessary is shown by the fact that it developed gradually during different periods, but at analogous stages, in all types of society. The adoption of a school structure in education appears essentially to be linked with the systematization and steady increase in the use of written language. Learning to read naturally entailed a master with young people gathered round him, in a 'classroom', in a school.

We do not in the least gainsay the immensity of the new powers which writing,[1] and later on the printing-press, conferred on man, or the value of the services so rendered to education, above all by the printed book. But we note that this revolution also had certain less beneficial effects. Whatever the place of rites and taboos in predominantly oral education, it involved direct contact with

Written tradition

things and people. Books replaced these direct methods of transmitting knowledge and nurtured the prejudice that the written word—and its oral repetition—was the embodiment of all knowledge worthy of the name, much superior to lessons learned from daily life.

This pre-eminence of the written over the spoken word remains deeply embedded in most school systems today.

Masters and pupils

The growing store of knowledge and tradition was handed down this way for thousands of years from master to pupil, accompanied by strict, authoritarian, scholastic discipline, reflecting societies which were themselves founded on rigidly authoritarian principles. This set the pattern for *the authoritarian master–pupil relationship which still prevails in most schools in the world.*

Almost everywhere, churchmen—depositaries and guardians of all knowledge—dominated education, which in addition to trans-

---

to generation, when techniques are relatively backward and essentially empirical, it (traditional African education) nevertheless offers no possibility for progress through the assimilation and spread of new experiences and knowledge, because facts had to be transmitted individually, and therefore in isolation' (Abdou Moumouni, *Education in Africa*, London, André Deutsch, 1968).

1. 'In no part of the world has civilization at any time advanced to any considerable height or achieved any permanence unless by the aid of writing; but just as civilization generally implies the development of city life so writing has never been introduced in any other than an urban society' (*History of Mankind, Cultural and Scientific Development*, Vol. I, p. 631, Paris, Unesco, 1962).

mitting religious dogma was used to train scribes and administrators, doctors and architects, astronomers and mathematicians.

Education in Asia developed according to similar patterns. Respect for the written word reached its high point with the Chinese mandarins. Entrusted with the task of training State officials, the Chinese educational system, at first more open and liberal than others, was effective in teaching the harmony of thought and action until excessive formalism and a rigid system of grades and examinations paralysed it.

The world's first universities were those of the Brahmins in India, where they presented a consummate example of education based on philosophy and religion while at the same time stressing the study of mathematics, history, astronomy and even the laws of economics. Subsequently, Buddhist education emerged as a reaction against the Brahminical doctrine of caste and their monopoly of education, yet it in turn became equally rigid.

Education in ancient Persia involved lifelong training, covering all an individual's activities until the approach of old age. In addition to imparting knowledge of the sciences, moral virtues and intellectual disciplines, it included civic training and apprenticeship in practical life.

Schools were highly honoured in classical Greece and Rome, where children and adolescents of the upper classes were diligent students. The school's ideal was to form harmonious personalities with balanced intellectual, aesthetic and physical development. Knowledge, intelligence, appreciation of the arts and spiritual virtues were supreme values in an education designed for and confined to the élite. This aristocratic conception was confirmed and adopted down through the centuries by imperial, royal, feudal and patrician societies structurally dedicated to *cultivating a selective education, frequently of high quality, for the benefit of the minority, conferring the stamp of nobility on an élitist doctrine which remains very much alive in certain educational systems of our time.*

Ancient Western societies regarded the sum of knowledge which went into making an educated man as a clearly defined whole. This was the seven liberal arts—grammar, rhetoric, logic, arithmetic, geometry, astronomy and music—which long remained the unshakeable foundation of a classical education.

This classical education enjoyed such prestige that it tended to withdraw into its own universe and only grudgingly has it admitted contributions from the so-called exact and the social sciences.

Asiatic tradition

Graeco-Roman tradition

7

Findings

In the times when Christianity reigned supreme over a large part of the world, religion made its authority felt in every sphere of life. And its empire spread, above all, to education. One could say that in Europe in the Middle Ages the Church and education, with few exceptions, were one and the same thing. This does not mean that education, permeated with religion as it may have been, was incapable of adapting itself to the particular purposes of princes and merchants, clerks or warriors. Mediaeval education was essentially a response to the conditions of feudal society as well as to religious ideas. Many Asian and Latin American societies, which long remained in a feudal stage of development, have had very similar systems that contributed to institutionalizing rigid social and cultural divisions.

Many of the hierarchical forms and discriminatory practices for which current systems are blamed are in reality vestiges of an education devised for a very different type of society from those in which they survive.

*Islamic
education*

In many countries, Islam—with its self-appointed universal mission—endeavoured to define the objectives and methods appropriate to an education which would be both lofty and far-reaching.[1] With its confidence in man's capacity to perfect himself through education, the Muslim world was among the first to recommend the idea of lifelong education, exhorting Muslims to educate themselves 'from the cradle to the grave'. Islam enjoined all men, women and children, to educate themselves in order to educate others in turn. Muslim education paid special attention to learning in the sciences, medicine, philosophy, mathematics and astronomy. However, through distrust of heresy and subversion, certain educational systems in the Muslim world finally retracted into a reticent attitude towards the innovative spirit.

*Mediaeval
model of the
university*

In Europe during the Middle Ages, large institutions for higher education, ambitiously labelled universities, came into being. The wealthy, industrious commercial cities, jealous of their franchise and fame, frequently set the example for such establishments, which quickly came under the direction of powerful representatives of the rising bourgeoisie. The universities spread first of all through Europe, and then to the Americas. Teaching concentrated on

1. 'To create such a society and also to believe in one single God, to attain a way of life which combines the love of this world with asceticism, and lastly to achieve spiritual and moral education, are the four outstanding ideals of Muslim education' (A. K. Kinany, 'Muslim Educational Ideals', *Yearbook of Education*, London, Evans, 1949).

8

scholastic philosophy and the humanities, and later gradually expanded to include the natural sciences.[1] The Arab and Muslim world deserves recognition in this respect, with a flourishing culture which extended through Asia, Africa and to Europe.

Despite many evolutions, higher education continues on the whole to abide by certain apparently immutable rules, such as its division into separate faculties. In earlier times, these patterns doubtless responded to objective requirements for the development of knowledge. But today, this legacy must be reappraised in light of contemporary needs. Universities are more directly open to the movement of ideas than other educational institutions and more immediately required to keep up to date in the fields of scientific and technical education.

Both force of circumstance and social and intellectual criticism are subjecting universities to increasing pressure, requiring the university establishment to adapt more dynamically to the realities and needs of a rapidly changing world.

From the Reformation to the Renaissance and until the early days of the modern era, post-mediaeval Europe exerted a powerful influence on the development of civilization, opening up vast horizons for knowledge, unleashing new social forces and redefining humanism. Yet, to a certain extent, this influence was slow to make itself felt on education, notwithstanding the fact that the development of philosophic thought, the new vistas in psychology and the promotion of living languages to the dignified status of academic disciplines did enlarge the horizon and, here and there, vitalize practice.

Advent of modern times

At the same time a crucial change had taken place in the material means for educational action; the introduction of the printing-press now made books, the containers of knowledge, available to the masses.

And, in fact, as economic progress created an increasing need for personnel capable of reading, writing and counting, education began to spread and be popularized, and in so doing necessarily took on many new forms.

1. 'Historians assessing the university culture of this period were struck by this artificial, wearisome technique, this verbalism, both of which were the price which had to be paid for its all-pervading dialectic. Yet scholasticism should not be judged on the basis of these decadent forms. It played an undeniably historic part: it enabled uncultivated, relatively unskilled minds to assimilate the immense heritage of ancient times which had been suddenly revealed to them, and to rely on a powerful intellectual instrument so as to produce original works of their own' (*History of Mankind, Cultural and Scientific Development*, Vol. III, Paris, Unesco, to be published).

Findings

The industrial
revolution

In countries which were taking their first steps towards industrialization, progress in industry began to have a very nearly direct
relation to the popularization of education. As the industrial revolution spread to more and more countries, it triggered an expansion in education leading to the concept of universal and
compulsory school-attendance, linked historically to the idea of universal suffrage. The social order—in which class conflict, far from
fading away, grew more sharply defined and acute—sought to confine this democratization of knowledge within narrow limits. It
was one thing to begin giving rudimentary lessons to children in
the cities and the countryside, to ensure that industry had a labour-
reserve sufficient for its needs. It was quite another to throw open
to the people those avenues of classical and university education
which were the fief of the well-born and the wealthy.

When, a quarter of a century ago, the United Nations proclaimed
that man has a right to education, they were endorsing a democratic
ideal several centuries old. Its application, however, continues to be
hampered in many places by conditions similar to those prevailing
at the time it was first expressed.

Transplanted
models

Yet, seen across the prospect of time, and however important
the economic eruption of the modern age may have been, nothing
seems to have had more significant consequences for the world than
the mark and orientation which the colonizing Europeans left on
modern education in Latin America, Africa and vast reaches of
Asia. Colonial régimes, whether British, Dutch, French, Portuguese
or Spanish, transplanted and distributed the various European
models of education—just as they were—to all lands under the
sun.[1]

In exercising sovereignty over a large part of the world until
recent times, Europe, with its political and economic power, set its
seal on educational institutions in the developing countries. And
just as the political and economic effects of colonialism are still
strongly felt today, so *most educational systems in American, African*
and Asian countries mirror the legacy of a one-time motherland or

---

1. 'The education provided by the colonial government . . . was not designed to prepare
young people for the service of their own country; instead, it was motivated by a desire
to inculcate the values of the colonial society and to train individuals for the service
of the colonial State' (Julius K. Nyerere, *Education for Self-Reliance*, Dar es Salaam,
Ministry of Information and Tourism, 1967). Likewise, the aim of British education
in India, in the nineteenth century, was to produce 'a class of persons, Indian in blood
and colour, but English in taste, opinions, in morals and intellect' (Lord Macaulay,
Minute on Indian Education).

10

of some other outside hegemony, whether or not they meet those nations' present needs.

Since the industrial revolution—and even more so after modern-day scientific and technological transformations—the very content of the ways of life and means of production, of man's hopes and fears, his cares and joys, has profoundly changed. The prospects for education have also changed and become greater, for a variety of reasons. Centralized, lay societies have called in new quotas of trained personnel to serve the State. Economic development has multiplied jobs for qualified men, making it necessary to train more and more technicians and professional executives. The right to education has come home to the workers, whose consciousness has awakened, as one of the major means to social emancipation. Accelerated modernization in many societies has led to more and more fundamental, quantitative and qualitative changes in primary, vocational and generalized education. Meanwhile the process of socialist revolutions begun with the October Revolution more than fifty years ago, and the national liberation movements which reached their zenith hardly ten years ago, have created new demands and new needs.

Entering the modern age

What general conclusions about education can we draw from this fragment of history?

First, education has a far richer past than the relative uniformity of its present structures might lead one to think. The Amerindian civilizations, African cultures, Asian philosophies and many other traditions are imbued with values which could become a source of inspiration not only for educational systems in the countries which have inherited them, but for universal educational thought as well. There can be little doubt that many eminently valuable possessions have been lost—in some cases even before the colonial era, through internal decline—or were destroyed or distorted through external action, especially through colonialism. It is relevant to note, however, that many nations which have undergone foreign rule—including some of those now most resolutely affirming their independence—have proudly taken over, particularly in education, the best part of the intellectual disciplines and so-called classical culture acquired in harder times.

Second, outmoded dogma and custom weigh heavily on education and, in many ways, the older nations suffer no less from anachronisms in their educational systems than the young States which inherited them in the form of imported models.

11

Although this view of the past has been fragmentary, the history of education seems to propose a dual task for the future—its restitution and renovation, at one and the same time.

Current characteristics

Since the end of the Second World War, education has become the world's biggest activity as far as over-all spending is concerned.[1] In budgetary terms, it ranks a close second in world expenditure of public funds, coming just after military budgets.[2] It is being asked to carry out increasingly vast and complex tasks that bear no comparison with those allotted to it in the past. It constitutes a vital component in any effort for development and human progress and occupies an increasingly important position in the formulation of national and international policies.

Three new phenomena

Three widespread current phenomena deserve particular attention, from both a doctrinal and a practical point of view.

The first point to consider is that for centuries educational development, especially in the countries of Europe which initiated the industrial revolution, had generally followed economic growth. Now, *probably for the first time in the history of humanity, development of education on a world-wide scale is tending to precede economic development.*

Education precedes

This trend first emerged, boldly and successfully, in countries

1. 'We can only grasp the extent of a country's effort and carry out international comparisons on an identical basis if our conception of education is a broad one. Concentrating only on the national education budget leads to underestimating that effort and, above all, to ruling out comparisons in space and time, for the content of and areas covered by budgets varies from country to country and, within one country, from one period to another, for political or administrative reasons' (Lê Thành Khôi, *L'Industrie de l'Enseignement*, p. 39, Paris, Les Éditions de Minuit, 1967).
2. The question of the relative proportion of financial allocation for education and for defence respectively is a controversial one. World-wide military expenditure in 1968 amounted to $182,000 million. Expenditures for education, including public spending in the education sector (which alone amounted to $132,000 million in the same year), plus funds for training in other sectors, expenses for educational programmes in mass communication, private expenditure, etc., are much higher. (In this connexion, see also page 41.)

   It is particularly interesting to note that the rate of increase (percentage) in spending on education is higher than that of military expenditure: military expenditure, $+10\cdot4$ (1965–66), $+10\cdot7$ (1966–67), $+6\cdot1$ (1967–68), $+0\cdot2$ (1968–69); State expenditure on education, $+11$ (1965–66), $+11\cdot3$ (1966–67), $+10\cdot5$ (1967–68), (figures lacking for 1968–69) (figures from the Swedish International Peace Research Institute and the Unesco Office of Statistics).

12

such as Japan, the U.S.S.R. and the United States. Many other countries, especially developing nations, have chosen to follow this path in the last few years,[1] despite the heavy sacrifices[2] and all the difficulties involved.

Another no less important fact for the future, of a sociological order, is that *for the first time in history, education is now engaged in preparing men for a type of society which does not yet exist.*

) *Education*
) *foresees*

This presents educational systems with a task which is all the more novel in that the function of education down the ages has usually been to reproduce the contemporary society and existing social relationships. The change can be easily explained if the relative stability of past societies is compared with the accelerated development of the contemporary world. At a time when the mission of education should be to train 'unknown children for an unknown world',[3] the force of circumstances demands that educationists do some hard thinking, and that in so doing they shape the future.

This trend may be seen in countries which are endeavouring to organize a radically different society, following profound changes and the accession to power of new social or political leaders. It also appears in countries possessing ample technological resources, which—without having undergone abrupt political changes—have devised a new 'human project'. Elsewhere, the political situation, domestic difficulties and conflict make it harder to achieve an overall vision of social targets. As a general rule, what is lacking is not willingness or clarity of vision, but necessary structures and resources.

The third significant fact is the contradiction arising between the products of education and the needs of society. Whereas, in the past, societies evolved slowly (except for brief mutations) and absorbed the products of education easily and willingly, or at least managed to adapt to them, the same is not always true today.

1. Such as the People's Republic of the Congo, where, in spite of a low national *per capita* income (about $220), one inhabitant out of four is at present attending free primary school; or Cuba, which, although possessing limited resources, has made rapid progress towards the universalization of primary education, adult literacy and the expansion of secondary education.
2. Cameroon, for example, increased its public expenditure on education from 1967 to 1968 by 65 per cent, while at the same time growth in its GNP was little more than 10 per cent.
3. 'We must place the future, like the unborn child in the womb of a woman, within a community of men, women, and children, among us, already here, already to be nourished and succoured and protected, already in need of things for which, if they are not prepared before it is born, it will be too late. So, as the young say, The Future is Now' (Margaret Mead, *Culture and Commitment, A Study of the Generation Gap*, New York, N.Y., Doubleday, 1970).

13

Findings

For the first time in history some societies are beginning to reject many of the products of institutionalized education.

This social, economic and psychological phenomenon is due to the fact that accelerating development and structural change tend to accentuate the gap which normally exists between structures and infrastructures and superstructures. This shows how easily educational systems can become out of phase. A system designed for a minority—when knowledge was slow to change and man could, without undue presumption, hope to 'learn' in a few years everything to satisfy his intellectual and scientific needs—quickly becomes out of date when employed for mass education in times of whirlwind change and when the volume of knowledge increases at an ever faster pace. The effects of multiple conflicts—unequal growth, discrepancies in social and economic development, movements and countermovements—all have a tremendous impact on education. The system finds it difficult to keep up with the demands of an expanding society;(the people it educates are not properly trained to adapt themselves to change,)and some societies reject the qualifications and skills being offered when these no longer answer direct needs. This is the consequence of unbalanced growth—stop and go development which creates equilibrium in one sphere by upsetting it in another. Even so, this process is not totally negative, although the readjustment and change it demands are distressing and tiring. The world of education today reflects these dilemmas.

Hence the need for change felt at the beginning of this century and especially since the end of the Second World War. Education had to adapt more to social and economic demands and to learners' wishes and aptitudes. At the same time, it had to provide more equal opportunities.

Common trends

Another phenomenon needs mention. Although exchange of experience is not particularly well organized in this field, education does display a number of common trends and characteristics. If these are more evident in some places than others, it is nevertheless significant that they appear in various guises all over the world. In spite of all the cultural, historical, economic and ideological differences that exist among countries, or even regionally or sectorally within a single country, it is interesting and comforting to note that the education enterprise has, in this respect, the character of a worldwide concern. Here are some of the more significant of these trends.

The first concerns the choice of educational models. When it comes to choosing between two basic options—restrictive selection

14

or open admission—the second more commonly finds favour. A number of developed countries are currently at grips with the transition between their earlier, highly selective systems and more open policies. Most developing nations opted at first for open educational systems, but lack of resources and demands of economic development have often led them to introduce more or less strict selection. They are concerned to avoid both the managed dictates of economic plans and the risks of *laissez-faire* anarchy. Accordingly, they seek measures that reconcile respect for man with the demands of society, and individualization with the socialization of education.

Another common trend is towards technocratic systems basically designed to train workers and qualified professionals and to promote scientific and technical advancement. Although such a model tends intrinsically to restrict the educative base and encourage a considerable degree of selection, its effects have been neutralized in many countries where general development concerns have required the partial retention of open systems.

A more recent trend noticed in educational policies is the response to aspirations for freedom expressed by the broad mass of society.[1] This liberating movement is particularly prevalent where economic and social development requires initiative and active participation by the whole population.

Another dominant issue is the change in responsibility for educative action. Until the turn of the century, education was dispensed mainly by the family, religious institutions, subsidized schools, apprentice guilds and independent establishments of higher education. Today, in most countries of the world, these responsibilities rest chiefly on public authorities and the State. There are three main reasons for this. First, a general tendency to rely on public bodies to satisfy social needs; second, in almost all countries—even where private initiative is encouraged—it is considered that the State alone is in a position to assume responsibility for over-all

---

1. '... a system which, for want of a better expression, will later be qualified as "liberating", and which should probably also be termed utopian. Its underlying objective is to pave the way for a new society. Its fundamental principle is disalienation. Its structure, which is open and flexible at every level, and its systematically compensatory teaching methods aim at preventing the recurrence, within the educative system, of differences resulting from the various social backgrounds. The desire to enable every personality to fulfil itself and to endow each individual with the faculties which will allow him to cast an intelligent, critical eye on society around him is the guiding factor in the choice of educative content, which combines art, science and politics, and of teaching methods which rely considerably on the pupils' and students' initiative and on their potential activity, both individually and collectively' (Jacques Fournier, *Politique de l'Éducation*, p. 172, Paris, Seuil, 1971).

educational policy; third, many governments, aware of the importance of education's ever-increasing political role, are determined to
keep control of it.

Among current developments in the structure of educational
systems, the following trends should be noted. Extension of pre-
school education remains limited and generally within the school
framework. The base of primary education is broadening and
children begin going to school at an earlier age. The time spent at
school is lengthening, and reforms often lead to incorporation of
primary education into the first years of secondary school. Enrolment is increasing, and not just at the first level. There is vertical
expansion as well, with growing numbers at higher stages. However, as the school population increases there are more drop-outs
and repeaters. In general, intake is at the lowest level of the system
and outflow halfway up—largely because of failures—or at the top,
after successful completion of studies. Admissions and departures mid-
way through programmes are still rare, but beginning to be accepted.[1]
The justification for strictly selective systems is questioned by critics
who want greater attention paid to relieving the handicaps suffered
by the most underprivileged social groups.

In spite of persistent opposition, school curricula are beginning
to be less burdensome. Variations formerly noticed in the programmes of different elementary schools—which were often a
reflection of social discrimination—are fading rapidly. More and
more, instruction is given in the mother tongue.[2] There is a tendency to raise the age at which choice of specialization is required,[3]

1. 'Throughout the world, educational systems . . . have common features. First, the
   number of pupils at entrance is larger than the number at final graduation. Second,
   the flow upward is regulated, and in some cases impeded, by horizontal barriers of
   required age and attainment. Third, the upward movement of pupils develops according to three patterns: (a) dual division of very high and very low educational attainment; (b) tripartite division of very high, medium, and very low attainment; (c) an
   open system of equivalent though varied levels of attainment for all' (George Z. F.
   Bereday, Essays on World Education: The Crisis of Supply and Demand, p. 98, New York,
   N.Y., Oxford University Press, 1969).
2. In the Soviet Union, for example, which practises the principle of giving instruction
   in the pupils' mother-tongue, education currently takes place in sixty-six languages.
3. In the socialist countries of Europe, the single school with eight-, eleven- and twelve-
   year teaching programmes provides a general polytechnic education on a wide range
   of subjects to children up to the age of 15, 16 or even 18 years. In the Scandinavian
   countries, the unified school with its nine-year programme puts off specialization until
   the age of 15 or 16 years, at the end of the period of general secondary schooling.
   Comprehensive schools in some countries (Canada, the United Kingdom, the United
   States, etc.) permit children to follow polyvalent courses, diversified according to the
   fitness, bent and abilities of each child, while the age at which children are steered
   towards conventional education, either modern or technical, has been put off until 16
   or 17 years (from Roger Moline).

16

which does not prevent more diversification of technical and professional education to fit the growing variety of jobs in modern industrial production. Links between various types of education are multiplying—between general and technical education, polyvalent cultural courses and specialized training and among the humanities, science and technology, which figures increasingly in general education.

In higher education, traditional institutions are in a state of transformation, and all of post-secondary education is expanding and diversifying. This diversification takes two opposite paths. One is the seemingly paradoxical grouping of multiple facilities in one large establishment or under one centralized administration ('multi-universities') and the second is towards smaller, more flexible and more diverse types of institutions to cater for particular audiences in local conditions.[1] Higher education is more and more staggered over several levels. Many new disciplines are being introduced, and interdisciplinary instruction is developing at the same time as higher education is becoming increasingly integrated with scientific research.

The scope of higher education has been enlarged to meet the new requirements of a larger student body, of research and community needs, and the appeals of those who want the university to act as a catalyst for social reform. New kinds of structures, students and curricula entail a thorough revision of selection and evaluation procedures. Student participation in the management of educational institutions and teaching programmes is growing.

All over the world teachers now constitute a very important socio-professional group; in some developing countries they form the largest group of wage-earners.

To all this must be added the general trend towards extending the non-school sector of education. Adult literacy campaigns are making headway, and the distinction between formal elementary education and literacy programmes is beginning to blur. Schools and universities are supplemented and sometimes replaced by a multitude of extra-academic or para-academic activities, calling for the use of methods long neglected or only recently introduced in traditional education. These developments are taking place in two

1. 'Some limit must be set to the size of educational institutions—but in that case some means must also be taken to provide for higher education outside the universities, at home, at the place of work, or in suitable local centres' (James Perkins, *Reform of Higher Education: Mission Impossible?*, New York, N.Y., International Council for Educational Development, June 1971, Occasional Paper, 2).

17

main areas. First, in the socio-professional milieu, with a whole range of activities designed to provide civic training and professional instruction, with schools and other educational institutions offering courses for improvement, retraining or catching up on instruction and universities admitting adults without any formal conditions. Second, in the socio-cultural milieu, through freer and more flexible structures, where self-learning is assisted by provision of new and varied sources of materials and data, by numerous leisure activities and by social and community programmes likely to promote participation and encourage mutual education.

Increasing stress is laid on the links between educational development and other developments in society and the economy.[1]

The concept of educational planning, admittedly limited essentially to school and university education, has been adopted by many governments in the course of the past decade. Effective in varying degrees, complex and technical—and sometimes seen as a magic solution—methodical planning contributes on the whole to a judicious use of available human and financial resources. Finally, education is generally trying to transcend its purely didactic role and set its sights on the full flowering of human faculties.[2]

It is true that most of the phenomena reviewed above are sometimes only trends, not widespread practice, and often appear in varied forms. The essential fact is that *even where these common trends have not yet emerged, or even when they lead to varying results, they are rarely opposed by contrary currents and there is little indication they will take a different course in the future.*

This does not mean there are not highly divergent and even contradictory movements to be seen at other levels. Educational development follows organic paths, some countries tending towards centralization, State control and a global system,[3] and others towards decentralization, loosening of State control and greater variety.

1. On this matter, commission member A. V. Petrovsky has called attention to the particular interest of educational development in the Soviet republics of Central Asia, 'which have made astonishing progress in the field of national education in a short space of time'.
2. 'The mission of the school is no longer—if it ever has been—purely and simply to transmit a certain sum of knowledge. The fundamental aim of a basic school, and one which should guide its teaching above all else, is to give each individual the possibility of developing his aptitudes and tastes freely' (Ingvar Carlsson, Minister of Education and Cultural Affairs, Sweden).
3. As in the Soviet Union. On this subject, commission member A. V. Petrovsky describes the basic principles of the educational system in the U.S.S.R. in the following terms: 'State control and centralized management of public education; universal and

The fact remains that many developments show a general consistency which is all the more remarkable in that they have sprung from very diverse ideas, criticisms and protest movements, which may be grouped into four major trends.

The first of these consists in reforming and reorganizing existing education structures and modernizing teaching methods. With or without attendant structural changes on the socio-economic level, reforms of this sort are on the agenda nearly everywhere. The measures and initiatives taken by public authorities, as well as scientific bodies and individual educators, have implicitly, if not explicitly, prepared the way for major innovations in a number of countries.[1] Numerous changes have taken place in developing countries,[2] largely as the result of central-government initiative, although the scarcity of means and a certain bureaucratic inertia sometimes dampen innovative enthusiasm and incline people to wait for confirmation of experiments undertaken elsewhere. In some countries possessing enormous intellectual and financial resources, the extent and gravity of problems—and the failures to date in confronting them—provide strong arguments for those who stress that fragmentary measures are ineffectual, and thus advocate total reform.

Educational reforms

In countries which more or less recently have gone through social and political upheavals, events have often led to profound structural changes in the educational world, affecting the student base, access to education at various levels, curricula revision and, although to a lesser extent, modernization of methods.[3] The establishment of close ties between schools and their milieu is a top priority in countries which view the education system as a vast mass movement, where each individual who has received an education has a civic duty to teach those who have been denied learning

Structural transformations

compulsory schooling; open entry, free of charge, at all levels; unity and sequence in all types of education.'
1. System-wide reforms and striking innovations can be cited from many countries, e.g. those in the United States and Canada, where locally generated reforms and experiments, notably in modernization of curricula and utilization of the most advanced technologies, are particularly impressive; the reform proposals in the Federal Republic of Germany focusing on democratization and introduction of comprehensive secondary education; the reforms applied or foreseen in Costa Rica, Finland, Japan, Mexico, the Netherlands, Philippines, Sweden (in higher education), Czechoslovakia in vocational education), etc.; and the educational policy launched in France in 1968 which focused mainly on higher education but has had repercussions in other sectors.
2. As, for example, in Bolivia, Brazil, Egypt, Iran, Rwanda, Tunisia and Venezuela.
3. In various ways, these are the objectives which have prompted the reforms undertaken in Chile, India, Indonesia, Peru and Tanzania.

19

opportunities.[1] Similar preoccupations are found in countries trying to separate education from the State by socializing it and making it the direct and active responsibility of those involved.[2] The problem of structural changes is predominant in countries which consider that education should be completely revolutionized, if necessary by outside forces.[3] Here, it is proposed that education and productive work should be completely integrated and that students must cease to form a distinct social category.

In these varied experiments, we should distinguish between specific aspects, determined largely by existing political structures and particular ideologies, and other elements less directly bound to these factors and, as such, susceptible of wider application.

Radical criticism

Belonging to the third movement are proponents of 'de-institutionalizing' education and 'de-schooling' society. Such theses, which as yet have no experimental basis, accordingly remain intellectual speculation.[4] They are grounded on an outright condemnation of 'institutionalized' education and lead either to intermediary formulae or radical plans for a total 'de-schooling' of society. This extreme thesis is developed from the postulate that education constitutes an independent variable in each society and a direct factor in social contradictions.[5] The school's position in society and the play of

1. This is so in Cuba, especially in the context of its literacy campaign, or in the Democratic Republic of Viet-Nam with its people's education experiments.
2. For example in Yugoslavia, where schools are run by councils of delegates representing teachers, pupils, parents and the local community, etc.
3. As in the People's Republic of China, where 'the linking up of educational institutions to the dynamic sector of society whether, in the economic sense, the production sector, or in the political one, that of the proletariat, is designed to create conditions of the most complete interdependence of every teaching unit and the socio-economic collective on which it depends, in such a way that one and the same spirit quickens productive work on the one hand, and on the other, the new culture that is forming. The main formula for this interdependence is a triple alliance, which at every level organically unites first the revolutionary representatives of the proletariat, then the political and military leaders, and finally teachers and learners' (L. Vandermeersch, *Educational Reform (People's Republic of China)*, p. 6, Paris, Unesco, 1971, document of the International Commission on the Development of Education, Innovations Series, 13).
4. The best-known promoter of these ideas is I. Illich, who meets with other critics at the CIDOC centre at Cuernavaca, Mexico, but people elsewhere have also taken up their ideas. They draw a clear distinction between the development of educational possibilities—which they favour—and the institutionalizing of these activities, which they are against. Discussing the part that education should play in future society, Illich has said that he is not opposed to placing an educational enterprise in the middle of a city with human dimensions, but that the real question is, 'Are we moving towards expanded education and programming with the idea that individual growth is a form of *praxis*, or are we heading for *scolae* in the original meaning of the term? . . .'
5. 'What is new about your statements is that education would no longer be dependent and reflexive but would become an independent variable, a causal element in society . . . In other times . . . political and educational theory functioned jointly, as if through symbiosis, the second always appearing as the dependent variable, with the idea that

forces to which it is subjected make it incapable, however, of being the instrument of a true education in the service of mankind or of promoting 'conviviality'.[1] On the contrary, it serves the purposes of repressive, alienating and dehumanizing societies. According to Illich, therefore, institutions should be 'inverted' and the school suppressed, so that man may regain his freedom in a society shorn of formal schooling, resume control of the institution and thereby recover his initiative in education. In their absolute form, these concepts do not seem to conform to any of the world's existing socio-political categories, but their authors think that de-schooling society would sooner or later lead to an over-all change in the social order likely to break the present vicious circle in which education is trapped. Even those who endorse these ideas recognize that while young persons can form their characters and learn by living within the community and performing practical tasks, some form of schooling is still necessary for certain kinds of learning. Be that as it may, these novel theories, which are close to other movements among young intellectuals, are interesting both for the controversies and play of ideas that they touch off and for the lively way in which they propound the problem of education. They help to throw light on possibilities from which other systems, even very different, may well draw inspiration.

A fourth movement, swelled by the dissent of the users themselves, has made its appearance in certain countries where education is of increasing concern to politicians, educationists, researchers and philosophers, as well as to the students themselves and the general public. *Dissent*

The analysis of reactions often seen among working-class people confronted by rigid educational systems—parents who notice negative reactions in their children or students sceptical of the value of the educational possibilities offered them—yields fruitful results. When the school system remains the exclusive preserve of an intellectual élite, the product of the bourgeois class which built the system and continues to dictate its laws and moral values, students become confused by the divorce between an outmoded education and the reality of the world around them. They become frustrated, dissipate their energies, grow bored or put their hopes in something else.

---

the function of the educational system is to cater to social needs' (extract from an interview with Illich in Cuernavaca).

1. By conviviality, Illich means the individual's endowment with the capacity for independent creative relationships with other people and the environment.

Student dissent made a niche for itself in history when widespread criticism infiltrated the heavily defended bastion of education. Despite its sometimes confused and naïve character, its two-edged radicalism, student protest opened a breach.[1] Apathy among the student population constitutes, in its own way, another form of dissent. Disaffection and lack of enthusiasm among students in many countries is undoubtedly a sign that antiquated education systems are being rejected.

Interest in education has never been greater. Among parties, generations and groups, it has become the subject of controversy which often takes on the dimensions of political or ideological battles. Education has become one of the favourite themes of empirical or scientific social criticism. It is easy to see why public figures are taken aback when their authority is challenged, not courteously—as in the past, by a few enlightened personalities—but massively by angry and even rebellious students. Also understandable is the wary reaction to many conclusions from present-day research, to the extent that they undermine the foundations of certain postulates once regarded as immutable. We believe that all these forms of dissent—overt or covert, peaceful or violent, reformist or radical—deserve consideration in one way or another when educational policies and strategies are being mapped out for the coming years and decades.

Where then are we to find the characteristic sign of the present moment, among this constellation of divergent or coincident trends, varying methods, teeming ideas and generous intentions?

For more than twenty years, attention has remained focused on a few major questions—how to obtain quantitative expansion in education, make education democratic, diversify the structures of educational systems and modernize content and methods.

A few years ago a new framework of problems took shape.[2] In

---

1. 'A major breach had thus been pierced, through student action, in the battlement of educational conservatism; and through this breach flared an irresistible torrent of long-standing issues, swelled by new issues and hastened by impatience and fresh hopes. As has happened in cases of destitution, oppression or injustice, the victims here ceased to be resigned to their fate. Those who still accept the defects and inadequacies of education as the outcome of a natural order of things are less and less numerous' (Paul Lengrand, *An Introduction to Lifelong Education*, p. 35, Paris, Unesco, 1970).
2. The document intended to serve as a working paper for the International Conference on the World Crisis in Education (Williamsburg, Virginia, 5–9 October 1967) considers that the world's educational problems stem from a historic conjunction of the following factors: an increase in the numbers of pupils, an acute scarcity of resources,

22

essence, it boils down to three questions. Are school systems capable of meeting the world-wide demand for education? Is it possible to provide them with the immense resources they need? In short, is it possible to continue the development of education along the lines laid down and at the rate we have followed?

To these very pertinent questions must be added queries of a different sort in order to throw fuller light on the dimensions of the problem as it affects man's future development.

We can and we must, given the present state of affairs, inquire into the profound meaning of education for the contemporary world and reassess its responsibilities towards the present generations which it must prepare for tomorrow's world. We must inquire into its powers and its myths, its prospects and its aims.

We conclude with the hope that national authorities responsible for education will avail themselves of assistance offered by international organizations, recognize the primordial necessity of placing educational problems in an over-all context, and seek answers to this all important question—does the educational apparatus, as now conceived, really satisfy the needs and aspirations of man and societies in our time?

galloping costs, the inability to adapt results, inertia and ineffectiveness (Philip H. Coombs, *The World Educational Crisis*, New York, N.Y., Oxford University Press, 1968).

CHAPTER 2

Progress and dead ends

The present state of education in the world is the product of many factors: traditions and structures inherited from the past, with their wealth of acquired knowledge and experience, and also some residual deadweight; new demands which present-day conditions make on education and the flux of ideas, initiative and experiment which they stimulate; and the results, although contradictory, of school development efforts in recent years.

The quantitative facts are ambiguous. Statistics disclose a dual picture. One shows the constant increase in the demand for knowledge and in the number of those who want (or who ought) to go to school, together with the unprecedented expansion of educational activities in recent decades. The other depicts the many dead ends to which this expansion appears to be leading, and the flagrant inequality in the geographical and social distribution of available educational resources.

Before seeking further conclusions, it is important to underline the precautions which must be taken with respect to statistics—their reliability and their validity for purposes of comparative analysis.

All statistics necessarily imply a selection, and any selection is by nature subjective. Statistics, furthermore, are used to express totals and averages, which necessarily mask differences and gaps, and these may be considerable. Statistics, however objective they may be, are worth no more, no less than the use to which they are put by those who present and study them.

Statistics on education come from two main sources: educational establishments and population census. In the case of institutions which are part of a closely supervised administrative system the data provided may be regarded as reliable. Such data can be subjected to tests and revised to ensure their validity over a period of time. However, they are still subject to error which can be significant when making inter-country comparisons. Uncertainty is far greater in the case of reports on literacy, educational attainment, etc., as derived from population census. These reports may be all the more imprecise in so far as they are not always obtained during objective interviews but provided in circumstances which do not usually allow them to be checked.

The uncertainty of quantitative data is not the only source of error in collating statistics for comparative purposes. Definitions of various categories of data often differ according to country, as do statistical techniques. This, combined with differences between the structures of various educational systems, means that the sets of figures to be matched are in many cases far from being comparable.[1] In addition to this, many developing countries lack the qualified personnel, technical equipment and the money required to set up adequately reliable statistical services.

Finally, we cannot ignore the fact that—given the political prestige attached to progress in public education—the authorities concerned are all too often prone to stretch the implications of figures, for both domestic and international purposes.

Keeping these precautions and reservations in mind, we may none the less draw certain conclusions following a quantitative analysis of available statistical material.

1. There are different interpretations of such terms as literacy, elementary schooling, qualified teacher, recurring expenditure, rural school, technical education, higher education, social sciences, etc., in the definition of statistical categories. There are also differences in reporting; for example, reports on enrolment can be made at the beginning of the school year, or at the end of the school year, when it is often lower, or even on the average attendance which could be even lower still. Compulsory schooling can be of four, five, six or even ten years duration; in some countries nearly all education is run by the State, in others, there is a large private sector. Data on expenditure therefore can be misleading. Some countries promote their students automatically, whereas in others students are likely to repeat. Any analysis of the efficiency of education must take this into account. In some universities the student does not decide on his field of study immediately on entry and is even free to change his university. In others, a firm decision has to be made immediately. Again, one cannot compare student flows without taking this into account.

Needs and demand

Definitions Educational needs and educational demand are terms requiring definition; we give them the following meanings.

Each society needs a certain number of educated citizens, more or less specifically qualified, at this or that level and with one or another prospect in view, including that of structural changes. Generally speaking, this need stems in the first place from the economy, but it may also be generated by a variety of other sources, including the State itself, which has to recruit administrative personnel and may also have manifold political motives for pushing educational development. The most positive among these is that of raising the people's cultural level and enhancing their consciousness, out of concern to create the conditions for greater mass participation in democratic processes.

Then there is the demand for education which—although voiced by individuals, including parents—becomes a collective phenomenon.

Four remarks Before making a closer analysis of these components of educational development, we must make four general remarks.

First, the correlation between needs and demand is not always naturally harmonious.

Second, disequilibrium may arise on either side. It is true that in many countries needs precede and exceed demand. But in many others, demand is greater than need.

Third, in many sectors and in most countries, these two factors fail to coincide (even where there appears to be an over-all equilibrium between needs and demand). It is an apparent paradox that these disparities are all the more marked when educational systems attempt to match economic fluctuations. They are less acute in cases where, following a preliminary effort to meet the needs of the economy, a country has gone beyond the phase of trying to adapt education mechanically to the situation and has begun assigning it broader, more complex tasks.

Fourth, educational needs and demand are both increasing enormously, however unequal their respective growth rates may be and whatever discords result. The effects of this increase may be seen nearly everywhere in the world, in the form of a massive increase in school attendance, a continuing tendency to prolong studies, growing recourse to out-of-school education and an ever-greater share of national resources being allocated to education.

Among the multiple causes of this expansion are population growth, economic development, increase in human knowledge, social transformations and psychological motives. Each has its importance, but the most decisive appear to be socio-economic and, as such, may be influenced and partly controlled by political choices and wishes.

But, demographic growth is a root cause; the much publicized and often feared 'population explosion' contains within it an even more portentous 'pupil explosion'. This is not the place to expound world demographic problems and—above all—not the place to discuss possible solutions to them, currently the subject of such heated scientific, sociological, political, ideological, philosophical and even moral controversy. *Demographic factors*

Two facts suffice to indicate the dimensions of this subject:[1]

1. During the first United Nations Development Decade, from 1960 to 1968, the world's population increased from just under 3,000 million to almost 3,500 million human beings. This was a jump of 17 per cent in eight years, an annual growth rate just under 2 per cent (see Fig. 1).

2. During this same eight-year period, the world's total school-age (from 5 to 19 years) population increased from some 955 million children to about 1,150 million, or by approximately 20 per cent, with an annual rate of increase of 2·35 per cent, that is to say at a rate nearly 20 per cent higher than the world population expansion rate.

For the remaining years of this century, predictions are that the number of people of school and university age will increase by more than 1,000 million. This represents an average annual increase of 36 million potential pupils and students!

Even these figures conceal the gravity of the problem, for they refer to world-wide data which, in lumping together figures for industrialized nations and those for developing countries, mask the real situation in most parts of the world.

1. All statistics used in this chapter were supplied by the Unesco Office of Statistics. The educational data do not include statistics from the People's Republic of China, the Democratic People's Republic of Korea and the Democratic Republic of Viet-Nam, but these countries are included when population data alone are mentioned and when literacy statistics are given. When the Arab States are presented in tables as a separate grouping, the figures are shown in parentheses as they are also included partly under Africa and partly under Asia. For further explanation of countries covered and sources of data, see Appendix 7, 'Educational Statistics, Explanatory Note'.

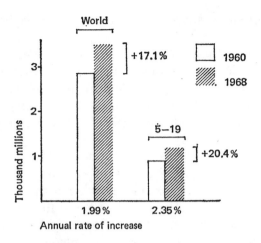

FIG. 1. Population growth: world total and age group, 5–19 years, 1960–68.

The demographic increase (which involves not merely an increase in births but a decreasing death rate and accordingly a lengthening of average life expectancy) is not the same in all countries. The problems it creates are felt far more acutely in some regions than in others (see Fig. 2), especially since the rate of increase is tending to rise even higher in those four regions where it already exceeds the average world annual increase rate (1·99 per cent), whereas in regions where it is approximately equal to, or lower than that mean, its pace is tending to slacken.

Economic development requirements

Another obvious cause of educational expansion stems from economic development. More men and women are directly involved in increasingly complex economic activities. Expanding economies need ever-larger numbers of skilled workers, and technological change transforms traditional trades or creates entirely new job categories requiring large-scale training or retraining. Any action aiming to spur the economy of a country presupposes a parallel effort in education. To this may be added the emergence of new demands from hitherto stagnant, traditional rural economies. This has led to urgent pleas for education from young people and adults, especially from the disadvantaged classes hitherto more or less entirely excluded from organized educational activity.

From the early workshop to the industrial revolution and from the Meiji revolution to the first Soviet five-year plans, *great economic movements have always been accompanied by an expansion in*

28

*education. The facts today confirm that the requirements of econ-
omic development and the appearance of new employment possibilities
are a strong stimulus to the expansion of education.*

Five major population groups present education with especially
serious problems from the point of view of the economy and employment. The first two groups comprise young people who have never
been to school and who are virtually devoid of any preparation for
work, and those who have left school prematurely and who are accordingly hardly better equipped. The situation of the other three
groups causes concern on another level. These are young people
who have successfully completed regular studies at a more or less
high level but find their training ill-adapted to the economy's
needs, adults employed in jobs for which they have not been trained,
and professional people whose training no longer meets the requirements of technical progress. The number of individuals in
each of the five categories has increased in recent years. This development shows that education is often out of phase with economic
trends and the needs of large sectors of society, so that in many
cases it is in fact producing more and more ill-adapted people,
despite increasing costs.

Development objectives in the course of the 1970s will be both

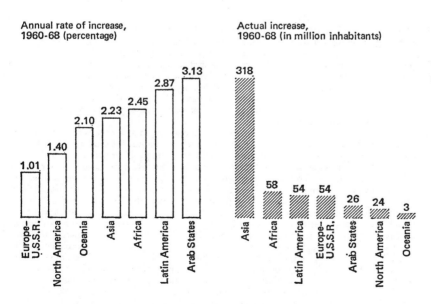

FIG. 2. Population growth by region: total population.

29

broader and more complex. It will be more and more difficult to dissociate economic from social objectives, and educational policies will have to make increasing allowance for their closer interaction. The 1960s were still dominated by the idea of poles of development, which led to technocratic overestimates of the effect of setting up 'islets' of industrialization. The different, predominant features of the years to come will highlight broader development efforts, stronger action to aid agriculture and rural regions in general, a more enlightened public opinion and more active participation of large segments of the population.

During the preceding decade, interest centred mainly on quantitative norms, on training professional and executive personnel and establishing administrative structures. But this present decade will probably be preoccupied with the already dramatic problems of unemployment and by the need to change social structures. Economic development has no meaning unless it results in abolition of privilege and more justice for all mankind.[1]

In these times of socio-economic, scientific and technological change, societies can no longer content themselves, as they are prone to do, with 'perpetually renewing the conditions of their own existence', as Durkheim put it. They need education enabling them to adapt to change and even assist it.[2]

1. 'The ultimate objective of development must be to bring about sustained improvement in the well-being of the individual and bestow benefits on all. If undue privileges, extremes of wealth and social injustices persist, then development fails in its essential purpose. This calls for a global development strategy based on joint and concentrated action by developing and developed countries in all spheres of economic and social life: in industry and agriculture, in trade and finance, in employment and education, in health and housing, in science and technology' (United Nations General Assembly, 17 October 1970: 'An International Development Strategy for the Second United Nations Development Decade').
2. In other terms: 'If in the 1970s education is looked upon as a means to a wider range of economic and social objectives, the efficiency of the educational system will refer to a wider range of objectives. The re-statement of the problem will be: how can education use resources so that it is effective in achieving whatever goals society sets for it?' (OECD, 1970). The following remarks by two Soviet specialists may be taken to have a similar meaning: 'One of the chief difficulties in forecasting educational development (quantitative development in particular) is that the basic method in this field is one of projection. Of course, projection from the most important past and present trends would be an ideal way of investigating the future if we could count on a smooth, evolutionary development of education within a stable system of economic and social conditions. There are, however, no firm grounds for supposing that such will be the case. This is why it is impossible to treat the forecasting of educational development as a separate problem: it is only a part, though a very important one, of the problem of social and economic forecasting for separate countries or groups of countries' (A. I. Markouchevitch and A. V. Petrovsky, *Where is Education Heading?*, p. 4, Paris, Unesco, 1971, document of the International Commission on the Development of Education, Opinions Series, 4).

Other concerns, resulting from more specific and deliberate considerations, also help to account for growing government interest in education. In many countries, education—and especially the reduction of illiteracy—appears to be the best way to forge and safeguard national unity. For newly independent countries, rapid educational development is a form of national emancipation, an essential aspect of the whole decolonization process. By modifying some pre-established features of the education system, authorities may endeavour to undermine the hegemony exercised by privileged social groups, or to create or re-create certain fundamental conditions for a quality of life which would enable a people in straitened circumstances to compare advantageously with materially prosperous nations.[1]

Political considerations

These manifold motives which governments may have for encouraging the development of education receive further impetus from pressure at the other pole—from parents and from potential or existing pupils and students. Whether it takes the form of demands, protest or even political hostility, its effect tends to run parallel to that produced by official policies for educational expansion.

Effects of pressure from the people

The social demand for education is constantly increasing. Pupils on one level strive for the level above. Parents generally want their children to have a higher degree of education than they had themselves. Education is regarded as the primary instrument in social mobility, even if the vistas it is reputed to open up turn out to be fictitious. In developing countries, university degrees and diplomas often take on the value of substitutes for titles and privileges customarily recognized in ancient, feudal-style societies, many of whose social structures survived despite changes in régime. These considerations of prestige and form sometimes strongly influence the orientation given to educational systems and the resources allocated to different disciplines.

1. 'The quest for the quality of life which is the essence of modern education offers new hope and opportunity to poor and materially deprived societies. With the right type of education a developing society can attain the satisfaction, harmony and comprehension that may elude a more prosperous community. Education could, indeed, be the most potent factor in eventually reducing the gap between affluence and poverty which is widening so alarmingly in terms of *per capita* income. Though education cannot do much in equalizing money incomes in the short run, it can certainly do far more in enriching the quality of life for the poor as well as the rich. The dazzling achievements of man in outer space have to be matched by an educational revolution affecting his inner space also; a new union of science and spirituality is the main challenge posed to those who seek a renewal of education' (Prem Kirpal, 'Modernization of Education in South Asia: The Search for Quality', *International Review of Education*, No. XVII, 1971).

Sociology of the demand for education

Thus, the growth in the demand for education, while remaining fundamentally determined by the needs of economic development, follows a sociological mechanism with a logic of its own, so that the law of supply and demand of the labour market is far from operating directly, at least in the short run. To understand why, we do not need to quit the field of socio-economic analysis and play the devil's advocate for irrational motives. There is, indeed, some justification for such behaviour. One does not embark on studies towards a degree with one's eye merely on the morrow but on an entire life-time—a lifetime which is likely to reach its high point somewhere around the year 2000. Who could be blamed for believing, even if unconsciously, that economic development will speed up, that employment possibilities will multiply, that the qualifications required everywhere will become steadily higher, and for conceiving those hopes to be a right, if not for oneself then at least for one's children?

Attempts to rationalize the organization of school systems by programming the production of qualified persons in a direct line with manpower forecasts and economic development plans are thwarted above all by the fact that parents do not agree to their children being refused the education required for the modern sector of the economy, even when this has only a limited or minimal capacity for absorbing them. It follows that political pressure, to the extent that it makes abundant allowance for parental aspirations, tends constantly to require the educational system to operate in advance of real employment outlets. These sometimes ill-grounded hopes and the ensuing disappointments have at least the merit of bringing those concerned to an often acute awareness of certain very real defects in educational systems, and of encouraging public opinion to voice criticism, which may have a salutary effect.

The combination of all these needs and interests accounts for *the unprecedented pressure of the demand for education at all levels and in all its forms.*

Regional distribution of demand

Although this pressure exists everywhere, it is not felt to the same extent in all parts of the world, because of the unequal regional distribution of people under 24 years of age, the different degrees of school enrolment achieved at different levels and the differences in socio-economic conditions (see Fig. 3 and Table 1).

The potential demand for education in developing countries remains enormous at the primary and secondary levels—which are the most crowded.

32

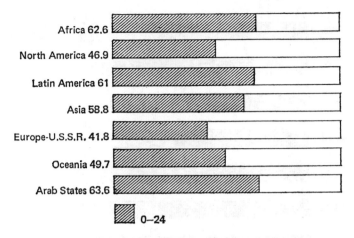

FIG. 3. Population 0–24 years old by regions as percentage of total population 1968.

In the developed regions (North America, U.S.S.R., Europe, Japan and part of Oceania[1]) the growing demand for education is concentrated on the secondary level and universities. Figure 4 shows that the proportion of all school-enrolled children attending primary school is between 54 and 68 per cent in developed regions, while elsewhere it remains about 80 per cent.

Universal school enrolment at the primary level has been virtually achieved in some developing countries and in the industrialized

TABLE 1. School enrolment rates (percentages) in 1967/68

Region	Children of primary-school age attending school (at any level)	Children of secondary-school age attending school (at any level)	Students registered for higher education in relation to young people aged 20–24
North America	98	92	44·5
Europe and U.S.S.R.	97	65	16·7
Oceania	95	60	15·0
Latin America	75	35	5·0
Asia	55	30	4·7
Arab States	(50)	(25)	(3·1)
Africa	40	15	1·3

1. Australia and New Zealand.

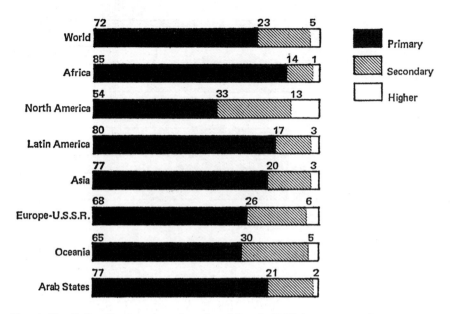

FIG. 4. Pupil distribution, by educational level, 1968 (percentages).

nations. Some of the latter have a secondary-school attendance in excess of 70 per cent, the most advanced reaching 90 per cent. Yet more than half the total population of developing regions have never been to school, less than 30 per cent of their young people go to secondary school and less than 5 per cent go on to higher education.

From the foregoing, it emerges that the multiple political, social, demographic and economic factors which have made such a powerful contribution to the quantitative development of educational needs and demand in recent times have also, despite their contradictory aspects, had a no less remarkable convergent effect at the qualitative level. They have brought about a decisive change in attitudes not only among societies and authorities but also among individuals themselves—taken *en masse*—towards education. We may say that from now on *if education has not yet assumed the place it deserves in the existence of all people it has at least come to represent something for each individual.*

The demand for education, characteristic of our time, is of unprecedented dimensions and strength. This evolution is taking place— for various yet concordant reasons—in all regions of the world, whatever their level of economic development, their demographic growth rate, population density, extent of technological progress, and whatever each country's culture and political system. It is incontestably a universal historical phenomenon.

All indications are that this trend will gather momentum. It seems to us to be irreversible. Future educational policies must be formulated on this basic fact.

Expansions and limits

Most governments have declared their readiness to do everything possible to meet this influx of demands and needs.

During the eight-year period from 1960 to 1968, the total number of those attending schools rose from about 325 million to some 460 million (see Fig. 5). This increase of 135 million, that is to say

Expansion speeded

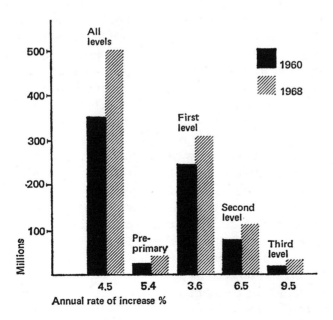

FIG. 5. School enrolments 1960–68.

of more than 40 per cent—an annual average of 4·5 per cent—is 100 per cent higher than the corresponding rates of increase in the population of school-attendance age and 135 per cent higher than the world demographic increase rate.

Moreover, expansion of schooling on a world-wide scale is probably even higher than world figures published by Unesco indicate. For although precise data on the People's Republic of China, the Democratic People's Republic of Korea and the Democratic Republic of Viet-Nam are not available, estimates of total school enrolments in these three countries come close to 150 million, which would swell the over-all world figures cited above by about one-third. If we include approximately 40 million pupils attending pre-school establishments, we may say with little risk of error that *the number of persons receiving formal, institutionalized education throughout the world borders on 650 million.*

Towards universal school enrolment

It is striking to note that the entire world is now moving towards one and the same objective: universal school attendance. The aim is at the primary level in countries where this has not yet been legally instituted or has yet to come into effect; or, in cases where basic schooling has been or is being broadly achieved, at the 'upper primary' or secondary level (see Appendix 9). Without gainsaying the earlier extension of certain traditional or religious forms of basic education which already existed in many countries, the above-mentioned fact is all the more remarkable in that the principle of giving every child an elementary education only goes back a century or even, in most regions, a few decades or years. The considerable progress made in such a short time is due essentially to developing countries' efforts, and those which have not yet officially instituted compulsory schooling (a total of twenty) are not necessarily the least diligent in this respect.

For laws do not necessarily create facts in this kind of activity. Decisions and plans are difficult to translate into reality. Many countries have undeniably failed to achieve educational targets contained in their short- or medium-term programmes or in legislative texts and solemn declarations, even when they have been written into the constitution (as may be seen from official figures themselves which—as we noted above—do not always provide every guarantee of objectivity).

While increase in elementary school enrolment has been considerable, world-wide progress in higher, secondary and pre-school education has been even faster than in primary education. Second-

36

ary education has progressed about one and a half times as fast as primary, and higher education more than twice as fast. Percentage growth rates by educational level during 1960–68 were as follows: higher education, $+107$; secondary education, $+65$; pre-school education, $+45$; and primary education, $+33$.

Numerically speaking, the problem of providing teachers to handle this expansion has in general been met. Whereas the school-enrolment rate increased an average of 4·5 per cent annually between 1960 and 1968, the increase in the teaching force not only equalled but overtook that rate, at an annual average of 4·7 per cent. The number of teachers rose from 12·6 million to 18·2 million, an over-all increase of 50 per cent.

Recruiting teachers

To have a complete view of the global situation in education, we must add to the school growth indicated above the increase in innumerable out-of-school activities. These comprise educational radio and television broadcasts (public or private), adult literacy programmes, people's universities, correspondence courses, a multiplicity of cultural activities, study circles, etc. To these may be added diverse educational activities on the vocational level, mainly in the industrialized countries: apprenticeship programmes, workers' promotion courses, advanced training and conversion courses, management training schemes and seminars, etc.[1] And media available or potentially available for educational purposes, in the broad sense of the term, are by no means limited to strictly defined educational activities and methods. These also include: the press (7,980 daily newspapers of general interest, with a total printing of 350 million papers, plus 615 million copies of periodicals); books (487,000 titles published in 1968); libraries (798,297 national, public, school, university and specialized establishments) containing some 5,000 million volumes; 14,374 museums, visited by hundreds of millions of people annually; 674 million radio sets, receiving programmes from 18,850 transmitting stations, and about 250 million television receivers picking up 13,140 stations; and films distributed to a network comprising some 252,000 cinemas.

Out-of-school potential

One's satisfaction, at first sight, at the growth rates and figures cited above is considerably tempered by the following two facts.

First, between 1960 and 1968, in absolute figures the number

Partly deceptive figures

---

1. In the Federal Republic of Germany, for example, industry itself handles 90 per cent of industrial training. In the United States, spending by industry on technical and vocational training is estimated to equal one-third of total public expenditure on education (or more than $10,000 million).

of children aged between 5 and 14 who were unable to attend school has increased by 17 million. This means that every year some 2 million more children were refused the right to an education.

Furthermore, a particularly deceptive illusion is created here by grouping all world statistics together. Results have been far more modest than either hopes or needs precisely in the four regions of the world lagging furthest behind the others. In fact, during the eight years in question, the proportion of school-age children attending primary or secondary schools rose by a total of no more than 4 percentage points in Africa, 9 points in Asia and 10 points in Latin America and the Arab States.

If we assume that the rates of population growth and school enrolment continue to develop in the 1970s in accordance with the rates recorded over the past decade, it follows that *in 1980 the number of children aged between 5 and 14 not attending school will total approximately 230 million.*

Literacy and illiteracy

Statistics on adult illiteracy, without which any status report on world education would be incomplete, are as shown in Table 2.

TABLE 2. World illiteracy statistics

Year	Estimated world adult population (over 15) (millions)			Illiteracy rate (%)
	Total	Literates	Illiterates	
1950	1,579	879	700	44·3
1960	1,869	1,134	735	39·3
1970	2,287	1,504	783	34·2

The percentage of illiterates has shrunk, but the number of illiterates has continued to increase. However, this at first sight discouraging result contains within it one positive fact: if literacy had only increased at the same rate as in the two preceding decades, the number of illiterate adults would have risen to 810 million by 1970; instead, it was 27 million less than that figure. This may be regarded as a turning-point, since it is the first time that the past trend has been reversed.

It would be a mistake, however, to harbour too many illusions as to developments in the real literacy situation in vast regions of the developing world merely after glancing at global statistics. For they reflect it less and less accurately, as the final outposts of illiteracy in the industrialized nations are conquered or absorbed. Estimates for 1970 are that in Africa and the Arab States only one adult (i. e. over 15) in four can read and write, while in Asia hardly more than half of the adult population is literate. In absolute figures, it is estimated there are 40 million illiterates in Latin America, 50 million in the Arab States, 143 million in Africa and more than 500 million in Asia.

As to the future, preliminary estimates by experts in education statistics predict substantially greater results in the 1970s than those recorded in the 1960s. This forecast is based on the combined effects expected from progress in primary school enrolment and literacy programmes, and from ageing in the population. None the less, given a world adult-population forecast of 2,823 million at the end of the 1970s, and assuming that some 500 million more individuals will then be able to read and write, it is thought that *in 1980, there will still be 820 million adult illiterates and a world adult illiteracy rate of 29 per cent.*

Yet the problem is of a different kind. Even in areas where campaigns against illiteracy appear to be producing results, these are frequently of a purely formal nature without any really significant consequences for educational development. All in all, few literacy campaigns have achieved what are generally agreed nowadays to be the real objectives of the struggle against illiteracy. The aim is not simply to enable an illiterate person to decipher words in a textbook but to become better integrated into his environment, to have a better grasp of real life, to enhance his personal dignity, to have access to sources of knowledge which he personally may find useful, to acquire the know-how and the techniques he needs in order to lead a better life. If we compare the enormous (the word is not too strong) human effort which many countries have devoted to campaigns of this kind in the past to the modest results obtained, and if we also consider the national and political prestige attached to the publication of victory bulletins on this subject which are often more real on paper than in fact, we may well take this disappointing experience as a timely warning against certain risks and perils threatening the school-expansion campaign currently under way.

Lessons from literacy campaigns

Many countries have been unable to achieve their objectives and many governments have made impractical promises. Among parents and young people, very many hopes—either prematurely aroused or, at least, insufficiently qualified—continue to be frustrated. Awareness of these disappointments should lead us to rethink many problems and to take care not to confuse even the most praiseworthy wishes with reality. If we fail to do so, we shall risk creating unhealthy situations and incurring the reproach that we are succumbing to demagogy in this particularly delicate field of social action.

But wisdom cannot be reduced to adapting plans, promises and hopes to the dimensions of available means. It also involves seeking not only more means, but other means, so that the limits of what is possible may be extended by introducing a new scale.

With this in mind, we may conclude these remarks with the following:

Since the end of the Second World War, an immense effort has been made to extend school enrolment for children and adolescents and to combat adult illiteracy. It has produced considerable results. However, it is becoming evident that even if this effort were increased to its utmost, using the same means as in the past, it would not enable foreseeable needs to be met.

Whence the question: should we rely only on existing educational systems to carry out the tasks which lie ahead? The present-day world is marked by a population explosion, the imperative requirements of economic development and the fight against hunger, the scientific and technological revolution, the multiplication of knowledge, the rise of the masses, the consequences and new expressions of the democratic idea, the extension and proliferation of information and communication media. This world is making and will make many new demands on education. Does it not contain new means which education may and must make use of, if it is not to fail in its task?

Resources and means

The expansion of education has required and will continue to require a massive increase in spending.

World expenditure   In 1968, public expenditure on education rose to about $132,000

40

million, as against $54,400 million in 1960–61, an increase of nearly 150 per cent in only eight years.[1]

These figures do not include expenditures by the People's Republic of China, the Democratic People's Republic of Korea and the Democratic Republic of Viet-Nam. Nor do they include credits allocated in many countries to private education or outlays for educational activities by various government offices such as the Ministry of Labour, the Ministry of Agriculture, the Ministry of Defence, etc., or by public bodies such as radio or television stations broadcasting educational programmes. Neither do these figures allow for the considerable cost of countless out-of-school and non-governmental educational activities in many countries, or for family spending on schoolchildren's equipment, food, clothing and transport.[2] An over-all estimate including all these factors would probably lead to a figure for world spending on education of more than $200,000 million annually.

As concerns public financing alone, the proportion of provision for education in State budgets is generally rising. By region, increases from 1960 to 1965 were as follows: from 14·5 per cent to 16·4 per cent in Africa; from 15·6 per cent to 17·6 per cent in North America; from 12·6 per cent to 15·4 per cent in Latin America; from 11·8 per cent to 13·2 per cent in Asia; from 13·5 per cent to 15 per cent in Europe and the Soviet Union; from 10·4 per cent to 15·7 per cent in Oceania. On the world level, the proportion of national budgets slated for educational expenses rose from 13·5 per cent in 1960 to 15·5 per cent in 1965; at present it is probably about

Budgetary expenditure

1. Any attempt to evaluate world spending on education runs into very great difficulty, due not only to the fragmentary nature of the data available but also to the fundamental problem of converting national currencies into one standard exchange currency (the U.S. dollar). Because of the lack of complete and reliable information, the value of the figures presented here must be considered to be that of approximate over-all estimates. Expenditure being expressed in terms of current prices, its increase may be imputed to a certain extent (some 5 to 6 per cent) to the effects of inflation. (Although inflation during the 1960–68 period was far greater in certain Latin American and Asian countries than in others, conversion into U.S. dollars corrects this difference to a large extent, since the exchange rate applied takes into account the real devaluation of national currencies in relation to the dollar. Apart from the technical difficulties which would have been involved in calculating expenditure at constant prices, expressing our estimates in terms of current prices seemed to us to be more appropriate to our argument, based as it is essentially on a comparison between expenditure on education and the over-all volume of national resources, or between the rates of increase of these and other indicators, also expressed in terms of current prices.
2. This expenditure, often overlooked, is substantial. A recent study (Pierre Daumard, *Le Prix de l'Enseignement en France*, Paris, 1969) states that, in 1964, a family's spending directly related to its children's school-attendance averaged 1,180 francs per child—a total of 7,700 million francs, more than 44 per cent of the total public expenditure on education (17,400 million francs).

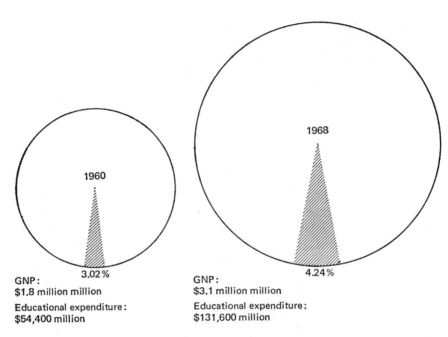

FIG. 6. Educational expenditure as percentage of world GNP, 1960 and 1968.

16 per cent. In 1967, eighteen countries allocated more than 20 per cent of their budgets to education expenses, whereas in 1960 this was true only of six.

Educational expenditure and GNP

An even more significant fact is that average world-wide public spending on education is increasing more rapidly than the average world-wide gross national product (the People's Republic of China is not included here), since it took up 3·02 per cent of world average GNP in 1960 and 4·24 per cent in 1968 (see Fig. 6). Among regions, it ranges between 3·6 per cent (for Latin America) and 5·9 per cent (for North America).

Comparative increase in costs

If we compare world increase in enrolment in traditional school systems for the three levels of instruction with that of spending on such instruction, we see that for the period between 1960 and 1968 the enrolment figure rose by 4·5 per cent annually whereas the corresponding annual increase in spending was 11·7 per cent. Proportions for the same period by region are as shown in Table 3.

School wastage

This increase in spending has not prevented traditional educational systems from displaying serious symptoms of inefficiency. One of the most flagrant of these is the extent of wastage, that is,

42

TABLE 3. School enrolment and expenditure, percentage annual rate of increase, 1960–68

Region	Enrolments at all three levels	Spending allocated to education
Africa	6·2	10
North America	3	12·1
Latin America	6·2	11·3
Asia	5·6	14·1
Europe and U.S.S.R.	3·0	11·0
Oceania	3·7	11·7
Arab States	(6·6)	(8·5)

TABLE 4. School wastage values in first-level education in various regions

Region	Extreme values for input/output ratio[1] in the region's countries	Mean value of the input/output ratio
Africa	1·24–3·55	2·00
Latin America	1·53–2·42	1·90
Asia	1·00–2·48	1·31
Europe	1·00–1·56	1·20

1. The cost of wastage in non-monetary terms is expressed by the relationship between the 'number of student-years invested' per successful graduate and the duration of the cycle or level of education. The result is an input/output ratio which is used as a measure of internal efficiency. For a system functioning under optimum conditions this ratio would be equal to 1; the wastage 'cost' is measured by the difference between the figure expressing this ratio and the figure 1. Figures given in this table were calculated on the basis of data received from eighteen African countries, thirteen Latin American countries, thirteen Asian countries and eleven European countries.

the rate at which students are repeating or abandoning courses. (Table 4.) The dimensions of this problem are typified in a 1969 Unesco inquiry covering the years 1960–61 and 1967–68.

In half the countries of the world, half the children enrolled in schools fail to complete the primary cycle. Even if we consider only those who leave school after their first, second or third year—that is, for the most part, having acquired little lasting benefit—the fact remains that in many countries the money spent on them absorbs between 20 and 40 per cent of the total State education budget.

This wastage is therefore, quantitatively speaking, a very serious phenomenon. But it has a further, symptomatic interest in that it points out the inefficiency and imperfection of the educational systems which give rise to it, and provides a clear illustration of the fact that the frequently cited antinomy between the nominal increase in expenditure on education and the relative decrease in yield from educational activity is due essentially to qualitative factors.

Distribution of financial resources

In seeking greater returns from educational expenditure, the total volume of financial resources is not the sole determining factor. In many respects, the way in which they are distributed is even more crucial. From this point of view, public spending on education continues to be concentrated on the institutionalized forms of teaching, reserved for children and adolescents attending schools.[1]

Despite oft-stated intentions, such budgeting is an expression of the enduring rule of allocating most public funds for the specific benefit of the school and university population. This reflects the old idea that schooling is the only valid education and that the time for learning is limited to traditional school age.

Special financial treatment for schools

It is increasingly evident that in most countries—and therefore for most people—this narrow conception, this unilateral method of financing needs, is fundamentally unjust. For hundreds of millions of illiterate people in the world, school can no longer be of help. In the developing countries, nearly half the children of primary school age today are condemned, no matter what happens, to grow up without ever having attended a class. Even if we acknowledge the pedagogic and didactic superiority of methodical, rigorous instruction in school, a concern for balance combined with the requirements of social and economic development, would seem to make it imperative to avoid sacrificing one person in every two among the present generation, and many of those in future generations, by providing for more immediate, more practical, more massive and also more lively non-traditional educational patterns. This might be accomplished—in terms of unit cost—at less expense than present systems; for the aim is to change as far and as quickly

1. The following figures (percentages) show as examples the budget breakdown of three countries to illustrate the uneven sectoral distribution of State spending on education: *country A*, primary education 39, secondary education 18·1, universities 18·1, subsidies for private institutions, 4, other programmes 6·8, general administration 10, other State institutions 4; *country B*, primary education 46·8, secondary education 13·1, higher education 15·8, technical and professional 10·2, normal 5·7, administration and other (such as spending allocated to popularization services and cultural activities) 8·4; *country C*, primary education 50, general secondary education 31, secondary technical education 6, professional 6, other 7.

44

TABLE 5. World rates of increase in public educational expenditure (percentages)

Region	Mean annual increase rate, 1960–68	Increase rate, 1967–68
Africa	10·0	9·2
North America	12·1	13·2
Latin America	11·3	10·8
Asia	14·1	12·6
Europe and U.S.S.R.	11·0	7·9
Oceania	11·7	3·6
Arab States	8·5	10·7

as possible the situation in which millions of adolescents, who have never been to school or who have left school prematurely, find themselves abandoned, and, further, to provide the great mass of adult illiterates with continual learning opportunities.

Does this mean that, from one day to the next, existing financial resources should be redistributed by reducing credits allocated to schools and turning over the difference to out-of-school activities? Assuredly not. But given the fact that State educational expenditure is increasing from year to year, we must decide what proportion of the additional increment should be used to develop and perfect formal school establishments and what amount should be allocated to other needs, especially to adult education, pre-school education and the development of educational technology. A decision to favour the latter would begin, through the usual operations of budget renewals and increases in credits, the process of gradually correcting the internal structure of education budgets.

This is all the more urgent inasmuch as an examination of the general trend of educational spending shows that while the increase remains considerable it has begun to slow down in the past few years (Table 5). (It is difficult, however, to ascertain, at least in general terms, to what extent this development is the cause and to what extent the effect of the simultaneous slow-down in the rate of increase in school enrolment.) Increases in spending fell from an average of 12·1 per cent between 1960 and 1965 to 10·5 per cent from 1967/68 (with school-enrolment increases falling from 5 per cent for 1960/65 to 3·6 per cent in recent times). More detailed analysis has shown that this phenomenon has occurred in five of the seven regions under consideration.

Slower rates of increase

45

This does not mean that educational expenditure will not continue to increase. In areas where this increase has begun to waver it would not appear, in general, to have reached a ceiling.

It seems, however, that many countries are beginning to realize the inadequacy of calculating increases in State education budgets merely on the basis of increased enrolments in the traditional school system. Official organizations called in to evaluate these matters have become more demanding on financial questions.[1] The fact is that justified criticism of the low yield from many traditional-style educational activities, in relation to their cost, is apt to clamp a brake on the current continuing expansion of resources devoted to education unless major reforms are introduced in the distribution and utilization of funds, thereby justifying the sacrifices demanded for this purpose from the entire society.

Criteria: rigid or variable?

Does this mean, then, that there may be predetermined criteria by which a 'rational' rate of educational expenditure may be mathematically ascertained, covering all circumstances and any country, which should be adhered to or which would be dangerous to exceed? We do not believe so at all, nor do we believe that any international body, this commission included, can claim to lay down rules and norms in this matter. All we feel entitled to say on this point may be summed up as follows.

Obviously at any given period, each country has limits which are for that country to ascertain, the 'intolerance thresholds' beyond which the burden of educational expenses could dangerously disturb economic balance. The question of the volume and even the distribution of budgetary expenditure goes far beyond the framework of educational policies, in the strict sense of this term, and that of budgetary techniques. Just as the educational yield, in so far as it may be quantified, can only be evaluated in socio-economic terms (which is not in the least to deny its qualitative evaluation in relation to culture, democracy and individual rights), so the price of education is not limited solely to the sum of accountable spending. It also comprises considerable social and economic cost in terms of labour, investments and priorities. Failure to allow for all these factors involves running the risk that the sacrifices any given society

1. cf. the report by the Indian Education Commission (*Education and National Development, Report of the Education Commission 1964–1966*, New Delhi, Ministry of Education, 1966), concluding that linear increase in education could only lead to failure, the report by the Commission on Educational Reform in Mexico (*Aportaciones al Estudio de los Problemas de la Educación*, Mexico, Secretaría de Educación Pública, 1971), and many others.

agrees to make for its educational system may not be accurately measured and programmed as a function of the variation in yield which that society expects, but as a function of the system's own intrinsic needs.

Highly different individual choices may be justified, in the light of these considerations, according to the country in question. A nation deriving most of its revenue from channelling a large quantity of manpower into the secondary or tertiary sectors of its economy can and must apply a different policy, even in budgetary matters, than a nation living essentially off exports of raw materials. For this reason, it may well happen that a country already spending a quarter of its budget on education may be taking healthy action, in the interest of technological progress or the development of public utilities, by deciding to increase educational spending still further. Another country, devoting a far more modest proportion of its resources to education, would be taking a great financial and economic risk, paving the way to inflation and/or sacrificing other investments by making massive increases in educational expenditure.

We have grown used to hearing political discussions on education being reduced to the question of how much it is reasonable and possible to increase credits allocated to school education for the current year or the plan period ahead. As a rider to this, we hear the subsidiary query as to what share of the credits so voted or decreed should be respectively allocated to the various educational levels, ranging from primary to higher.

Restructuring expenditure

However, this debate is changing. Until now, the school as an institution and symbol has had its prestige strengthened, its position confirmed, through the extension of school systems in accordance with the combined wishes of public authorities, parents and young people and also by the extent of the sacrifices which society made on its behalf. But now the massive demands being made on schools, the often vehement calls for a more equitable sharing of the existing educational potential and the growing insistence of all the people who have never had, or fear they will never have, access to instruction, would appear to be leading to a reappraisal of the school's supreme, or reputedly supreme, hegemony in the world of education. It is hard to see how States can continue setting aside with impunity an ever greater proportion of their resources for an activity which, in spite of everything, remains confined to a fraction of their population, without endeavouring to devise forms

47

of education which would assure a better return on their money.[1]
The concept of global education (in school and out of school) and
of lifelong education (all through life as well as during childhood
and adolescence) is emerging clearly as a conscious aspiration. It
is a response to multiple requirements, both in countries suffering
from a stagnant, traditional economy and in those undergoing
dynamic evolution. It seems logical to deduce that governments,
harassed by difficulties and contradictions in their school programmes, will in the fairly near future respond to this current (fed
by both frustration and hope, like all social movements capable of
engendering historic changes) by adapting and substantially restructuring their educational systems.

---

*There has in general been broad agreement on making the financial
sacrifices needed to cover the demand for education. They have increased at an even faster rate than has the number of pupils.*

*There is no absolute theoretical 'ceiling' or 'floor' for educational
spending. In order to find the 'optimal' level for such spending, it
must be determined less in terms of the volume of available financing
resources than by rigorously applying the fundamental political and
economic options of State and society, even to public education hitherto
regarded as sacrosanct.*

*In this respect, increasing financial resources, however necessary
this may be, is not the only possible solution. A no less effective expedient
may be to make more judicious budgetary choices and to apportion
effort and means in more productive fashion, in particular by innovations in the use of supplementary resources allocated to education.*

*With a few possible exceptions, governments are facing a dilemma.
On one hand, it is or will eventually become impossible or at least
irrational to mobilize financial resources in direct proportion to the*

1. 'When a country reaches the point of having to make over a considerable portion of
its budget to education, and when that education yields few diplomas and even fewer
productive citizens, it can no longer be content with solutions devised merely to improve the "quality" of instruction in school or of teachers' training or even to adapt
professional training to employment requirements. Such a country is compelled to tap
new resources, no longer measurable in budgetary terms since—by definition—the
budgetary resources have been exhausted. At this point, "educational resources" takes
on a new meaning: from then on, the entire means of the community are made available to all its members. Even if officials are drawn from ministries other than the
Education Ministry, even if students and pensioners are brought in, aided by communication media, transport, housing, all human and material means must be enlisted and
"optimized", the better to serve that community's ultimate aims' (Sylvain Lourié,
statement during the fourth meeting of the International Commission on the Development of Education, Paris, Unesco, 6 October 1971).

total demand for schooling. On the other, the demand for education is already or soon will be of far greater dimensions than traditional educational systems have the capacity to handle, even when operating at optimum levels. Under these circumstances, governments can hardly fail to question whether trying to satisfy this demand uniquely through existing institutions and budgets is reasonable, and whether it would not be more appropriate to use other forms and other means.

Imbalance and inequality

The ever-growing gap between industrialized and developing countries has produced the fundamental drama of the contemporary world.

Certainly, this division is due partly to differences—variations in culture, values, goals, paths—which imply no notion of 'being ahead' or 'lagging behind'. It is a good intellectual rule in treating this subject to exclude words such as 'outdistancing' and 'catching up' from one's vocabulary. There is even a logical snare in the very expressions 'developed country' and 'developing country', for they may suggest that the condition towards which nations in the 'third world' aspire is by definition what is found today in allegedly developed countries, as if they too were not involved in a process of continual development.[1]

The fact remains that whatever idea each nation forms of its own future, it will foresee abundant development of its natural and human resources. The history of industrialized societies shows how science and technology make immense contributions to such development. Here, essentially, is the objectively negative and harmful imbalance between the plenty enjoyed by some and the penury suffered by others. And it is difficult to see how this division can ever be overcome—quite the contrary—without an organized, rational transfer, an equitable redistribution, of the scientific and technological stockpile which has accumulated at one pole of the community of mankind.

1. The world-wide distinction between two groups of countries in terms of their levels of development is in any case an obvious simplification, and one could hardly presume to make any categorical deductions from it as to this or that country's possible responsibilities towards others, in present circumstances, and the extent of its duty to show solidarity.

49

Findings

*Regional
inequalities*

Clearly, education, as the mediator of knowledge, has a major role to play here. One of the basic conditions for preventing this division from growing even greater is to eliminate the disparate availability of the right to education for people in different parts of the world. But once again, exactly the opposite is happening.

In 1968, the developed nations' expenditure on education rose to more than $120,000 million, and that of developing countries to less than $12,000 million. With about one-third the population and only one-quarter of the young people in the world, industrialized countries spent ten times more money on education than the developing countries.

The most serious aspect of this enormous difference is that it is growing larger. From 1960 to 1968, industrialized nations' educational expenditure increased from 3·52 per cent to 4·80 per cent of their gross national product, which in turn, during the same period, increased by 78 per cent. Developing countries' educational expenditure also took up a larger percentage of their GNP (at a slower rate of increase, however, the figure rising from 2·73 to 3·91 per cent), but their over-all revenue itself increased only by 62 per cent. The consequence is that industrialized regions' educational spending increased by 145 per cent and that of developing countries by only 130 per cent (see Fig. 7).

In other words, there is an absolute increase in educational expenditure in the developing countries, but they are allocating a decreasing percentage of world-wide expenditure in this area. (The figure in 1960 was 9 per cent; in 1968, 8·6 per cent.)

This means that large-scale efforts, financial sacrifices and considerable results—in the education race as in the march to economic progress—have all failed to prevent the continued widening of the gap between industrialized and developing countries.

During this period, about half of the world's school enrolments were recorded in developed countries, where those of school age (5–24) form only one-quarter of the world total for their age group.

Conversely, the developing countries, twice as populous and containing three times as many children and young people as the developed countries,[1] have hardly more than half of the world's school pupils.

In Europe, the U.S.S.R. and North America, the increase in primary and secondary school enrolments between 1960 and 1968

1. Twenty-two per cent of the world's children under 15 are in developed countries; 78 per cent are in developing countries.

50

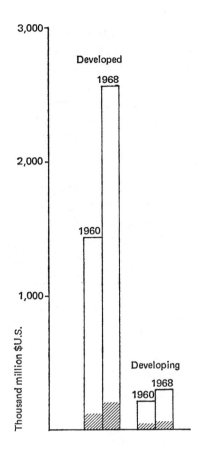

FIG. 7. Educational expenditure as part of total GNP, developed and developing regions, 1960–68.

ran parallel to the increase in the population of young people between 5 and 19 years of age. In developing countries, the population in that age group increased by 36 million more than the increase in school enrolments.[1]

Figures on higher education show that in North America nearly

1. The enormous disparities concealed within regional averages must not be forgotten. For example, in Africa, the mean primary-school enrolment rate is 46 per cent but ranges according to country from 8·7 per cent to 92 per cent; the average annual growth rate of the secondary-school system varies between 0·3 per cent and 11·8 per cent: in 1967, national budgetary allocations to education varied, according to figures available, between 11·3 per cent and 23 per cent, the GNP moving between 1·4 per cent and 6·7 per cent; unit costs for primary education ran from $18 in one country to $126 in another. In Asia, State spending on education in 1968 amounted to 3·7 per cent of the regional GNP; one country spent less than 1 per cent; three countries spent between 1 and 2 per cent, two countries between 2 and 3 per cent, six countries between 3 and 4 per cent, two countries between 4 and 5 per cent, and three countries more than 5 per cent. These differences make it claer that regional averages and forecasts have no more than a relative value, while national strategies and forecasts accordingly become even more important.

51

half (44·5 per cent) of the people who have reached post-secondary age are in fact enrolled at that level. The attendance rate is markedly lower in Europe but remains considerable (about 15 per cent), whereas in Latin America and Asia this proportion is greatly reduced (about ten times less), falls sharply again among Arab States (fourteen times less) and is infinitesimal by comparison in Africa (thirty-four times less). All in all, there are nearly two and a half times as many students in the European and North American higher educational systems than in all the other regions of the world combined. In North America, one learner in eight attends a higher educational establishment, and the ratio in Europe is 1 in 20. Corresponding ratios in developing regions are: 1 in 38 in Asia, 1 in 45 in the Arab States, 1 in 49 in Latin America and 1 in 90 in Africa.

Distribution of teachers

The favoured and less favoured nations reveal a similar disparity in the number of teachers, even without taking into account differences between primary-school teachers' professional training levels. Developing countries have 65 million more pupils than Europe and North America but approximately the same number of teachers. The primary-school situation, by region, is as follows: in Europe and the U.S.S.R., one teacher for 25 pupils; in North America, 1 for 26; in Latin America, 1 for 32; Asia, 1 for 36; Arab States, 1 for 38; Africa, 1 for 40.

Education for girls and women

Again, differences are marked in education for girls and women. In North America, Europe and Latin America, school enrolments of boys and girls at primary and secondary levels are approximately equal. But grouping Africa, Asia and the Arab States together, we find 50 per cent more boys than girls in primary schools, and 100 per cent more in secondary schools. World illiteracy figures show further the extent to which women are at a disadvantage; some 40 per cent are estimated to be illiterate, compared with 28 per cent of men.

Information media

No less striking is the unequal distribution of resources in out-of-school information and communication media, which are increasingly essential instruments for educational action. The developing countries are less favoured right from the start in this area as well. In Africa, newspapers print only eleven copies per 1,000 inhabitants, and in South Asia and the Arab States, eighteen per 1,000, which is about one-twentieth the figure for Europe and North America. Similarly, there are no more than forty-five radio receivers per 1,000 inhabitants in Africa and thirty-three in South

Asia, whereas in North America, with 1,339 sets per 1,000 inhabitants, there are already more radios than there are people. There are more than 250 million television receivers in the world; fewer than 5 million of this total are in Africa, South Asia and the Arab States. It is obvious that much ground remains to be covered before mass-communication media earn their title.

In the 1960s, Unesco organized a series of regional conferences[1] grouping education ministers. In many respects, these meetings achieved their aim. They sharpened awareness of needs and enabled energies to be better mobilized for developing and improving school systems, helping to set up a body of doctrine which has great ethical and practical value. They also became the occasion for outlining ambitious regional targets for school enrolment.[2]

Setbacks

Despite considerable success, which in some cases even exceeded forecasts, it must be admitted that results in other cases are still quite far from these targets. The target agreed on at the first Asian conference, Karachi, 1960, was to achieve universal compulsory primary education by 1980. By 1970, the adjusted enrolment ratio in grades I–V was calculated to be 83·2 per cent. In 1961, the Addis Ababa Conference on Education in African States also agreed on a target of 100 per cent enrolment by 1980, with an intermediary stage of 71 per cent in 1970; by 1965, the latest reporting year, a figure of 44 per cent was recorded against the 47 per cent targeted for that year. The Santiago Conference in 1962 called on Latin American countries to achieve 100 per cent primary enrolment by 1970. This enrolment ratio was achieved by 1968 in many countries of the region but some countries are still considerably below it. In 1966, in Tripoli, Arab States confirmed that enrolment of all primary-school-age children by 1980 remained their goal; by 1967, however, they were still only at 62·1 per cent.

These figures prove the outstanding achievements which have been made in relation to the targets set, but it must be pointed out that they mask serious deficiencies. If one includes in the num-

1. Karachi (1960), Beirut (1960), Addis Ababa (1961), Santiago (1962), Tokyo (1962), Abidjan (1964), Bangkok (1965), Tripoli (1966), Buenos Aires (1966), Vienna (1967), Nairobi (1968), Marrakesh (1970).
2. The primary-school enrolment targets established at the ministers' conferences are in terms of adjusted enrolment ratios, calculated by dividing all-age primary enrolment by the population of the age group corresponding to the normal duration of the course. Thus, in Asia, for example, the all-age enrolment in grades I–V divided by the population 6–10 yields the adjusted grade I–V enrolment ratio; in Africa, the Arab States and Latin America, the all-age enrolment in primary schools, grades I–VI, divided by the population 6–11 yields the primary enrolment ratio.

bers enrolled only those children falling within the age group[1] corresponding to the government-established length of primary schooling, it provides a much darker picture by showing just how many children in the regions are not receiving the prescribed schooling. Enrolment ratios calculated on this basis show that, in 1968, only four out of ten primary-school-age children in Africa were actually in classes. In the Arab States, only half attended school. Forty-five per cent of Asia's children and 25 per cent in Latin America were similarly not enrolled.

In the socialist countries and the industrialized nations of the West, the quantitative objectives decided on in the early sixties have been achieved. In member States of the Organisation for Economic Co-operation and Development (OECD), for example, the figures confirm that educational expenditure has greatly increased. In half of the countries studied, this increase exceeded 10 per cent, while only four countries recorded rates lower than 7 per cent.[2]

Quantitative progress made by countries which are already very advanced is all the more significant compared to the inevitably slower pace in developing countries because it accentuates existing imbalances in the world.

Despite the hopes conceived some twenty years ago, education has so far been no exception to the harsh rule of our times which tends to increase the unequal distribution of goods and resources in the world.

This is all the more serious because education is the indispensable instrument for the propagation of science and technology which is fundamental to the success of developing countries' current endeavours.

While educational programmes to aid the underprivileged are being undertaken at national level, we may ask whether the international community should not at the same time exert itself more energetically to eliminate the persistent and worsening educational disparities among the nations of the world.

---

1. Thus excluding over-age pupils who, if counted, produce the statistical aberration of some countries reporting more than 100 per cent enrolment.
2. An OECD document points out that so far as its member States were concerned, this progress clearly exceeded forecasts at the 1961 Washington Conference (*Comparative Study of Educational Expenditure and its Trends in OECD Countries since 1950*, Paris, 1970, Conference on Policies for Educational Growth, Background Study 2).

CHAPTER 3

Education and society

The urgency of the tasks related to the expansion of educational systems has led planners to concentrate mainly on the quantitative aspects of the effort required, of the obstacles to be overcome and the disequilibria to be corrected. But we are becoming aware that the essential questions—questions of substance—concern the relationships between education and society, education and the learner, education and knowledge, between aims avowed and aims achieved.

Education is both a world in itself and a reflection of the world at large. It is subject to society, while contributing to its goals, and in particular it helps society to mobilize its productive energies by ensuring that required human resources are developed. In a more general way, it necessarily has an influence on the environmental conditions to which it is at the same time subjected, even if only by the knowledge about these which it yields. Thus, education contributes to bringing about the objective conditions of its own transformation and progress.

When history is seen in sufficient perspective, there is no reason why this dialectical process—and this optimistic view of it—should not be quite clear, with its relationships of cause to effect and effect to cause.

What is even clearer, however, at the level of social phenomena, is that until the present, education as we have known it through all the forms of society which have lasted for any length of time has been the select instrument by means of which existing values and balances of power have been maintained and kept in effect, with all the implications of both a positive and negative character which this process has had for the destiny of nations and the course of history.

So far as teachers', learners' and parents' personal experience is concerned, the social function of educative practice—in its many pedagogic forms and as it actually takes place in a wide variety of different contexts—is infinitely complex. While its practice illuminates the liberating power of education, it also demonstrates the limits to its powers, its shortcomings and its oppressive, coercive effects.

The contradictory nature of the basic facts in this situation helps to account for the widely differing opinions on the relationship between education and society. Broadly speaking, they may be grouped into four schools of thought:

Education and society: four schools of thought

Idealism, which considers that education exists in and for itself.

Voluntarism, consisting in the conviction that education can and must change the world, independently of any changes which may take place in the structure of society.

Mechanistic determinism, according to which the form and future of education are directly controlled by and more or less synchronized with surrounding environmental factors.

Finally, the school of thought which derives from all three of these, and which postulates that education necessarily reproduces and even exacerbates and perpetuates the vices inherent in the societies which supporters of this school are currently criticizing very sharply. Their view is that there can be no conceivable remedy for education apart from radically changing society. However, in apparent contradiction to this, they maintain that the educational world may well set the stage, with an interior revolution of its own, for a subsequent social revolution.

For one reason or another, each of these positions has at least some logical justification. None of them however seems to us to be capable of providing a complete account of the real situation, or fully able to inspire action which would be sufficiently concrete and discerning.

In our view, there is a close correlation—simultaneous and delayed—between changes in the socio-economic environment and the structures and forms of action of education, which we believe makes a functional contribution to historical movements.[Moreover, it seems to us that through the knowledge it provides of the environment in which it operates education may help society to become aware of its problems and, provided that efforts are centred on training 'complete men' who will consciously seek their individual and collective emancipation, it may greatly contribute to changing and humanizing societies.]

Traditions and constraints

The correlations and interactions between society and education are so complex that simplified explanations cannot possibly give an adequate account of them. This remark is valid for the tasks which education assigns to society and society to education, reciprocally, and also for statements concerning the objectives to which such tasks are designed to lead. As to these, it should be noted, as elsewhere on the subject of development objectives, that they cannot be expressed in the neat and simple rhetorical terms used for objectives in the past decade. Ready-made solutions are less helpful today than ever.

This is equally true of judgements on present-day forms of the relationship between education and society, for any criticism voiced in general terms can only take on meaning when applied to a specific situation.

Education, which both reproduces and renews itself, is often accused of immobility. It is certainly not the only institution against which such reproaches are levelled. In fact one of its essential functions is that of repetition, to repeat to each generation the knowledge that the previous generation inherited from its forebears. It is therefore normal for educational systems to be given the job—as in the past—of handing down traditional values. This is why they are inclined to form closed systems, both in time and space, and to be largely concerned with their own existence and success.[1]

Self-perpetuating function of education

So the system looks inward and backward. This viewpoint helps to consolidate existing structures and to form individuals for living in society as it is. Therefore, and we do not mean this pejoratively, education is by nature conservative.

All education, beginning with family education, has the task of socializing children and adolescents. Schools continue and will continue to carry out the duties of civic training (especially in countries which recently acquired or recovered their national ident-

Use and abuse of civic training

---

1. 'To what extent and at what speed are educational systems capable of adapting themselves to changing circumstances? They are endowed with a considerable built-in inertia. If the function of teaching is considered as the reproductive function of a society, it should not be forgotten that genetically speaking the primary quality of a reproductive system is to reproduce its type as exactly and as faithfully as possible and to ensure what a biologist has called "the reproductive invariance of living beings" conducive to the conservation of the species' (Pierre Bertaux, *Factors Influencing the Development of Education*, p. 7, Paris, Unesco, 1971, document of the International Commission on the Development of Education, Opinions Series, 11).

ity) and of ideological training (in countries where leaders of a revolution consider it their duty to capture minds and to topple all the bastions of the past). The important thing is not the position which instruction of this kind has in education, but its aims—at least the implicit ones. Does it encourage self-fulfilment in individuals with a healthy idea of their relationship to the world, or does it condition individuals, make them follow set examples and become easy to govern? Does it encourage the development of people with independent minds and sharp critical faculties, or cultivate unthinking respect for hierarchies? The fact is that in very many situations children and adolescents need above-average strength, an exceptional capacity for escape, or an unshakeable character if they are to maintain intact the curiosity and inventiveness which are man's primordial faculties.

Hierarchies

Hierarchies, whether official or merely residual (depending on the society in question), are apparent in the structures of education. The very terms 'primary', 'secondary', 'higher', 'professional', 'technical', or 'scientific' are loaded with discriminatory overtones. The teaching profession itself is too hierarchical. People still often think that a teacher's rank and status is measured by the age and mental level of his students. The school-master giving 18-year-old youths a classical education enjoys grater respect than his colleague teaching 15-year-old boys in a technical college. There is certainly more prestige attached to teaching mathematics than to teaching toddlers to read and write. Cock of the roost, of course, is the university professor.

Finally, there is an over-rigid hierarchical relationship between teacher and pupil.[1] When this relationship becomes too strict, it suffocates the learner's awareness of his own responsibilities and excludes a potentially positive free response.

Élitism

The term 'élitism' is a rather poor definition of the condition it describes. Theoretically, it does not generally mean—or no longer does—that first-class education is reserved to a specific caste. It really consists of separating the 'cream' of society from the rest.

1. Many people, of course, defend opposite theses and promote differing interpretations. The director of the London University Institute of Education has expressed himself on this subject in forceful language: 'The fight against the old authoritarianism led us to neglect the degree to which the teacher's function must be positive, and has left us in a poor mental state to deal with the different problem of our own time. Our problem is not too much guidance of the young, but too little. This point is crucial. And all the fears we may have of being labelled "authoritarian" must not prevent our saying it' (Lionel Elvin, 'The Positive Roles of Society and the Teacher', in: R.S. Peters (ed.), *Perspectives on Plowden*, p. 87, London, Routledge & Kegan Paul, 1969).

It is a system which aims not at excluding people on the grounds of their social background, but rather at co-opting 'the best', as defined by the existing élite. Hence the school acts as a sieve, starting in the elementary classes and operating through successive stages of filtering with an eye to selecting the future élite. And if social mechanisms inevitably favour the academic success of children from privileged social and cultural backgrounds, this must be seen as a consequence and not as an aim of the system. Moreover, the word élite implies a small number. But the system does not cease to be 'élitist' simply because it grows quantitatively. The determining factor is the principle of selection, however many are chosen, and the exclusion of all others on the basis of criteria laid down by the existing élite, which continually makes these restrictions more stringent.[1]

This conception of social advancement through education is typical of blocked societies[2] whose sole purpose is their own perpetuation. But it also affects societies in evolution, both in developing and industrialized countries. The established élite has a convenient and apparently equitable method of recruiting its successors from one generation to the next, namely by taking most of them from among its own offspring, which is a very pleasant thing to be able to do, while at the same time it picks out a selected few from the less favoured classes. This machinery has a triple advantage. It gives society a safety-valve, it gives the ruling class a good conscience and it makes sure of fresh blood for the élite. It is surely less scandalous than other selection systems based not on competitive examination but on ethnic, racial or ideological discrimination. It must above all not be concluded from the vices of élitism as practised in blocked societies that a healthy conception of élitism and educational democratization are incompatible. These two terms only come into contradiction when allegedly élite intellectual groups are selected in terms of non-democratic criteria and structures. Élitism of the kind which forges a power-equals-class link into the system will prevent the emergence of an authentic élite, but democratically

Blocked societies

1. For example, in order to become a member of the élite in most African countries ten years ago, secondary-level studies were sufficient; five years ago, a university degree became necessary; the only studies that count today are post-graduate ones. It is useless multiplying opportunities for access to education, since this does not necessarily increase equality of opportunity, the level of criteria for success moving steadily higher, so that it is always just beyond the masses' grasp.
2. 'The blocked society secretes a blocked educational system which in its turn maintains and perpetuates the blocked society by the conditioning of the young which it imposes' (Louis Ruillen, 1970).

59

widening the bases of education to enable all individual aptitudes to find fulfilment stimulates the rise of a 'natural' élite. But the fact remains that *even a broadly based élitist system has a different stamp from a truly democratic one. A vital task for our time is to seek fundamental, non-discriminatory models. On all sides, the search will run into political and financial obstacles, psychological resistance and, above all, the rigid stratification of society. Only in those. societies in the process of achieving integration through a widespread dismantling of their social barriers can the tasks of education to select and distribute lose their negative, filtering aspect and take on the positive feature of promoting human achievement.*

Education an image

Education, being a subsystem of society, necessarily reflects the main features of that society. It would be vain to hope for a rational, humane education in an unjust society. A bureaucratic system, habitually estranged from life, finds it hard to entertain the idea that schools are made for children, instead of children being made for schools. Régimes based on authority from the top and obedience from the bottom cannot develop an education for freedom. It is difficult to imagine school imparting a taste for creative work in socio-economic conditions in which work is generally an alienation. And how can one imagine a society woven out of privileges and discrimination developing a democratic education system?

Education renews

It by no means follows that for lack of being able to modify and correct social conditions by itself that education must remain their passive offshoot. The subordinate relationship of education to the socio-economic system is not such as to make it impossible to act, if not on the entire complex, at least on this or that particular element. Pressure is being brought to bear to renew educational structures and content so that they become able to contribute more or less directly to social change. This is certainly possible, provided that we have a clear image of society in light of which educational objectives may be formulated. We should like to see wider acceptance of this dynamic attitude.

Facts prove the correlation between contradictions in social systems and the comparative impotence of educational systems. There are close links between societies' major objectives and the aims assigned to education. It is also evident that it is almost impossible to break out of the vicious circle of underdevelopment and the inequality in educational development without an attempt to deal with both of these problems together.

Two conclusions follow from this. First, it is far more necessary today than in the past for reforms in education to have social and economic development objectives.

Second, it is hard to conceive of society developing without a renewal in education. This is valid for all societies, of whatever type, whatever their predominant doctrine and however they envisage their future—whether reformist or revolutionary.

Methods and content

Education and educational methods are coming under fire nearly all over the world. The content of education is criticized because it is irrelevant to individual needs, because it holds back scientific progress and social development, or because it is divorced from contemporary problems. Methods are criticized because they overlook the complexity of the educative process, fail to learn from research and are not sufficiently directed at training minds and attitudes.

However, the first question which arises here (and it lends itself to controversy, as we shall see) is that of the choice and use of the various media for communicating knowledge—the spoken word, the written word, the visual image. Media, in fact, condition the methods and, to a greater or lesser degree, the character and content of education.

Cultural communication

Speech is regaining some of the importance it had in communication before printing was invented. A huge amount of information is transmitted by word through the mass media, radio and television. The spoken word is still primordial in vast regions of the world where illiteracy still prevails. The number of jobs based on the spoken word is on the increase. And among the peoples of former colonies the rehabilitation of the indigenous mother tongue is a means of reasserting a personality smothered by the hegemony of imported written language.[1]

The spoken word

1. 'The colonial culture "names" the world in its own way, substituting for the "word" that the colonised individual desperately needs, in order to express his own world, the word which it uses as an instrument of domination. In most countries, the school, instead of being a centre for genuine dialogue—that is, an exchange of genuine words between teacher and learner in order to arrive at a still better understanding of the world—reflects colonial relationships. As the undisputed authority and source of knowledge the teacher "deposits" knowledge with the pupil much as the investor deposits his money in the bank' (M. Mardjane).

61

The written word

This strong comeback of oral expression does not mean that the written word is withering away. With more children going to school and adult literacy programmes developing, more and more people have learned to use the written word to express their thoughts, to communicate. Furthermore, the written word becomes indispensable when knowledge has to be structured, and ordered or information assembled for reference in convenient and permanent form. Finally, verbal communication itself draws very liberally on written texts.

Yet written expression is far more exposed to the dangers of abstraction than oral expression. The world seen through the printed word tends to shed its concrete elements and become a set of ideas and symbols. We know the damage done by 'bookish' culture, which fosters the habit of seeing the world through printed volumes and newspapers and creates a gap between reality and its interpretation that is hard to bridge.

The former distinction between 'noble' professions, implying knowledge of '*belles-lettres*', and manual occupations virtually excluding that knowledge, is tending to disappear. An increasing number of activities require possession of culture in the true sense of the word, but except for a very few professions, this can no longer be reduced to an essentially verbal culture. The popularization of science and technology is increasing the number of people who, in the course of their professional activity, have to deal with things as much as with words. This requires a whole new set of tools other than language. Technological training necessarily uses other methods as well as the spoken word, such as demonstrations, experiments, practical work and the acquisition of routines, reflexes and skills. It is important to recognize that this sector of modern man's training is as much a part of his culture as the conventional 'civilization of letters'.

Pictures

Communication through pictures has developed on an unprecedented scale. All manner of visual representation is invading everybody's world everywhere, infiltrating all forms of modern life. Today, the image is present at all the various levels of cultural experience, either as a vehicle for information, as entertainment, or as a tool for scientific research.

Misusing media

In a world where powerful means of mass communication place the farthest corners of the planet at one's finger-tips, it is just as necessary to avoid systematically belittling the spoken word and the picture in order to glorify the written word, as to

62

beware of the temptation to make almost exclusive use of speech and vision.

Instead of setting various methods against each other, it is more constructive to list the resources they offer and determine methodically the conditions in which each may be used to supplement the others.

The problem applies to all kinds and all levels of teaching, but it is of particular relevance to the millions of people who can neither read nor write. It is not, in the least, to propose abandoning the attempt to introduce vast masses of people to the written word for the first time to note that in remote and inaccessible regions of the world, wherever literacy campaigns are making only slow progress, the visual image and the spoken word provide a short cut for communicating information, which it would be wasteful not to use. And indeed, in mass literacy campaigns undertaken today, there is too often a tendency in practice, to take sterile either-or positions. Either rudimentary, traditional teaching methods are discarded altogether and replaced by modern audio-visual means or instruction in reading and writing is attempted with chalk and notebook, to the exclusion of the powerful new media. But, in addition to the immediate benefits they can produce, the fact is that audio-visual methods can also pave the way—by imparting practical information and prompting social action—to greater cultural awareness, stimulating the desire for learning and for acquiring other styles of communication, including that of written expression.

On this issue, we are in entire agreement with the Director-General of Unesco[1] when he said that *the written word must not be pitted against the image, for a truly modern education, from the level of elementary literacy training to the top levels of higher education, should integrate word, sound and image.*

The discriminatory grading of the means of transmitting culture and education goes hand in hand with a no less negative grading of what is transmitted.

1. 'There can be no contradiction between means and end, or between means towards the same end. There would be a contradiction if an education exclusively based on audio-visual means were contemplated. Let us leave these paradoxical musings on modernism to the visionaries in the "ikonosphere". The written word must at least follow, or, better, hold together or buttress, and in any case go side by side with broadcast, televised, acted or mimed instruction. True modern education is not something which pits the image against the written word, but one which integrates both for the same purpose of training minds in a synthetic process characterized by a constant transition from one system to the other. . . . This is the only way to ensure that mankind does not lose its unity, and is not split into groups of educated peoples, sole custodians of the Word, and "informed" or rather conditioned peoples' (René Maheu, *La Civilisation de l'Universel*, p.104, Paris, Laffont-Gauthier, 1966).

Findings

Subject hierarchies

For essentially historical reasons, the subjects of traditional curricula are given a value that often bears little relation to their educative or social usefulness. Literature and history are generally invested with greater prestige than geography or economics, and the study of classics takes precedence over learning about the contemporary world. Even science as a whole suffers from such prejudice: pure science is often more highly regarded than applied science.

Anachronism and omissions in programmes

An understanding of the world is one of education's major objectives. More often than not, however, this concern is expressed in abstract explanations, so-called universal principles, or in a narrow utilitarianism, none of which offers satisfactory answers to young people asking questions about reality and wondering about their own future.[1]

Outdated curricula

The fact is that many school programmes are ill-adapted to provide knowledge of the real universe, as the present generation sees it, and to the problems facing people today:[2] military, social and racial conflicts, world-wide famine, pollution, the status of youth and women and the condition of minority groups. Educators often feel that they do not possess sufficiently accurate information on these subjects or the right kind of teaching material. There is also a fear of tackling thorny questions if not outright refusal and there is the difficulty that these topics involve many disciplines which would be hard to include in strictly subject-based time-tables.

1. 'Not only does the child lose all feeling of the unity of knowledge, but he may well no longer understand why he is being taught and why he is being asked to spend a good deal of his time at school. Teaching is abstract, theoretical, conditioned by a certain conception of knowledge, and divorced from real life, just as the school is cut off from its environment. The finality of school life is lost sight of, and it is forgotten that a school's basic function is to prepare a man for life—to form his character in a specific way. But education loses sight of the sort of man it wants to turn out; nor does it for all that centre on the child at which it is aimed. . . . There is a clear parallel between the compartmentalization of disciplines and the barriers between school and life, just as there is between the disintegration of knowledge and the fact that the school is in no way integrated with its environment' (extract from the final report of the Unesco seminar on the training of teachers by the interdisciplinarity system, to use this system in schools, Bouaké, Ivory Coast, 24 March to 4 April 1970).
2. 'Students must be taught how to take advantage of information sources for their own training, and how to use a certain number of tools to that end: this completely changes knowledge-transmission structures and authoritarian pedagogic attitudes. For that is based on a statutory gradation between the generations which separates independent and responsible adults from the dependent and irresponsible young. We must avoid this separation. We must also avoid separating the world of school, apparently linked to respectable if conventional norms and to its own internal aims, from the concrete universe in which the requirements of work, personal commitments and responsibilities frustrate each and every attempt to remain aloof and saintly' (Armand Biancheri, *La Rénovation Pédagogique*, Centre de Recherche et de Formation en Éducation, École Normale Supérieure de Saint-Cloud, 1970).

The utilitarian attitude sees the spread of science and technology as the means of achieving short-term material goals. It neglects the other dimension of science, that it is a means to objective knowledge helping man to define his choices—even in the field of applied science itself. It tends to pit man against his environment, presenting him as master and overlord of nature, instead of placing him in a state of harmony and balance within that environment.

School curricula often gloss over social studies. But man has to become aware of his place in society over and above his role as producer and consumer. He should be made to understand that he can and must play a democratic part in the life of society, that he is able as an individual or as a member of a group to make society better or worse than it is. The child must be offered a vision of the world in which he has to live so as to enable him to decide on his approach to the future.

Social education

Traditional scientific teaching makes little effort to relate classroom knowledge to the practice of science where hypotheses are not taught, but tested, where laws are not learned but discovered. Such curricula rarely reveal the degree of creativity, intuition, imagination, excitement and doubt involved in scientific activity. Nor should the ability to observe, collect, categorize, and relate evidence to conclusions be the business of scientists alone. The demystification of science and the popularization of scientific practice should not be seen as a decline, but rather as a step in the right direction.[1]

Scientific education

The dichotomy in education between the exact and natural sciences and the human and social sciences encourages this attitude. It is diametrically opposed to the now forgotten humanistic approach, which Marx expressed as follows: 'The natural sciences will one day incorporate the science of man, just as the science of man will incorporate the natural sciences; there will be a *single* science.'

Human sciences are often particularly neglected. Generally

---

1. The foregoing criticisms are unfortunately only too true in the majority of cases. They are brought into even sharper relief by the attempts of some, if not most, countries to correct the situation. The reforms are concerned with the aims, methods and content of science education. Understanding principles and analysing concepts are stressed in preference to learning formulae and facts by rote. Greater use is made of experiments, and newer teaching methods are used. An attempt is being made to provide a tangible link between science teaching and the milieu in which pupils live. Some experiments are determinedly innovative, like the Harvard Physics Project or the work of the Physical Science Study Committee in the United States, or the Nuffield Foundation Science Teaching Project in the United Kingdom, or the introduction of modern mathematics at the secondary-school level in France. Initiatives of this sort are however exceptional.

speaking, most education systems do not help their clients—whether they be youngsters or adults—to discover themselves, to understand the components of their conscious and unconscious personalities, the mechanisms of the brain, the operation of the intelligence, the laws governing their physical development, the meaning of their dreams and aspirations, the nature of their relations with one another and with the community at large. Education thus neglects its basic duty of teaching men the art of living, loving and working in a society which they must create as an embodiment of their ideal.

Technological education

One of the basic objectives of science teaching should be to underline the interdependence of knowledge and action. This concern should lead to dovetailing science teaching and the teaching of technology, to highlighting the relationship between research and practical development and application. But just the opposite is happening today, with education systems generally introducing a sharp separation between the two—a separation which is damaging to both. In general education, curricula are far too prone to make room for sciences rather than technology. By shearing it away from the practical side, a part of science is sterilized on the pretext of giving it greater prestige, and as a result it loses much of its effectiveness as an educational tool.

An understanding of technology is vital in the modern world, and must be part of everyone's basic education. Lack of understanding of technological methods makes one more and more dependent on others in daily life, narrows employment possibilities and increases the danger that the potentially harmful effects of the unrestrained application of technology—for example alienation of individuals or pollution—will finally become overwhelming. Most people benefit from technology passively, or submit to it, without understanding it. They cannot, therefore, control it. Education in technology at the conceptual level should enable everyone to understand the ways in which he can change his environment.

On a practical level, rudimentary understanding of the processes of technology will enable a person to evaluate, select and make more effective use of technological products.

In present-day general education, technology is not treated in a systematic, conceptual fashion. No attempt is made to develop an understanding of the uses of technology to individuals, society or the world at large.

For a grasp of technology, it may be viewed as a process through which materials are transformed, and this always requires both

66

energy and information. Following this, a unified approach should analyse the principles underlying all processing, simple or sophisticated, and show that technology deals with everything man does to modify his world.

Artistic experience—in creation of art forms and aesthetic pleasure—is, along with scientific experience, one of the two roads that lead to a perception of the world in its eternal newness. Like the capacity to think clearly, the individual's imaginative faculty must also be developed; imagination is at the source of scientific invention as well as artistic creation. Any education which for rational reasons concentrates on teaching so-called objective facts rather than stimulating creative desire is going against the grain of what Albert Einstein experienced. 'The most beautiful thing we can experience is the mysterious. It is the source of all true art and science.' *Artistic education*

From an educational viewpoint, the tangible result of artistic activities is not the only thing that matters. The state of the mind and heart that creates is also important. What really counts is the awakening of creative enthusiasm which helps lift man to a higher level of existence. Seen in this light, the traditional distinction between 'fine' and 'popular' arts loses any significance and disappears.

One fundamental and necessary personality component is an interest in beauty, the capacity to perceive and to integrate it into one's make-up. However, artistic education can and should assume another function; it is a means of communicating with the natural and social environment, of understanding it and, the case arising, of protesting against it. This element has so far been little more than timidly approached in educational practice.

The content of traditional education curricula generally has little relationship to vocational needs. The humanities still exert their prestigious influence on the path chosen by many pupils at school or university, although the majority of developing countries need more specialists and technicians in the applied sciences. *Vocational training*

The idea of preparing for careers is undergoing a change. At the rate technology is advancing, many people during the course of their working life will hold several jobs or change frequently their place of work. In some countries, half the wage-earning population are in jobs that did not exist at the beginning of the century.

Education rarely equips the individual for adapting to change, to the unknown. The world has not yet widely accepted the principle of a general, polytechnical education at secondary level—an

67

education which would guarantee professional mobility and lead to lifelong education.[1]

As regards the role and responsibility of education in the labour market, two kinds of imbalances between manpower supply and demand must be distinguished. There is an over-all quantitative imbalance and there are structural imbalances in the sense that while supply may meet demand in terms of quantity, the jobs offered may not match either the capacities or the requirements or preferences of those seeking work. Although—contrary to the generally held idea—education can contribute to correcting over-all imbalance, especially in rural regions, the kind of imbalance which it mainly helps to attenuate (or exacerbate) is structural; and this depends on whether or not it endeavours to adapt to the needs of the economy, and also on whether or not it panders to aspirations, attitudes and hopes of the kind which are largely irrelevant to the real conditions of professional life.

These problems illustrate the dual functions of the school. The school's task is not merely to seek out aptitudes, train them and give them a seal of approval. It must above all develop personality and attitudes. Such problems are common to all countries, but are particularly acute in developing countries where salary scales often contribute towards a search (or wait) for certain kinds of jobs, for which the supply exceeds the demand, or which have little effect on development. This is especially the case in public service, where administrative posts are traditionally rated higher than technical jobs.

Manual education

The education systems of a number of societies, both in the industrialized countries as well as in developing nations, contribute towards perpetuating the distinction between intellectual training and practical training and underestimate manual work as a calamity which must be avoided at all costs through education. All too often, curricula are so graded that training in manual work is reserved for the academically less endowed.

Physical education

It is readily agreed that physical education should go beyond the exercise of muscles, nerves and reflexes which is its primary concern. But stress is generally given to the value of the competitive spirit and the relation between physical exercise and character-building, more often asserted than demonstrated. Essentially people should

---

1. And acceptance is withheld despite the positive results it seems to yield in a number of cases, especially in highly industrialized countries such as the United States and the Federal Republic of Germany, and in most of the socialist countries.

68

learn to adapt fully to their bodies, the basic foundation of personality. Physical education suffers less from theoretical inadequacies than from the general indifference which, in practice, is still far too prevalent.

The neglect or disdain from which some elements of educational programmes continue to suffer, the deficiencies and imbalance of curricula appear to us to be among the most serious symptoms of the disease of which education is both the victim and the cause. The separation of its intellectual, physical, aesthetic, moral and social components is an indication of alienation, undervaluation and mutilation of the human person.

Education suffers basically from the gap between its content and the living experience of its pupils, between the systems of values that it preaches and the goals set up by society, between its ancient curricula and the modernity of science. Link education to life, associate it with concrete goals, establish a close relationship between society and economy, invent or rediscover an education system that fits its surroundings—surely this is where the solution must be sought.

For far too long education had the task of preparing for stereotyped functions, stable situations, for one moment in existence, for a particular trade or a given job. It inculcated conventional knowledge, in time-honoured categories. This concept is still far too prevalent. And yet, the idea of acquiring, at an early age, a set of intellectual or technical equipment valid for a lifetime is out of date. This fundamental axiom of traditional education is crumbling. Is not this the time to call for something quite different in education systems? Learning to live, learning to learn, so as to be able to absorb new knowledge all through life; learning to think freely and critically; learning to love the world and make it more human; learning to develop in and through creative work.

Seemingly abstract words. But education is such a huge undertaking, it has so radical an influence on man's destiny, that it will be damaging if it is only considered in terms of structures, logistical means and processes. The very substance of education, its essential relationship to man and his development, its interaction with the environment as both product and factor of society must all be deeply scrutinized and extensively reconsidered.

69

The path to democracy

For several years critics have accused schools of being hives of injustice, authoritarianism and discrimination. This has understandably caused some surprise, since it amounts to blaming the school for being what society has made it, through the successive mandates given to it over the centuries. However different these may have been, there was general agreement that schools should be hierarchical and authoritarian.

This vehement criticism can, however, be explained. Primarily, it expresses strongly felt needs, in tune with the mood of the day. It is also sparked by what many people regard as hypocrisy, namely, the use of a smokescreen of pseudo-democratic phrases to cloak real injustice.

Progress in democratizing education

It is certainly true that educational authorities usually declare that their ambition is for schools to help equalize opportunity. Economic requirements in some countries, ideological goals in others, the struggle for national liberation in many parts of the world and even, in some cases, the fear of social unrest, all contribute to the pressing need to make education more democratic. And there are signs of considerable progress. Both modern and traditional societies have created conditions to enable more people to attend school. Nearly all societies are trying to extend the time spent at school. Industrialized countries, whether socialist or capitalist, are continually expanding secondary and higher education. Introduction of general examinations, competitive tests and uniform methods for assessing educational achievements has abolished, *de facto* if not always *de jure*, traditional privilege. This is undeniable progress attesting to the capacity of democracy to improve education in structure, dimension and pedagogical practice.

Persistent privilege

Yet injustice still exists in many different ways in the educational world. We are not referring here to disparities between countries but to inequalities inside countries.

Regional differences can reach such considerable proportions that figures relating to the educational situation in two different geographic sectors, for example, may vary by more than 50 per cent in relation to the national average for the same item.[1] Other

1. In India, for example, significant disparities may be seen in comparisons between the average school enrolment rate for the 6–11 year old age group, which is some 80 per cent, and regional rates, such as 121 per cent in Nagaland, 77 per cent in Andhra

70

examples of inequality include the concentration of educational facilities in the major cities and towns to the detriment of vast rural zones,[1] and their concentration—even more flagrantly unjust— near city centres to the detriment of shanty towns, *favelas* and other poor districts lacking the schools available to their richer neighbours. Add to this the numerous cases of ethnic or racial inequality, which is sometimes outrageous, even in countries with ample material means to remedy the situation.[2]

Certain sectors of education are highly privileged, others are but poor 'country cousins', depending on the social status of the classes to which they cater. Children of the poor or those who belong to groups suffering racial or social discrimination are in a difficult position from the outset, whether from lack of due care for physical and mental requirements of early childhood or lack of pre-school education. They are handicapped, sometimes irremediably so, in comparison to children of the wealthier classes or from backgrounds more favourable to proper growth and development. Where school places are increasingly limited as pupils mount the promotion ladder, a more or less arbitrary selection process prevents many who are capable of continuing their studies from doing so. The inadequate development of literacy programmes and out-of-school vocational training means that those who missed their chance of entering the school network at the outset find it less and less possible to educate themselves as they grow older.

Thus, the universal right to education—in which contemporary civilization takes such premature pride—is often refused, by a complete reversal of justice, to the most underprivileged. They are the first to be denied their right in poor societies; the only ones deprived in the rich.

However, equal access to education is only a necessary—not a

Equal access— unequal opportunity

Pradesh, 68 per cent in Punjab and 57 per cent in Madhya Pradesh. The differences in the upper group are much higher; the average percentage of 36 per cent (enrolment in classes VI–VIII to total population in the age group 11–14) was 22 per cent in Bihar, 31 per cent in Assam, 43 per cent in Gujarat and 71 per cent in Kerala.

1. In one country in Latin America, for example, 66 per cent of primary schools in urban areas offered the full five years of the elementary educational cycle, whereas only 6 per cent did so in rural areas; and 59 per cent of village schools provided only two years of schooling.
2. 'In 1964, black students constituted approximately 5 per cent of the total national enrolment; by 1969 the proportion of black students had grown to 6 per cent, although blacks made up 12 per cent of the college-eligible age group' (*Campus Unrest*, Report of the President's Commission on Campus Unrest, Washington, D.C., United States Government Printing Office, 1970).

71

sufficient—condition for justice. Equal access *is not* equal opportunity. This must comprise equal chance of success.[1]

But chances of this kind, on the contrary, are very unequal. Proof of this lies in the systematic distortion, found at the beginning and end of educational cycles, in the comparative social background of those entering and leaving school.

The negative correlation between the financial, social and cultural status of families and the opportunity of access to the varying types of education, and thereafter of succeeding, is far from having the same weight in every country, although it remains a universal phenomenon.[2] The reasons for the most part are obvious. Children from poor backgrounds are compelled to go to work prematurely, students who work have to do so in addition to studying. Elsewhere, hygiene is poor, food bad, homes overcrowded, etc. Other equally important if less obvious causes have been abundantly highlighted of late,[3]

1. A number of authors who have studied the conditions required for a true equalization of chances point out that if the means of school education alone are equalized, and all other considerations apart, this in fact results in unequal results. 'It was recognition of these facts which led the British Plowden Committee to the principle of positive discrimination. This principle in the end, however, points to the most radical definition of equality of educational opportunity. The aim can be defined not as equal educational *inputs* but equal educational *outcomes* (again for groups, of course, not individuals). . . . Coleman's most dramatic and most disputed finding is most relevant: what accounts for poor academic performance is not so much unequal educational provision but the character of schoolmates. In other words, the most significant correlate of achievement test scores is the social class climate of the school's student body' (A. H. Halsey, *Education and Social Change*, Paris, Unesco, 1972, document of the International Commission on the Development of Education, Opinions Series, 51).
2. 'Since the change in régime, both a spectacular boom in the total numbers of school-goers and a deep upheaval of the social strata whence these come can be seen in all the socialist countries. . . . This unusually widespread dual movement, which is increasing the number of pupils and recruiting them more democratically, constitutes an original feature of the socialist systems' (Robert Castel). The fact remains that in Hungary (according to S. Ferge) and in Yugoslavia (according to M. Mastić and R. Supek), for example, average marks obtained by children whose parents are high-level executives, professional people or intellectuals far exceed the averages obtained by children of skilled workers, manual or farm labourers.
3. Educational systems, '. . . inevitably tilt the scales on the side of children whose parents are educated and who thus provide their children with a good vocabulary and a culturally rich environment' (Coombs, op. cit., p. 32). 'The chances of succeeding at school, and later of succeeding socially, are unequally distributed among children from varying backgrounds. . . . No longer able to incriminate a purely economic heritage, since free education is becoming more and more widespread and the numbers of pupils and students in secondary and in higher education have become as large as we know them to be, sociologists are turning against the cultural heritage. The school system is such that it works on behalf, and in favour of, inherited status. It claims to be equalitarian, but its function consists in upholding prerogatives, in ensuring that today's social order of things is maintained, by concealing under the most sovereign hypocrisy the means whereby not only it selects the élite, but also forces the children of the most underprivileged classes to drop out' (A. Girard). 'One of the most important recent achievements in the field of educational sociology consisted in showing that success or failure in acquiring learned culture could not be evaluated without reference to the sub-culture of the groups from which the pupils or students come' (Robert Castel).

TABLE 6. Enrolment in higher education by parents' occupation in selected countries

Country[1]	Liberal professions and management		Workers	
	Students (as percentage of total enrolment)	Group (as percentage of total active population)	Students (as percentage of total enrolment)	Group (as percentage of total active population)
Austria	32·4	7·4	5·5	63·7
Italy	11·6	1·7	15·4	59·6
Japan	52·8	8·7	8·7	44·2
Norway	33·6	10·4	23·9	55·4
United Kingdom	62·9	21·5	27·2	71·5
United States of America	52·4	22·9	26·6	57·4
Yugoslavia	17·9	8·8	19·0	28·0

1. At varying years between 1960 and 1966.
Source. The Social Background of Students and their Chance of Success at School, International Conference on Education, twenty-third session, Geneva, 15–23 September 1971 (doc. Unesco ED/BIE/CONFINTED/33/3, 7 June 1971).

beginning with cultural—especially language—conditions that determine the level and content of academically useful pre-school knowledge.

These facts may be deplorable but facts they are, and educational systems are not able to eliminate them. But at least they should not make them worse.

Whatever power education has, or has not, to alleviate in its own domain inequalities among individuals and groups, a resolute social policy to correct unfair distribution of educational resources and effort is the obvious pre-condition for any progress in this respect.

The disparities in question, especially the uneven degree of success achieved by various social classes in primary and secondary schools, are very clearly reflected in higher education, as may be seen from Table 6.

Inequalities at university level

Highly complex socio-economic processes govern these phenomena and, to a large extent, they are not immediately determined by educational policies. Measures such as organizing university campuses, implicitly or explicitly fixing university enrolment quotas for specific groups or even expanding scholarship systems,

Palliatives

are merely palliatives, unless they are incorporated into a resolute, long-term cultural promotion strategy, backed by a comprehensive effort to bring about political and social democracy.

Educational democracy does not reside solely in mutiplying schools, extending opportunities for access to the various levels and prolonging the period of study. Reducing the problem to this neglects the fact that other methods are available by which individuals can develop their aptitudes and find their future path.

Internal obstacles   In reality, many other questions arise. How do the various branches of education fit in with each other? Have the desired relationships been established between education for the young and that for adults? Have the conditions for a real horizontal and vertical mobility between institutions of all types and at all levels been created? Are there any dead ends in the system? Does it enable everyone to 'catch up' at any moment by acquiring whatever knowledge he or she may lack? Can people of all ages enter and leave the system at will; enter it, even belatedly, on the basis of whatever personal experience they may have acquired in private or social life?[1]

Furthermore, an educational system cannot be described as democratic, even when students and pupils are recruited on a democratic basis, if its fundamental approach is not democratic; if it is open, broadly speaking, but run by narrow-minded people; if it endeavours to break down social barriers but restricts and impoverishes the subject-matter taught; if it offers learners many paths but bars them access to truth.[2]

Democratizing education will only be possible if we succeed in

1. 'In order to be truly democratic, education should have the kind of structure which would enable individuals not only to prepare themselves to play a part in society, but also to have access to education after having been able to test their aptitudes in social life. But, today, exactly the reverse is true: education ceases precisely as society acknowledges an individual's right to behave as a responsible person, socially speaking' (J. R. Gass, OECD, Paris). A second remark is along the same lines: 'The most recent studies and inquiries show that the democratizing process of the school system (including university) has come to a dead end. Now, it is the principle of lifelong education which aims at helping people to resume study at any age in terms of later, better defined goals, in accordance with aptitudes better measured through experience in life, with well-considered motives and which, through effective guidance, makes it possible to break the deadlock . . .' (Henri Janne, Brussels, 1971).
2. 'Broadening the social base for recruitment is far from being a sufficient criterion for democracy in education. A school which recruits its pupils from among the entire population and guarantees them equal opportunity for social advancement, yet which is founded on intolerance, the glorification of power, national or imperial chauvinism, the absence of man's universal acknowledgement of man, and on racism will not be a democratic school' (Georges Friedmann, *La Puissance et la Sagesse*, p. 435, Paris, Gallimard, 1970).

74

shaking off the dogmas of conventional pedagogy,[1] if free and permanent dialogue is set up within the educational process, if this enhances individual awareness[2] of life, if learners are guided towards self-education and, in short, change from objects into subjects. Education is all the more democratic when it takes the form of a free search, a conquest, a creative act; instead of being, as it so often is, something given or inculcated, a present or a constraint.

Equality in education requires personalized pedagogy, an attentive investigation into individual aptitudes. Equal opportunity does not mean levelling. It must not at any cost entail the denial of the fundamental freedoms of individuals, attacks against the integrity of the human person or technocratic, bureaucratic abuse of power.[3]

Equal opportunity for all does not mean nominal equality, the same treatment for everyone, as many still believe today; it means making certain that each individual receives a suitable education at a pace and through methods adapted to his particular person.

Pedagogy could improve immensely if it were to acknowledge two fundamental weaknesses that all too often make it a hard taskmaster. The first is ignoring, not to say purely and simply denying, the subtle and complex workings of a personality, the multiplicity of its various forms and means of expression. The second is failing to allow for the infinite diversity of individualities, temperaments, aspirations and vocations.

Nowhere does this lack of understanding appear more clearly than in the inordinate importance given to selection, examinations and diplomas. The system rewards the strong, the lucky and the

Marking systems, selection, examinations and diplomas

1. 'Dominant in conventional pedagogy, is the concept of a model student, of a type of person who serves as a reference. The driving force of this kind of pedagogy is not to develop the person, which would entail continuing concern for his freedom, his self-responsibility, but to acquire the maximum amount of knowledge' (Bernard Courcoul, 'Nécessité d'une Pédagogie Nouvelle', *Cahiers Pédagogiques*, No. 60, April 1966).
2. 'To the extent that an active method gradually helps him to become aware of his problems, of his condition as an individual, as a subject, man will acquire instruments enabling him to make choices. . . . Knowledge cannot be "popularized", "imparted" by someone who considers that he knows to those who consider they do not know; knowledge is built up through relationships between man and the universe, relationships shot through with change, and critical problem-solving within these relationships continues its development' (Paulo Freire).
3. 'For the young, democratization has been made synonymous with uniformity and rigidity, whereas if there is to be educational progress, the range of options offered, the reform of conditions of access, a fair distribution of opportunities according to the socio-professional division of the country should constitute the *minimum aims* of this progress' (Thierry Lemaresquier, *Education from the Point of View of the Young*, p. 5, Paris, Unesco, 1971, document of the International Commission on the Development of Education, Opinions Series, 46).

conformists; it blames and penalizes the unfortunate, the slow, the ill-adapted, the people who are and who feel different.

A reassuring ideology has arisen, based on the idea of merit. This, historically speaking, is democratic in the sense that the rights of merit are set against privileges derived from birth and fortune. But its effect is to give those on the right side a good conscience while concealing the other side of the problem. That is, are those who have the advantage of socio-cultural conditions which are favourable to linguistic and abstract expression—or even those who have an above average IQ—more deserving, from the human and moral point of view, than their peers?

It remains true that it is usually in society's interest to select its most capable members for performing difficult or responsible tasks. While this narrow conception of human capacities and of the relationship between the individual and society can and must—and, at any rate, will—be superseded, it has its validity in countries where urgent needs for trained executives in the economy and administration lead to a meritocratic process of selection. This appears all the more justified when it is the only way to block nepotism or favouritism.

Methods of selection are open to criticism not only from the point of view of the principles and philosophy of education, but from a practical standpoint as well. There is little evidence that selection procedures are capable of predicting accurately whether an individual has the aptitudes required for a particular career. Generally speaking they test a narrow range of activities which relate to the hierarchic curriculum. So little do they take social and economic handicaps into account that these often appear to be considered as an additional cause of inaptitude constituting valid grounds for rejection.[1] While the marking system does in general enable an individual's achievement to be compared to that of his peers, it rarely considers his progress in relation to his own starting level.[2]

1. 'Educational systems, by grading students, also degrade. Those who "fail" to qualify in examinations ... become frustrated because the expectations which the system itself kindles in them cannot be fulfilled. Social seniority is bestowed because of the level of schooling achieved. The reckless competition among the educants is the result of such a system which acts as a patronage of an élite' (C. M. Labani, *Ends and Objectives in Education*, p. 4, Paris, Unesco, 1971, document of the International Commission on the Development of Education, Opinions Series, 7).
2. It has been said that the widespread system of examination and selection which consists in making each examinee's chances as 'objectivized' as possible is based on a 'principle which may be expressed as follows: "Above all, to form a valid judgment about someone, the main thing is not to know him!" And who can fail to realize that this is one of the fundamental rules for any bureaucratic system?' (Robert Bazin).

The theoretical purpose of examinations is to measure past · achievement and assess an individual's future capacities. Schools are naturally qualified to carry out the first of these tasks. But should they wield the heavy responsibility of deciding who is to enter professional life? The fact that relations between schools and the various spheres of activity for which they conduct this selection process are often highly tenuous makes their competence in this respect even more questionable.

Despite the damage done by rigid, formalistic and depersonalized selection systems at every stage of the educational process, they are still used almost everywhere, with a few rare exceptions and apart from occasional experiments. Real solutions to problems arising from such systems can only be found in a sweeping reorganization of the structure of educational procedures on the lines of lifelong education.

Once education becomes continual, ideas as to what constitutes success and failure will change. An individual who fails at a given age and level in the course of his educational career will have other opportunities. He will no longer be relegated for life to the ghetto of his own failure.

Beyond questions of form and method, and without debating at this point the teacher's general function in any educational process, the teacher–pupil relationship, the cornerstone of the edifice of traditional education, should be fundamentally reappraised, especially when it becomes a dominator-to-dominated relationship. This is entrenched on one side by the advantages of age, knowledge and unchallenged authority, on the other by a position of inferiority and submissiveness. A wave of rejections of this obsolete state of affairs in human relationships has swept the world of education in our time, expressed by passivity and rebellion, drop-outs and protest, as well as by independent-community teaching schemes and attempts at self-management in schools and universities, all of which is to be added to the deeper political, social and cultural causes of the so-called 'crisis of authority' making itself felt in certain educational systems.

Teacher–pupil relationship

From the standpoint of lifelong education and in the present state of human knowledge, calling teachers 'masters' (whichever of its meanings we give the word), is more and more an abuse of terms. The teacher's duty is less and less to inculcate knowledge and more and more to encourage thinking; his formal functions apart, he will have to become more and more an adviser, a partner

77

to talk to; someone who helps seek out conflicting arguments rather than handing out ready-made truths. He will have to devote more time and energy to productive and creative activities: interaction, discussion, stimulation, understanding, encouragement.

Unless relations between teachers and learners evolve accordingly, there can be no authentic democracy in education.

Co-management
and
self-management

Ensuring that people will be able fully to exercise their democratic rights in education also means guaranteeing their right to participate in the management of their educational establishment and in the definition of its policies.[1]

This is fully in line with a requirement expressed very forcefully today in political and economic affairs. Applying it to education raises two questions.

First, who among participants, users and others concerned should share this right to guide and manage education, as a joint enterprise? They could include teachers and parents; scientists, pedagogues, psychologists, paediatricians and others; students and pupils as from a certain age; administrative and other staff; employers—in certain branches of training—and representatives from various youth, labour, political and other organizations.

Second, at exactly what level should co-management and self-management operate, and to what extent? Possible activities might be to fix educational policies and objectives, establish and organize institutions, finance and distribute resources, define subject-matter, handle problems of method and pedagogy, recruit teachers, deal with salaries and regulations and supervise results.

1. 'Democratizing education does not only mean giving more education to more people, but also involving more people in educational management. Traditional education is failing to adapt itself to the needs of a growing number of people. It must be recreated. But who will recreate it? Not the administrators and the officials in education, but the people, all of them. They know their own needs and aspirations best. The question of democratizing education must be taken to the people in every country, that is to say, discussions on education and teaching must be organized, or rather unleashed at all levels in the population. Let democratizing education begin again with a real democratic act: as many people as possible must help to recreate education' (document presented by students for a debate at the Young People's Forum, Geneva, September 1971). 'Although the scope and intensity of the process of overcoming the phenomena connected with the educational crisis of society depend largely upon the economic power of each individual country, the key solution must be sought in a total transformation of the social position of education, the status and role of those directly concerned with the activities of the educational system, development policy and the administration of educational finances, as well as of the entire life and work of educational establishments, with the active participation of those directly concerned with education' (Stevan Bezdanov, *Unusual Ideas in Education*, p.2, Paris, Unesco, 1971, document of the International Commission on the Development of Education, Opinions Series, 35).

At this point it is hard to predict how far participation and co-management will be extended, despite the interest and scale of experiments which many countries have already undertaken. But we may be certain that the movement will grow, even if changing structures and abolishing age-old taboos, as such a reform presupposes, may seem unrealizable and illusory in this world.

In this section of our report, we have stressed failures, deficiencies and distortions in our educational systems, in what may be judged an excessive fashion. It may well be true that the picture we have sketched is not fair, in being incomplete and deliberately slanted towards criticism. A balanced stock-taking should present other aspects.

But our intention was not so much to set ourselves up as impartial, impassive judges as to try and contribute to taking action, by showing how necessary it is.

Education follows the laws of every human undertaking, growing old and gathering dead wood. To remain a living organism, capable of satisfying with intelligence and vigour the requirements of individuals and developing societies, it must avoid the pitfalls of complacency and routine. It must constantly question its objectives, its content and its methods.

Only in this way will it be able to contribute to its own democratization, while aware that this does not depend on education alone.

It is an enormous task. Conceptually, it presupposes that *we cease confusing, as people have more or less consciously done for a long while, equal access to education with equal opportunity, and broad access to education with democracy in education.*

Foreseeing the advent of democracy to the world of education is not an illusion. It may not be a perfect democracy, but when has this ever existed? Yet it will at least be a real, concrete, practical democracy, not inspired and built by bureaucrats or technocrats, or granted by some ruling caste. It will be living, creative and evolving. For this to be achieved, social structures must be changed and the privileges built into our cultural heritage must be reduced. Educational structures must be remodelled, to extend widely the field of choice and enable people to follow lifelong education patterns. Subject-matter must be individualized; pupils and students must be aware of their status, their rights and their own wishes; authoritarian forms of teaching must give way to relationships marked by independence, mutual responsibility and dialogue; pedagogical training must be geared to knowing and respecting the multiple aspects of human personality; guidance must replace selection; those making use of educational institutions must participate in their management and policy-making; the bureaucratic aspects of educational activity must be broken down and its administration decentralized.

Old concepts and new needs

In the preceding chapters, we have tried to show the need for a basic reconsideration of the structures and even the concepts of education. But in this field, as in many others, recognition of this need is obscured by certain received opinions about the conditions of social and economic progress.

The pride derived by industrialized nations from their own superiority and the envious admiration inspired among the poorer nations by that success have convinced both groups that the path to progress (considered in terms of development of forces of production and growth of national income) must necessarily lie in the direction followed in past years by the major developed countries. The only conceivable aim for the less developed nations was to 'catch up' the more advanced nations by passing faithfully, at an artificially accelerated pace, through each one of the phases tradition-ally covered by the developed countries. Similarly, we were tempted to think that social progress was universally automatic, or that social problems could be simply resolved by a change of régime. This led to underestimating the scope and complexity of the problems created by structural changes in societies; disregarding the con-sequences of the tensions and distortions provoked by discrimination and disparities of income; concealing the fact that economic and social transformations are essential to the resolution of conflict be-tween groups and peoples; and, above all, not appreciating the vital importance of the part which must be played in the process of development by the direct participation and active co-operation of the people.

The lessons that education should draw from a more sober view of social progress are many. Since education by itself is incapable of remedying the evils of society, it should strive to increase peoples' capacity to control their own destiny. It should endeavour, through helping every individual to develop his personal faculties, to free the creative powers of the masses by realizing the potential energies of hundreds of millions of people. And, in view of the fears regarding the long-term effects of immoderate technological progress, it should take steps to prevent the danger of a progressive dehumanization of existence by proclaiming ultimate aims of a humanistic nature.

Expenditures on education are usually regarded as special investments, governed by requirements which are fundamentally different, if not diametrically competitive with those of agriculture, industry and so on. However, it is becoming clear that development projects can achieve their aims only when they are invested with the proper human as well as material resources.

So long as tight distinctions are made between different investments, so long as they are regarded as rival and opposing, it will be impossible to break down the barriers between areas and adopt an intersectoral approach, combining and balancing the different parts of large programmes.

During these past ten years, the less developed countries and, to a smaller extent, certain industrialized nations have experienced a shortage of skilled manpower. This led people to conclude that there was an unlimited demand for technical personnel, that anyway, all technical training was useful for its own sake, and that the appearance of a surplus on the labour market was a transitory phenomenon, since this surplus would be absorbed automatically in any economy in process of industrialization. But it is generally observed today that the shortage has been either reduced or eliminated and that the number of diploma-holders unemployed often remains unchanged, or is sometimes even increasing.

As long as we believe that there is a direct correlation between the rate of growth and the structure of education, we shall not understand the need for devising systems of vocational training which are not based on the immediate needs of the labour market. A student's future working life depends on following vocational courses or certain training for immediate employment and, above all, on the indispensable general preparation required to give him maximum vocational mobility.

The most unquestioned dogma in education is that related to the school: Education equals School. Of course, it is true that schools, in absolute terms—by numerical expansion and qualitative improvement—continue to develop their fundamental role in the education system. But the school's importance in relation to other means of education and of communication between the generations is not increasing, but diminishing.

In fact, this equation between school and education will persist until we have a society where people will go on being educated more or less continously, for a long time or at intervals. We must see more clearly the image of education as a continuous project for society as a whole, not only with its schools but also its transport and communication systems, its multiple means of communication and the organized, diversified interactions of all its free citizens.

Other uncritical generalizations about education persist and multiply. People say education cements national and social unity and equalizes opportunity. School life promotes attitudes of solidarity and co-operation. All this is undoubtedly true, but the reality is not so one-sided or clear, and is full of ambiguity.

Even if it is incontestable that in numerous countries national unity has been forged by an education common to all people, it is also true that schools tend to strengthen the élite and to increase the advantages of the urban as opposed to the rural population. It is true that schools often provide the best means of escaping from the deficiencies of many rural areas, casting off the social stigma attached to manual work, or even rising to join the privileged élite. But, it is equally true that educational systems too often favour the members of the socially and economically privileged classes and the children who are academically most gifted, and by this destroy or compromise the future for large numbers of pupils. Moreover, while teaching the virtues—such as solidarity and co-operation—schools can also, by the very contradiction of their methods, nourish a rather unhealthy spirit of competition.

People still believe that the educational process is limited, by choice, to the period between infancy and adulthood. And that it should aim to provide everyone, on leaving school, with knowledge and skills which will stand them in good stead for the rest of their lives.

Contemporary psychological research raises questions about the truth of the first of these views. As to the second, accelerated change is killing it once and for all. But, if these narrow doctrines should continue to be upheld, it will be impossible to devise genuinely modern methods postulating firmly that education must be designed not only for the young but also must provide a means of enriching

83

the human experience of adults, and that the process of schooling need not necessarily be a continous one.

But discussion of such subjects still degenerates all too often into virtually vain disputes. Fruitless, at all events, in the case of those which life itself will settle, for old, outmoded ideas cannot withstand new needs very long.

PART TWO

Futures

CHAPTER 4

Challenges

Educational systems are subject to internal and external pressure.

Internal pressure results from malfunction and contradiction within the system. As we have seen, current deadlocks will make it necessary to reorient strategy and revise many options in the course of future educational development. However, past experience shows that these internal pressures and tensions are not by themselves enough to spur changes in educational structures.

External pressure is particularly powerful in our time. It is assuming new forms, setting off evolution in fits and starts, which then backfires, again changing and rearranging the basic facts of the situation. At present, it seems obvious that we can no longer continue along the same path, but people are still hesitating over which new path to choose. Future action will derive its orientation mainly from these outside factors.

The leap

Science and technology have never before demonstrated so strikingly the extent of their power and potential. During this 'second twentieth century', knowledge is making a prodigious leap forward. Research and innovation are being institutionalized, while change is accelerating boundlessly, as is the capital of human knowledge and the number of people working in science. (More than 90 per cent of scientists and inventors in all of human history are living in our times.) Equally remarkable is the constantly diminishing gap between a scientific discovery and its large-scale application. Man

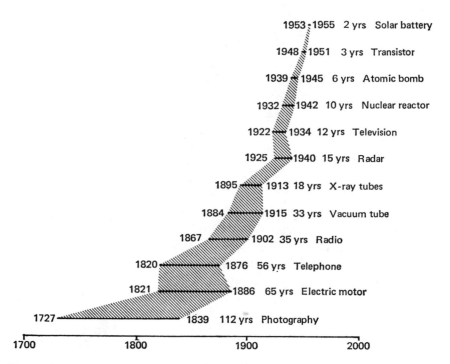

FIG. 8. Interval between discovery and application in physical science (after Eli Ginzberg, *Technology and Social Change*, Columbia University Press, 1964).

took 112 years to develop practical applications of the discovery of the principles of photography. Only two years separated the discovery from the production of solar batteries. Figure 8 shows the ever shorter time required for the application of eleven great discoveries made between the end of the eighteenth and the middle of the twentieth century.[1]

Another diagram (Fig. 9), covering a period of 250,000 years, indicates the drastic acceleration of four of the world's activities: travelling, communications, killing and calculating.[2]

For thousands of centuries man travelled at walking pace. Then came the wheel. Towards the end of the nineteenth century, the invention of the internal combustion engine enabled him to reach a speed of 140 kilometres per hour. By 1945, jet aircraft were already

1. John McHale, *The Future of the Future*, p. 60, New York, N.Y., Braziller, 1969.
2. Diagram prepared by the former British Minister of Technology, Anthony Wedgwood Benn, who used it during a lecture at London University on 25 April 1970.

88

travelling at ten times that speed. Today, astronauts move through space at speeds on the order of 40,000 kilometres per hour.

Twentieth-century speeds and world-wide availability of modern vehicles have made travel commonplace and distance inconsequential. Last century, the average man hardly ever ventured from his birthplace. Modern man is a nomad. In 1967, 108 million Americans took 360 million trips involving overnight stays more than 100 miles from their home. And in 1971 1 million foreigners voyaged to the United States, while 1½ million Germans took vacations in Spain. In 1970, airlines flew 310 million passengers 4,500 million miles.

Migrations from country to town, labour-force transfers, business and tourism—the consequences of such mass movement are enormous. Individual equilibrium, stability of community life and

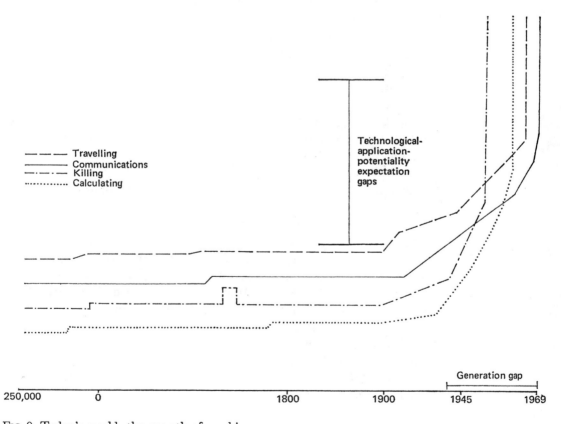

FIG. 9. Today's world: the growth of machines.

institutions, and traditional values are all subject to shocks and alterations which—whether beneficial or harmful—require man to be adaptable to change on an unprecedented scale.[1]

In communications man was limited for thousands of years to the distance his voice or a drumbeat could carry or the time it took to deliver a written message. In the 1960s, hundreds of millions of people heard astronauts speaking from space and saw them the moment they stepped on the moon.

The dizzying future

There is every reason to believe that this progress in human knowledge and power, which has assumed such dizzying speed over the past twenty years, is only in its early stages. It is likely to gather still greater momentum as teaching in all countries becomes more democratic and particularly as educational progress in developing countries produces many more researchers in fields related to man's knowledge and his control over the environment.

Further qualitative leaps forward may be predicted not only in inventive activity but in productivity, reliability and quality. Progress in electronics, coupled with the coming of computers, is the basis of a revolution comparable to the invention of writing. Prospects for industrial production have been radically renewed. Until quite recent times, industry used natural raw materials. But we now produce 'composite bodies' from certain microstructures, from atoms and molecules, which are stronger, tougher, lighter and able to withstand greater extremes of temperature than traditional materials. This revolution is freeing industry from some of its dependency on traditional 'natural resources', enabling it to draw the materials it needs from various organic or inorganic elements.

Scientific discoveries are innumerable and have tumultuous impact. There is virtually no aspect of our physical and social universe whose basic conditions are not modified or revolutionized, at ever-closer intervals. This scientific and technological revolution affects all countries, without exception. Probably more than any other factor, it has set its distinctive seal on the contemporary world by imposing on all men everywhere a concern with similar crucial problems and a rapidly increasing number of similar habits and practices. Linked to this revolution, cultural and aesthetic movements are forcing changes in values and ethics, in the transmission and perception of messages, in artistic creation and cultural de-

1. For a detailed study of the social and psychological consequences of modern man's mobility, cf. Alvin Toffler, *Future Shock*, New York, N.Y., Random House, 1970.

90

velopment. All these movements come into play simultaneously so that people talk about 'the double cultural revolution of the industrial age'. Its driving energy springs from a combination of reason and imagination, of the irrational and the emotional. Present-day educators are, in fact, faced with a fascinating task: that of discovering how to attain harmonious balance between rational training and liberation of sensibility.

Prospects for scientific development are exalting, impressive and at the same time terrifying. To consider only the past twenty-five years, during which humanity has been so prodigiously endowed with new elements for material progress, the question arises whether man's growing power, and the expansion and diversification in what he produces, have made him any happier. And whether the almost unlimited possibilities for developing the planet and being one day free of it are providing any vision of this happiness.

Exciting and terrifying prospects

It is commonplace to say that science and technology may be used both beneficially and harmfully, but there is a complex, knotty and subtle problem underlying that apparent platitude. It might well turn out to be the central moral problem of our time. It is also commonplace to reiterate that the consequences of scientific and technological activity depend fundamentally on the socio-economic and political system within which it takes place. It will doubtless be a long time, however, before man can entirely rule out the possibility of harmful applications of science. The science-technology complex not only justifies hope for solutions to humanity's problems; it also provides cause for world-wide anxiety.

Developing countries should learn a lesson, here, from the experience of industrialized societies, in order to avoid their excesses. The problem for such countries is less to be forearmed against the misuse of science than to integrate scientific values into their cultures.

Unquestionably, development—which all countries admit is necessary—implies adopting a scientific frame of mind. Developing countries can only achieve their own renewal yet retain their national features by integrating science into their traditional cultures, and by integrating universal thought into their own national life. A culture can only survive by being able to change.

A scientific frame of mind

Man's future is ineluctably linked to scientific advances and the development of productive capacity, whatever meaning we may give to the word progress itself—and whether we are optimistic,

91

pessimistic or merely etymological about it. Modern man is greatly dismayed to find that these processes evade him, that they obey their own logic and that their logic is inhuman. Matters are not changed by the fact that man himself set up these processes and controls each of their separate phases and sources, from research to consumption, by a chain of decision-making: to apply, undertake, invest, produce and distribute.

Whether we deem man's ability to re-establish mastery over the decisive elements in his fate to be great or small—and this is one of the most significant issues for contemporary thought, especially political thought—we can only conclude that a reasonable educational doctrine must be based on the following postulate: present and future societies have, or will have, the capacity to prove that science and techniques are not ends in themselves, their true object being mankind.

Science and technology must become essential components in any educational enterprise; they must be incorporated into all educational activity intended for children, young people and adults, in order to help the individual to control social energies as well as natural and productive ones—thereby achieving mastery over himself, his choices and actions—and, finally, they must help man to acquire a scientific turn of mind so that he becomes able to promote science without being enslaved by it.

Gaps

In 1961, the United Nations launched the First Development Decade and thereby drew the world's attention to the growing separation between a little cluster of wealthy nations and the two-thirds of humanity living in very precarious conditions.

As we begin the Second Development Decade, the gap dividing the privileged countries from the rest of mankind is far from having closed. On the contrary, it is still widening, a fact which hardly helps ease tension in the world.

Disparate factors

Population increase is one cause of the gap. The annual demographic growth rate in non-industrialized countries is 2·5 per cent. At this rate—if it continues, the population of the world in thirty years' time will be double its present figure of 3,600 million.

92

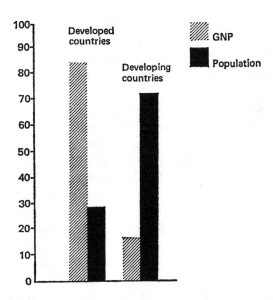

FIG. 10. The gap between rich and poor nations: population and GNP distribution in 1970.

As we know, economic growth in developing countries, especially in relation to demographic growth, is far from adequate. The annual figure during the 1960–68 period was only 4·9 per cent. During the same period the annual growth rate in developed capitalist countries was 5·2 per cent and in developed socialist countries it reached 6·8 per cent, while the population in these countries is increasing, on the whole, at a far slower rate. The average annual rate of increase in income per inhabitant was 2·4 per cent in developing countries. However, this average figure fails to highlight the fact that of all people living in developing countries (apart from the People's Republic of China), 22 per cent live in countries where individual incomes rose by less than 1 per cent, and only 30 per cent of people are in the countries where it rose by more than 2 per cent per annum.[1] The widening of the gap is, apparently, inexorable. (Fig. 10.)

The same trend may be seen in world trade. Since exports from developing countries consist mainly of raw materials, the demand for which grows less rapidly than for manufactured goods, the division between the two groups of countries is likely to grow more marked.

1. Lester B. Pearson, *Partners in Development*, New York, N.Y., Praeger, 1969.

93

The highly eloquent maps printed here (see Figs. 11 and 12) depict two singularly different versions of the world in 1980, according to whether we measure each country on this planet in millions of inhabitants (Fig. 11) or in terms of its national revenue (Fig. 12).

Unemployment

One particularly important consequence of this situation is that it makes the employment problem more acute. From 1960 to 1970 the active population in developing countries rose by 22 per cent as against 12 per cent in industrialized countries; from 1970 to 1980, the ratio is expected to be 26:11 per cent. Forecasts in absolute figures indicate that during this second period some 268 million people will make their first appearance on a labour market, in developing countries, while only 56 million are expected to do so in the industrialized countries.

If to the declared unemployed we add the 'hidden' unemployed, including all those who do not look for work because labour market prospects discourage them, and the underemployed (also either declared or 'hidden') including those who work less than thirty hours per week and endeavour to work longer or would do so if opportunities offered—then unemployment may be described as hitting a possible 40 per cent of the active population.[1]

One particularly disturbing feature is unemployment among young people, including an increasing number of graduates with degrees and diplomas. Such unemployment is two or three times greater in this group than among adults over the age of 25. It affects people who have had an elementary or secondary education more than the illiterate, on the one hand, and more than those with higher education diplomas on the other.[2]

The least favoured

Disparities between rural and urban areas, between those who work on the land and those who do not, are becoming more marked. Development of industry and services has helped to increase national revenue, but the attempt to achieve a maximum growth rate for the gross national product (GNP) has also produced economic disequilibrium and accentuated social inequality. In this process, agricultural workers, living at or below the minimum subsistence level, are among the least-favoured classes—requiring urgent political, social and educational action—as are the young people, educated or not, looking in vain for work. It is becoming

1. ILO, *World Employment Programme*, p. 42, Geneva, 1969; *Towards Full Employment: A Programme for Colombia*, p. 13–28, Geneva, 1970; D. Turnham, *The Employment Problem in Less Developed Countries*, p. 41–72, Paris, OECD, 1971.
2. Turnham, op. cit., p. 48–52.

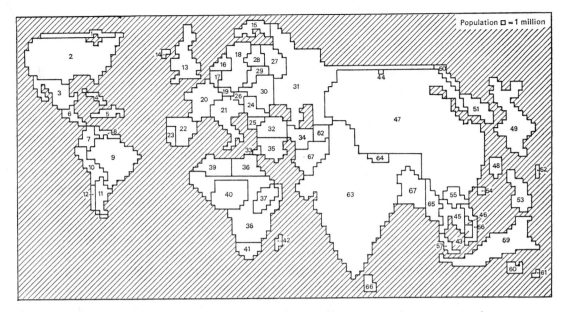

FIG. 11. The world in 1980 drawn in terms of millions of inhabitants (see code below).

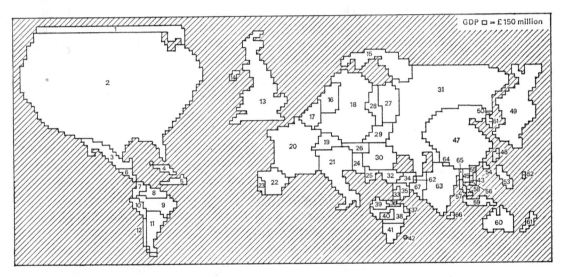

FIG. 12. The world in 1980 drawn in terms of national revenue (see code below).

CODE

Afghanistan (62)	Czechoslovakia (29)	Khmer Republic (43)	Poland (27)	Yugoslavia (24)
Argentina (11)	Egypt (36)	Korea (Republic of)	Portugal (23)	
Australia (60)	Ethiopia (37)	(51)	Singapore (58)	Arab Middle East (35)
Austria (26)	France (20)	Korea (Democratic	South Africa (41)	Oceania (52)
Belgium and	Federal Republic of	People's Republic	Spain (22)	Other African
Luxembourg (17)	Germany (18)	of) (50)	Switzerland (19)	countries (38)
Brazil (9)	German Democratic	Laos (46)	Thailand (45)	Other Caribbean
Burma (65)	Republic (28)	Madagascar (42)	Turkey (32)	countries (5)
Canada (1)	Greece (25)	Malaysia (57)	U.S.S.R. (31)	Other Central
Ceylon (66)	Hong Kong (54)	Mexico (3)	United Kingdom (13)	American countries (6)
Chile (12)	India (63)	Mongolia (44)	United States of	Other East European
China (People's	Indonesia (59)	Nepal (64)	America (2)	countries (30)
Republic of) (47)	Iran (34)	Netherlands (16)	Venezuela (8)	Other North African
China (Republic	Ireland (14)	New Zealand (61)	Viet-Nam (Republic	countries (39)
of) (48)	Israel (33)	Nigeria (40)	of) (56)	Other South American
Colombia (7)	Italy (21)	Pakistan (67)	Viet-Nam (Democratic	countries (10)
Cuba (4)	Japan (49)	Philippines (53)	Republic of) (55)	Scandinavia (15)

Source. Godfrey N. Brown, *Towards an Education for the 21st Century—A World Perspective* Keele (United Kingdom), University of Keele, 1970 (an inaugural lecture).

Widening gap

more and more obvious that developing countries possess great wealth in their abundance of labour, provided they put the requisite policies into effect.

Yet the essential problem is to gain some idea of the likely course of development over the next few decades. There is general agreement there will be many serious consequences if it continues on current lines. The world may find itself in a deadlocked and unbalanced situation in the comparatively near future, with effects on both industrialized and developing countries. Also, mankind would appear to be exhausting its resources, which may slow down world development. Finally, the gap between the highly industrialized and less industrialized countries will widen, even if the objectives laid down in the Second Development Decade are achieved 100 per cent. In fact, even if we were to suppose that annual population growth rate in developing countries levelled off at 1·8 to 2 per cent (that is to say, at well below its current rate), that the GNP in these countries reached an annual increase rate of 5 to 6 per cent, corresponding to an average increase in the product per inhabitant of 3 per cent (instead of the present 2·4 per cent) and if we assume, furthermore, that the increase in product per inhabitant continues—as highly likely—at the rate recorded over the past twenty-five years, the gap would none the less be 15 per cent greater by the year 2000.

Need for economic expansion

This should not be allowed to discourage effort. Quite the contrary. Development does not come about in a day. The United Kingdom and France took a hundred years to reach industrial maturity, the Soviet Union and Japan fifty. But in present conditions, developing countries cannot afford to take so much time over their economic expansion.[1] Countries industrialized earlier doubtless showed better economic progress, on the whole, or at least so it seems when one looks at their record. But neither, probably, did those countries suffer from problems arising in our time out of the division of labour on a world-wide scale. Their economic progress was accordingly due to the operation of a certain number of

1. The incisive opinion of one highly regarded economist on this subject is of interest: 'If the countries now at advanced stages of development took a long time to get where they are, why should not the Latin American countries keep to the same rhythm? Cannot time perhaps solve their problems too? . . . The economy's lack of the required dynamism cannot be corrected by the mere passage of time, and the longer the time that goes by, the harder will this weakness be to cure, and the greater will be the social and political cost, or, in a word, the cost in human terms' (Raúl Prebisch, *Change and Development*, report presented to the Inter-American Development Bank, Santiago de Chile, 17 April 1970).

historical laws which now seem beyond question. This led to people overlooking the differences between these nations. Thus it is hardly surprising that countries now in the process of development should have to think out—or rethink—their economic policy, not in terms of models provided by the advanced nations, but in terms of their own special situation.

Some analysts find fault with both the prospects and direction of the Second Development Decade. Their criticisms follow two lines of thought, at once contradictory and complementary. *Search for solutions*

There are those who believe it is not impossible to reverse development disparities by accelerating economic growth rates in the Third World. If these could climb to 7 per cent during the 1970s, 8 per cent in the 1980s and culminate at 8·5 per cent in the 1990s, the gap between the two groups of countries would begin to diminish. In 1970, an inhabitant of an industrialized nation had an income twelve times greater than his fellow man in a developing country, but—applying this theory—in the year 2000 it would only be eight times greater. Some seek the solution in a fresh world-wide distribution of resources and in the transfer of large financial and technical means to the developing countries, using different methods from those applied or recommended nowadays.[1] Others say the solution lies in changing development policies in their entirety, in concerted effort, in radically overhauling current approaches and in working towards a 'condition of global equilibrium'.[2] Some advocates of the global policy would appeal to

1. One author favouring this solution, Angelos Angelopoulos, proposes the following means to reach this end: 'If we consider that the GNP increases by 5 per cent annually, we would be able to carry out the proposed financing plan by taking 0·5 per cent of the GNP, that is to say less than half of the percentage recommended by international organizations, on condition that this contribution were provided *free of charge*. This complies with the new policy we are recommending, under which developed countries should adopt, towards the poorer countries, the system of redistribution of the national income which they apply in the domestic domain to improve the standard of living among their own less-favoured classes' (*Le Tiers-Monde Face aux Pays Riches*, p.143, Paris, Presses Universitaires de France, 1972).
2. Commenting on the Meadows Report, the executive committee of the Club of Rome, grouping educators, scientists and industrialists, said in a report: 'We recognize that world equilibrium can become a reality only if the lot of the so-called developing countries is substantially improved, both in absolute terms and relative to the economically developed nations, and we affirm that this improvement can be achieved only through a global strategy. Short of a world effort, today's already explosive gaps and inequalities will continue to grow larger. ... A goal would be for them (for the economically developed countries) to encourage a deceleration in the growth of their own material output while, at the same time, assisting the developing nations in their efforts to advance their economies more rapidly (*The Limits to Growth*, p. 191, 195, a report for the Club of Rome's Projection on the Predicament of Mankind, New York, N.Y., Potomac Associates, 1972).

developing countries to take measures to decrease their birth rates. Simultaneously, they urge industrialized nations to slow down their economic and technical growth and reorient their consumption patterns, which should permit a marked increase in aid to developing countries.[1]

A world approach

Whatever may be thought of such proposals (and we do not consider ourselves in a position to favour one or another) they appear to have the merit of expressing problems in global terms. Objective observers are inclined to consider them as a combination of factors, not to be separated by placing developing countries' needs on the one side and aid which industrialized nations could extend to them on the other. They believe these problems should be related to the facts of the world's economic situation, which covers evolution in all countries seen as one single set of problems, in all their complexity and interrelationships.

New meaning of 'gap'

It is worth noting however that these various proposed solutions all rely on exclusively quantitative data, hitherto usually reduced to the problem of the 'gap' between industrialized and developing countries. This idea may assume fresh significance if considered on an essentially qualitative level, that is to say if we give up using GNP or over-all growth rates as our main terms of reference. In fact, to the extent that a given developing country uses its resources so as to obtain the maximum yield from them, this notorious 'gap' loses most of its significance and is reduced to the status of a statistical comparison. From this point of view, the essential criterion becomes the use of an authentically national development model and to ensure that the entire population participates democratically in the development effort.

Inspiration for education

There are analogies between the foregoing general considerations and others more directly related to education:

If we agree that disequilibrium between resources and the use made of them must be eliminated, educational development should then play an ever-greater part in a policy designed for economic progress.

If social inequality holds up the advent of tomorrow's societies,

1. Paul Bairoch writes, for example: 'In macro-economic terms, this would consist in progressively reducing (in five to ten years) developed countries' growth rates per inhabitant per annum by 0·5 per cent to 1 per cent, and in transferring some 2 to 3 per cent of their gross product to developing countries, which could use these additional resources to produce a growth rate of some 4 to 5 per cent per inhabitant, leading to parity in levels of economic development in the two regions before the year 2050' (*Le Tiers-Monde dans l'Impasse*, p.344, Paris, Gallimard, 1971).

educational strategies must necessarily make a more determined effort to disseminate more widely the ways and means of learning.

If regional disparities within each separate country as well as between one country and another hamper world development, then it is only rational to encourage all efforts to educate the less favoured sections of the population, the rural regions and the least-favoured countries.

If countries clearly require an over-all policy and a common philosophy for development, then educational evolution would become more effective if it were founded on a common approach, which in turn could help to form national policies.

These are the directions that education should take, since it undeniably suffers from growing social and economic gaps and disequilibrium—which it can help to overcome, given a serious effort.

Environment in peril

Technological development has enabled man to solve many problems, but it has had harmful effects on a number of aspects of contemporary life. All over the world, it contributes to environmental deterioration.

This deterioration does not date from yesterday. During his 7,000 years of recorded history, man has had to tackle the environment and control it. But, through carelessness or ignorance, he has at times impoverished it. Fire, used for hunting and itinerant agricultural purposes, laid forests bare. Irrigation of arid regions increased salinization, which later led to the loss of cultivable land when drainage was inadequate to carry salts away from the irrigated zone. In North Africa and the Middle East, this process turned much formerly fertile land into desert.

Since the nineteenth century, spoiling processes have gathered speed as populations increased and industrialization developed. In former times it took centuries to exhaust fertile land; now a few decades are enough. In North and South America, as in Africa, intensive forest clearing, together with the disappearance of grass and other vegetation covering the soil, have led to erosion, floods and drought. The soil, no longer protected, is blown or washed away.

Disorderly expansion

99

According to United Nations estimates, 'Five hundred million hectares (1,235 million acres) of arable land have already been lost through erosion and salinization, two thirds of the world's forests have been lost to production and 150 kinds of birds and animals have become extinct because of man. Approximately 1,000 species or races of wild animals are now rare or in peril. Erosion, soil deterioration, deforestation, watershed damage and the destruction of animal and plant life continue and in some areas are increasing'.[1]

The growth of cities has aggravated this destruction. In the United States, some two hectares (five acres) of land per minute are absorbed into highways, urban expansion, airports, car parks and other 'modern requirements'. Forty per cent of the world's population now live in urban areas. If this trend continues, by the beginning of the twenty-first century about three-quarters will be living in urban areas overflowing their present limits, merging into each other to form 'megalopolises' of the kind stretching from Boston to Washington or from Tokyo to Yokohama.

Ecological disequilibrium

Until the nineteenth century, towns remained in direct, fairly close contact with the countryside or the sea, enabling man to satisfy his physiological and psychological needs. With the advent of industrialization, urban development was solely a function of economic or political imperatives, in the belief that man was master of his environment and capable of liberating himself from his natural biological limits.

The consequences of that disorderly expansion are now upon us: pollution of the air, the soil, lakes and seas; physiological and psychological disturbances; calm a memory, violence a constant menace. Noise—upsetting city-dwellers at work, in the streets and at home—interferes with mental concentration, provokes a new form of fatigue[2] and increases the risk of vocational illness and disorders, such as deafness. As the cities become more over-populated and anonymous, so man becomes more nervous and aggressive.

The developing countries, it would seem, have yet to learn this from the industrialized societies' experience. They have permitted (or solicited) elements derived from a totally different technological

1. U Thant, 'Man the Killer of Nature', *Unesco Courier*, p. 48, August–September 1970. See also, *Use and Conservation of the Biosphere*, Paris, Unesco, 1970.
2. According to Constantin Stramentov ('The Architects of Silence', *Unesco Courier*, p. 10, July 1967), studies in post offices showed that when the noise level rose from 75 to 95 decibels productivity immediately dropped by 25 per cent, while mail-sorting mistakes increased fourfold. When acoustic sound-screens placed round workers lowered noise-levels by 10 and 15 decibels, however, productivity increased by 5 and 18 per cent respectively.

universe to invade their accustomed way of life, speeding their 'development'. Its dualistic nature seems to be forcing them into a pattern of life in which they are becoming increasingly insensitive to the dangers of cultural and ecological disequilibrium. This phenomenon has already dragged many developing countries into a situation in which pollution of their towns and cities and, especially, the irreversible deterioration of their vital countryside are destroying the natural harmony of the setting in which their own culture has evolved over the centuries.

It is not only man's environment but—in the near future—his very fate which may be threatened, and he has already begun to suffer. Rapid changes are winding up tension in people, increasing insecurity, nervous disorders, antisocial behaviour, delinquency and criminality.

Technology has already produced gross harmful effects. It has jeopardized and is still disturbing the balanced relationship between man and his environment, between nature and social structures, between man's physiological constitution and his personality. Irreversible ruptures are threatening mankind. The job of confronting these multiple dangers falls largely on education. Work to remedy the situation involves an all-out attempt to prevent such division, to forestall and counteract the dangers deriving from the technological civilization. Stimulating awareness of such dangers is a demanding new task for education, but particularly appropriate to it for many reasons and, too often, one that is much underestimated.

Threats

The future of our societies lies in democracy, development and change. Our societies must accordingly train men for democracy, humanistic development and change.

But history is not an idyll. Democracy has to blaze a path through a mass of obstacles and snares. Technical progress, the relative abundance of goods already available in some places, and the plethora likely in the future, all hold out great promise for justice. But that progress is also a source of iniquity, alienation and new tyrannies.

Progress in information and communication techniques is

providing both governments and private groups with more and more extensive methods of intervening in individuals' lives and shaping their opinions. Meanwhile research on the brain and the learning process afford increasing possibilities for influencing human behaviour.

People today may also have far more information available and possess far more knowledge than their predecessors. But this knowledge often obscures a person's perception and understanding of reality rather than shedding light on it. The real reins of political power which most constitutions confer on the peoples, with sincerity or at any rate with great pomp and circumstance, are slipping more and more out of their grasp. Their participation in the decision-making process is beset with obstacles.

Fortunes and misfortunes of democracy

Progress in management sciences and cybernetics, as well as in education and the spread of information, radically changes fundamental aspects of democratic practice and leads people to claim a greater say in public life.

This means that democratic education must become a preparation for the real exercise of democracy.

Education in democracy can no longer be separated from the practice of politics. It must equip citizens with a solid grounding in socio-economic matters and sharpen their judgement. It must encourage commitment and vigorous action in all spheres of individual concern and endeavour—politics, public affairs, trade-union activities, social and cultural life—and help them to retain their own free will, to make authentic personal choices. It must teach everyone to fight against the abuse of propaganda, against the omnipresent messages and temptations of mass communication media, against the risk of estrangement and even of 'anti-education' which those media may bring.

Upheavals in private life

Profound changes are taking place not only in public life and work but also in the daily lives of more and more men and women. Leisure itself has become a complex phenomenon, offering new opportunities but triggering new problems.[1] People are plagued by doubt and scepticism, by the decay in time-honoured values, by

1. 'The individual is demanding the right to a space of time during which he may satisfy his own personality needs, regarded as an ultimate end and not as a means of social commitment which the community imposes on him. . . . Leisure has in fact (become) the crucible for new values in post-industrial society which are transforming the values of work, of politics, of faith and family' (Joffre Dumazedier, *Pour une Réévaluation Radicale de la Politique Culturelle de Peuple et Culture, 1971–1975*, Paris, Peuple et Culture, 1972).

102

the latent threat of nuclear cataclysm and all it could lead to: cosmic disturbances, earthquakes, degeneracy. It is often said that science and technology, industry and organization prevent harmony between life and work. The emotional content and security derived from family and community life are losing their importance and being replaced by impersonal relationships in a factory, an administration or a plantation. The individual, anonymous among the city crowds and the hordes of migrant workers, feels more and more lonely, helpless and 'unidimensional'. Material goods have increased but, at the same time, so has people's frustration. Advertising not only informs consumers, it also tends perpetually to create new needs, to drive customers to consume. A new alienation within the consumer society may accordingly be added to the individual's traditional alienation within his work.

Various forms of rebellion in our time, particularly among young people in certain countries, are directed against this 'warping' of values in the consumer society, against deterioration of the environment, against injustice, against war, against encroachments—apparent or not—on freedom and individual fulfilment. This must not be seen primarily as an expression of the traditional conflict between the generations. (In fact, that conflict—the 'generation gap'—is tending to fade away. Physically and psychologically, humanity is younger than it was; more than half the world's population today is under 25 years of age.)

The causes and forms of assertion or protest among young people vary according to the country in question and its stage of development. Some agree to work within the institutions to develop them, some to try to change them; but others refuse any integration into the 'old order', particularly those who accuse the establishment of letting millions of children die of starvation while it stockpiles atomic bombs and perpetuates unjust ruinous wars. Many demand different paradigms for their adult years from those society offers them. They seek new values, a new way of life in a peaceful, non-violent world, where pursuit of spiritual wealth will displace the race for material profit.[1]

At the same time a certain conservatism is working against the phenomena of the technological age accused of forcing the pace of

1. 'What makes dissent among young people a cultural phenomenon rather than a simple political movement is that it transcends the ideological level and attains to that of the conscience, striving to change our profoundest conceptions of the self, of others and of the environment' (T. Roszak, *The Making of a Counter-Culture*, New York, N.Y., Doubleday, 1970).

evolution or producing abrupt upheavals. The 'establishment', traditions, customs, hierarchies, the obsession with status, the reluctance to relinquish power or social position, all play their part in slowing down changes in our time.

Threats are growing more serious, clashes are intensifying and so are conservative reactions. Failure to grasp the essential contradictions in our world will make it harder than ever to find one's bearings in it and, especially, to discern the necessary paths for future educational action.

Education must recognize itself for what it is: it may be the product of history and society, but it is not their passive plaything. It is an essential factor in shaping the future, particularly at the present moment, since in the last resort education has to prepare mankind to adapt to change, the predominant characteristic of our time.

There are many, complex changes. Varying greatly in nature, they affect virtually every human community, and they are equivocal, opening new vistas and creating new threats.

Education, in this context, also has two dimensions. It has to prepare for changes, show people how to accept them and benefit from them, create a dynamic, non-conformist, non-conservative frame of mind. Concurrently, it has to play the part of an antidote to the many distortions within man and society. For democratic education must be able to provide a remedy to frustration, to the depersonalization and anonymity in the modern world and, through lifelong education, reduce insecurity and enhance professional mobility.

These aspects of educational action are all too often neglected, although it is unreasonable to expect more of education than it can give or count on education alone to produce solutions to the basic problems of our time.

But this does not in the least diminish the importance of efforts undertaken to renew methods of education and rethink its functions, duties and ultimate aims. On the contrary, the real dimensions of these efforts will be enhanced if they are seen against the background of this age of man and its challenging drama.

CHAPTER 5

Discoveries

The malfunction of much educational practice[1] makes renovation in education *necessary*. Changes in socio-economic structures and the scientific and technological revolution[2] make it *imperative*. Scientific research and technological progress related to education, combined with growing awareness among the peoples of the world, make it *possible*.

Both inside and outside the pedagogic universe, there is quite an arsenal of scientific, technological, social, cultural and structural innovations which could profoundly modify the basic conditions and organization of educational systems. Recent illuminating research on the brain, progress in the theory of information, systematic work by language and psychotechnical institutes, results obtained in group psychology and by teams of cultural anthropologists, models produced by systems analysts and cyberneticians are among the new acquisitions which often need little more than the appropriate administrative machinery and information transferral in order to increase the efficiency of traditional school systems.

New forms are emerging within the sphere of education itself. Rigid organizations are becoming more flexible, the educational institution is linking up with the social environment in new ways, internal roles and functions are being redistributed, authoritarian patterns are being replaced by structures allowing more 'participation', the concept of the total educational environment is taking root. Other developments include individualized teaching and modular systems and programmes.[3] These are partial innovations,

1. See Chapters 2 and 3.
2. See Chapter 4.
3. The world 'module' is used in computer-assisted teaching to mean a 'block' of knowledge, an element which may be incorporated in a logical assembly forming the

still mainly in the experimental stage. The pressure of circumstances may lead to their large-scale introduction in educational systems, or at least their use as demonstration models that could be widely reproduced in order to match resources more adequately both to needs and to individual and community aspirations.

This over-all view of scientific and technological aspects highlights the fact that in the present-day world, the educational enterprise has new dimensions far exceeding its traditional domain. This cannot be overlooked when developing educational strategies and policies or training professional personnel.

In fact, anyone responsible for educational practice and working with its daily problems will from now on be confronted with this or that new possibility discovered or indicated by science and technology. At a time when education must meet demands which appear to exceed its resources, it is being offered new tools, new powers on all sides, and finding new ways to carry out its ever-growing responsibilities. Failure to make reasonable allowance for these features when drafting educational policies and strategies and in teacher-training programmes would be tantamount to putting oneself deliberately in an impossible situation.

New findings from research

Brain research   The breakthrough achieved in recent years in our knowledge of the brain and in the biochemical sciences has led to a clearer and more objective understanding of human behaviour, of mental mechanisms and the learning process. One striking fact emerged from these new discoveries. The human brain has a very large unused potential which some authorities—more or less arbitrarily— have assessed at 90 per cent.

Cerebral neurophysiology has already opened up a number of prospects for improving the training process, by throwing light on

---

learner's personalized course of instruction. A modular chain is the series of modules selected by or imposed on a student according to his or her inclinations and aptitudes. An imposed modular series is known as a path and a freely chosen modular series is known as a way.

the mechanisms of mental attention, on the biochemistry of memory, the phenomena of fatigue and the optimal learning ages. We can control the condition and functioning of the brain through electric action and can also use biochemical substances to act directly on certain neuromechanisms.[1]

Laboratory research is currently studying the possible existence of 'memory molecules' in the brain enabling information to be stored in linear fashion and, consequently, the possibility of molecular models capable of expressing the learning process in other terms. It seems that some form of chemical supplement could improve defective or senescent psychological functions, but not to the extent of entirely replacing normal intellectual functions. The general opinion today would seem to be that chemical intervention has so far yielded more results at the affective than at the cognitive level. For this reason *current research does not aim to replace educational action by some form of pharmaceutical treatment, but merely to study biochemical aids to education.*

Experiments studying ways and means of reducing entropy in brain cells and guaranteeing a permanent consolidation of protein for memory-functions support the considerable progress already achieved in the practical field concerning the role of malnutrition, both qualitatively and quantitatively speaking, in the individual's mental activity, especially during the immediate post-natal period. Cerebral development having an irreversible character, deprivation in the course of its evolution, would seem to lead to irreversible consequences. Undernourishment in the mother can make the new-born baby's nervous system more fragile, and may lead to serious damage later on. Premature weaning can compromise the process whereby the neurones acquire myeline. The critical period for the brain's physical growth being between the fifth and the tenth month following birth, malnutrition at this time may reduce the number of cells in the brain, which has virtually finished growing by the end of the second year. Longitudinal development

Infant malnutrition

1. Research over the past ten years has been informative on the role of ribonucleic acid (a genetic substance controlling protein synthesis) in memory. The distinction is now drawn between immediate or 'telephonic' memory, a simple electrochemical mechanism lasting only a few minutes, and long-term memory, for which chemically coded neuromechanisms are recorded in the structure of the brain cells. Such memory involves the production of specific enzymes in the brain cells, and this can be facilitated or even provoked. More generally, it has been found that small quantities of ribonucleic acid are secreted in the brain cells during the learning process, and it would appear that any chemical substance capable of accelerating the cells' production of RNA could thereby facilitate the learning process.

studies[1] carried out in various countries, especially in Central Africa and Central America, show that malnutrition during the first four years of life leads to mediocre intellectual performance when children reach school age.

It is therefore during the pre-school period (and more particularly up to the age of 4) that society could adopt efficient nutritional measures which would improve the performance of its educational system.

Malnutrition[2]—social and economic aspects corroborate the ethical argument here—derives first of all from inadequate resources in the group to which the child belongs. If there are other deficiencies in the environment, he or she clearly runs greater risk of suffering from other handicaps when the time comes to go to school: psychological conditions, family situation, irregular school-attendance, etc. Nutritional and socio-economic shortcomings are not the only ones involved. The wrong kind of education and, worse, the lack of education, even among children living in comfortable material conditions, may have disastrous consequences for cerebral development. It has been established that 'educational deficiency' has a prejudicial effect on growth of the cortex. This introduces the idea of a real social crime, which to date has received scant attention: *the damage inflicted on human brains through negligence and lack of attention.*

Conversely, it is reasonable to assume, given the present state of research into cerebral biochemistry and the latent possibilities of the brain's approximately 10,000 million neurones, that if it were to benefit from more favourable conditions and a new kind

1. That is, studies covering all of an individual's lifetime, or carried out with an individual's history in mind.
2. The United Nations' concern over the problem of malnutrition in the world is closely linked to its concern over educational development, since 'protein-calorie malnutrition in early life can lead to physic and mental retardation which may not be reversible. If such damage has been done, the consumption of extra protein in adult life will not repair it and if such damage is widespread in a country, it will likely impede that country's future development in almost every respect' (U Thant, Secretary-General of the United Nations). This correlation, which is also important for educational strategies, is based on specific findings by experts in this subject: 'Protein malnutrition is an important cause of infant and young child mortality, stunted physical growth, low work output, premature aging and reduced life span in the developing world. Recent research has also revealed a link between malnutrition in infancy and early childhood and impaired learning and behaviour in later life. The widespread occurrence of protein malnutrition especially among infants, pre-school children, and expectant and nursing mothers in many developing nations spells grave danger to the full expression of the genetic potential of the population of large sections of the world community' (*Strategy Statement on Action to Avert the Protein Crisis in the Developing Countries*, New York, N.Y., United Nations, May 1971).

108

of educational action and environmental influence, the human brain could develop its creative capacities to unimaginable limits.

Current psychological research is producing ever more thorough studies of problems of knowledge, no longer regarded as a primitive, unchanging store of forms, but as a process of development. Contributions by experimental laboratories of psychology to the phenomena of learning and memory, clinical studies and epistemological investigations, studies in the psychology of form have all amassed a body of material which, put into proper order, could greatly increase the yield of school systems by making it possible to renovate organization and methods.

Contributions from psychology

Research in psychology is currently proceeding in the following particularly significant directions.

The first, mechanistic and reductionist, is that of the behaviourists, whose aim is to construct a psychology which does not depend on 'mental' elements. Their goal is to 'predict' rather than to 'understand'. Their laboratory studies concentrate on direct relations between stimuli, or inputs, which can be manipulated at will, and responses or outputs. The 'black box' branch of behaviourism does not concern itself with the 'internal connexions' between stimulus and response.[1] Theoretical considerations apart, psychologists studying the learning process use carefully controlled mechanical apparatus for distributing stimuli. They use only positive reinforcement for these, excluding any kind of punishment, each piece of information supplied by the machine presenting the 'subject', the learner, with choices. The choice testifies to the understanding acquired, especially—as in programmed teaching systems—in the case of linear learning and straightforward training, rather than in learning processes involving comprehension and discovery.

Behaviourism

Genetic epistemology endeavours to show that comprehension itself is subordinate to invention, which it sees as continual structure-building rather than as the mere discovery of already existing realities. From this point of view, intelligence consists in executing and co-ordinating actions in an interiorized, reflective fashion. These actions, as processes of change, are logical, mathematical operations, drives for judgement and reason. Knowledge is derived from action; less through simple associative responses or sudden

Genetic epistemology

---

1. The most recent American research in this field tends to abandon the 'black box' principle in favour of ascertaining the mental phenomena occurring between the entry of a physical stimulus and the expression of an observable response.

intuitions of forms than through the assimilation of reality into necessary, general co-ordinates for action. Pedagogy is accordingly assigned the task of encouraging the individual to organize reality into action and thought, and not merely to copy it.[1]

Forming the cognitive process

The psychopedagogic theory linked to the name of the Soviet scientist L. S. Vygotsky is based on the idea that work, an activity using instruments, prompts behaviour in the individual of a type determined by the nature of this activity and emerging indirectly through the symbols, words and figures, used for that purpose. Man's development is closely associated with the assimilation of systems of signs during the learning process. This is why it is the central component of the system of organization in the life of the child and has a decisive influence on his psychological development. On this basis, Soviet psychologists have worked out a strategy for active training of the cognitive faculties and the personality. They believe that the faculty of considered thought is not innate in man, but that the individual learns how to think and to master reflective operations. Pedagogues must learn to expand these processes and to supervise not only the results of mental activity but the way it unfolds as well. Data collected following applications of this psychopedagogic system have modified our ideas of the age limits to assimilating knowledge; for example, aptitudes among very young schoolchildren would appear to be far greater than previously believed. The system has made it possible to modify greatly the content and method of primary education.

Algorithms

This school of mathematical logic rejects behaviourism and endeavours to define a stable set of schemes and rules to be acquired. It replaces the 'black box' principle with that of the 'transparent box', whereby a programmed system of collective action directs the training of cognitive activity. To this end, these psychologists propose that optimal algorithms for learning activity be determined on the basis of formulae for the identification and solution of given classes of problems. Operational, descriptive models of the solution to given problems are established experimentally; they consist of a series of elementary intellectual operations which are functions

1. Jean Piaget, originator of this scientific school, describes it as 'of a constructivist nature (attributing the beginnings of language to structures formed by the pre-existing sensory-motor intelligence). It recognizes neither external preformations (empiricism) nor immanent preformations (innateness), but rather affirms a continuous surpassing of successive stages. This obviously leads to placing all educational stress on the spontaneous aspects of the child's activity' (J. Piaget, *Where is Education Heading?*, p. 3, Paris, Unesco, 1971, document of the International Commission on the Development of Education, Opinions Series, 6).

of the decisions to be taken. The aim is to teach procedures and not solutions, according to an 'operative-structural' method by means of which mental processes are taken in the direction of mathematical logic.

The structuralist approach, which concentrates on the psychology of form, gives the study of assimilation precedence over that of association, both in the fields of perception and of intellectual drives and social relations. The psychology of form, or *gestalt* psychology, seeks definitions for the basic unity in perceptual structures and in schemes of behaviour, the components of which form a complementary whole. Structuralist psychology examines choices between means and ends. An individual undergoing a learning process may choose between making a more intense effort, or adopting a slower procedure; he may even choose to move away from the goal or end, adopting an escapist form of behaviour and diminishing his application to the task in hand. Underlying the psychology of form are intuitive methods based on perception; the most modern versions of these may be found in audio-visual pedagogy, which uses ready-made configurations and ready-formulated results of mental operations. The structuralists define 'fields', that is to say organized wholes, according to geometric, algebraic, dynamic models of mental life. They stress the importance of certain relations such as subordination, interlocking and correspondence in the organization of mental life. They tend to lay down rational correlations between the mechanisms of perception, the content of consciousness, neural structures and logical and causal forms. Finally, they try to delimit areas of behaviour and study the paths taken—more or less direct or devious, independent or connected—by a goal-seeking individual.

Structuralism

The extent of the lag between progress in research—especially in experimental psychology—and the applications of its results to daily practice in schools is often deplored. Research workers' reluctance to give wide publicity to their discoveries combines, here, with the effect of scepticism among teachers who, as practitioners, work empirically and whose nature and function somewhat disincline them to modify structures and procedures. None the less, developments in science and technology have enabled substantial changes to be made. Audio-visual presentation and recording techniques have modernized language teaching; genetic epistemology underlies new teaching systems in the sciences; behaviourist laboratories have radically changed learning methods; new com-

Pedagogical applications of psychological research

munications technologies have made it possible to develop new patterns of instruction, such as open systems and self-service; and the combination of operational research and differential psychology is leading to individualized teaching, etc.

But some lessons may be learned from these scattered applications. Whether we have in mind merely the improvement of existing systems or the development of new learning strategies, scientific or technological developments can only exert an over-all influence on the current orientation of educational systems if:

1. Interdisciplinary contacts are systematically organized between the various researchers in the 'education sciences'.
2. Educational development institutions enable new findings to move from the laboratory or pilot project stage to large-scale utilization, taking into account the requisite strategical and logistical problems.
3. Efficient networks disseminate information to educational workers, and above all through institutes which train educators of all kinds and at all levels.

General and applied linguistics

Originally a discipline for studying language—the instrument itself and its functions—linguistics has invaded vast areas of knowledge over the past fifteen years: psychoanalysis, anthropology, sociology. Pedagogy itself has integrated a certain number of contributions from linguistics into its daily practice, in activities such as teaching children their mother tongue (systems for changing 'syntagmatic' combinations), foreign-language teaching by both oral and audio-visual methods (total structure approach), and the development of bilingualism.

Certain fundamental ideas in linguistics which throw fresh light on education are even more important. Assuming that learning to speak a language does not take place in the same way as learning other subjects, then attention must be focused on the creative quality of language,[1] a grasp of which enables the child to gain an understanding of sentences in his own language—even if their number is infinite—and then to do well in elementary education. Other research workers[2] use cybernetic combinations of 'transfunctional' grammar as part of this approach. In particular it includes research into the automatic synthesis of algorithms, grouped according to areas of change. Meanwhile psycholinguistics is currently endeavouring to explain how the child acquires an aptitude

1. cf. Z. Harris (transformational grammar) and N. Chomsky (generative grammar).
2. Soviet researchers, in particular Soumian.

112

for logical mental operations; to define the interiorized grammar of a speaking, listening individual; to evaluate affective or emotional content, and to devise new linguistic structures incorporating change and enabling irrational elements in the unconscious to find expression in everyday speech.

Beyond these differences in schools of thought, the directions which the discipline of linguistics has charted for the position of language and language training in mental activity would appear to be of considerable interest to the future of education.

Anthropology has close ties with linguistics due to its studies of the transition from 'nature' to 'culture', in which language plays the part of primary mediator. Anthropology contributes to pedagogic exploration through its qualitative and direct approach to reality, its descriptions of phenomena in visual, physical fashion, and its comparisons of the various forms of discourse among individuals and the community.

Contributions from anthropology

Highlighting the unified nature of knowledge, general anthropology (whose conclusions in this respect are disputed, however, by a number of scientists) provides strong arguments supporting the idea of interdisciplinary educational methods. It provides material on which to base a reappraisal of school programmes, the constitution of curricula adapted to the education of minority groups and heterogeneous classes of people and the definition of a universally acceptable body of subjects designed for the development of cultural 'pluralism' and international awareness.

Cultural anthropology[1] also throws light on the functions of education, by recording and explaining what it transmits. It describes

---

1. American cultural anthropology has been concerned of late with the meticulous study of the way school establishments function. Laurence W. Wylie has studied deductive pedagogy and its social constraints in a French primary school (*Village in the Vaucluse*, Cambridge, Mass., Harvard University Press, 1957). Richard L. Warren has analysed the rationalized bureaucratic order in a German rural school (*Education in Rebhausen, a German Village*, New York, N.Y., Holt, Rinehart & Winston, 1967), and John C. Singleton the personalized, hierarchical order in a Japanese village school (*Nichu: A Japanese School*, New York, N.Y., Holt, Rinehart & Winston, 1968). These works are in the same tradition as current analyses by the European Centre for Sociology of educational systems and the reproduction of authority and class-relations (Claude Grignon, *L'Ordre des Choses. Les Fonctions Sociales de l'Enseignement Technique*, Paris, Éditions de Minuit, 1971). Other recent studies in Burma, Ghana and Liberia have dealt with pre-literate societies and the part played in these by the family circle, initiation ceremonies, secret societies and their possible significance for school systems even beyond the frontiers of developing countries. Erich Fromm and Michael Maccoby have studied the apparently disastrous impact of imported culture and institutionalized school on the cultural life and identity of the inhabitants of a Mexican village (Erich Fromm and Michael Maccoby, *Social Character in a Mexican Village*, New York, N.Y., Prentice Hall, 1970).

the ways and means of such transmission and its consequences for the integration of the individual into society. In particular it illuminates the affective, non-cognitive aspects of education: school rituals, games, master–pupil interaction—especially the question of the docility and passivity of pupils—the importance of messages transmitted unconsciously in relation to intentional teaching and, finally, the propagation of innovations.

Political anthropology, involving the study of power and conflict in primitive societies, and economic anthropology, which studies means of production and trading in primitive and rural economies, and the relationships between economics and ecology, also provide material for reflexion on the role of schools in development.

Anthropology may help to re-establish the position of education in developing countries, to build systems both for transmitting cultures and for aiding development. Taken further, anthropology may help countries and communities to define the educational content or subject-matter to be transmitted.[1]

In general, anthropology makes a fruitful contribution to redefining the role of education and reorienting its action.

Theory of information

Information theory is drawing educators' attention more and more to the anatomy of communication.

Research of this kind has considerable application, not only to the construction of teaching-sequences and daily communication between teacher and pupil, but also, more generally, to the formulation of educational messages and schemata, whatever the means of transmission involved. (These may include teaching manuals, educational radio and television networks, audio-visual presentation, teaching machines, various methods of language teaching and the organization of mathematical discourse.) Among recent laboratory results, experts stress the definition of an 'optimal' level of redundancy for a given quantity of information, the consequence of excessive redundancy on the number of solutions found by the student or receiving individual, the speed of presentation regarded as a significant variable and the close relationship between data processing and memory processes.

1. 'Anthropology reminds economics of the limits of its theoretical validity, and Western culture of the background to its ideological prejudices. The primitive peoples of the world are, in fact, not poor. The goods they need are not *scarce*. Their existence is not limited to *subsistence* [in the sense of survival]. Anthropology, like any science, must break up ready-made truths and invent new modes of thought in order to penetrate the profound logic in man's history' (Maurice Godelier, *L'Anthropologie Économique*, Paris, Denoël, 1971).

114

Applications of information theory to pedagogic research show that the most important criteria are not transmission time or economy of means in the transmission of a message, but its efficacity, that is to say its intelligibility.

Research into non-verbal visual communication points up the interrelationship of diverse media combinations. Semeiology is the study of the use of signs in communication. Road traffic signs, cartography, schematic anatomical drawings, exploded views, diagrams, wiring plans, administrative or business hierarchy charts, graphs, comic-strip cartoons and visual publicity make no use of 'linguistic' processes—any more than do bees, which communicate through movement. In this field, *learning how to interpret and construct such sets of signs has special didactic interest both because of their technological content and their many practical applications to the educational process.* *Semeiology*

Information theory relates to cybernetics. Cybernetics is gradually becoming a science of organisms, a method of fundamental concrete training, in contrast, say, to mathematics. Seeking to define models for self-adapting totalities, cybernetics contributes to the solution of complex logistic problems arising from the organization of learning conditions. Cybernetic pedagogy (in the United States and even more in the Soviet Union) operates at the level of self-regulating individual micro-systems such as adaptable teaching machines, and also among macro-systems such as institutions confronting an infinite variety of individual differences among pupils. In tasks of this kind, it uses computers to present a varied range of programme units appropriate to different learning levels and aptitudes. *Cybernetics*

Research by biologists, neuropsychologists, linguists, anthropologists and cyberneticians constitutes an invaluable potential and justifies great hopes for the future. But the results of this research are still for the most part in the laboratory stage.

Nevertheless, the seeds for the most essential elements in the renewal of education systems will be sown and grown in these laboratories, institutes and research workshops. We therefore suggest to all those responsible for making decisions in this field to consider *channelling an increasing proportion of financial resources allocated to education into scientific research, in multiple disciplines, so as to clear more and bolder paths for pedagogic and didactic innovation. It would be in their own interest if industrialized nations*

115

were to arrange for scientists and educators from Third World countries to co-operate in this research so as to help them acquire the elements they need in order to continue original research in their own countries.

New developments from science and technology

Pedagogy, ancient art and new science

As in all sciences, our time has witnessed sweeping changes in pedagogy, to the point where the concept itself has changed. A body of related disciplines has led to reinforcement of the scientific aspects of pedagogy. What once was an art—the art of teaching—is now a science, built on firm foundations, and linked to psychology, anthropology, cybernetics, linguistics and many other disciplines. However, the application of pedagogy by teachers is in many cases more of an art than a science.

The concept and field of application of the education sciences are both becoming broader in scope. Pedagogy appears to have been confined, in the past, to giving instruction to the young, as its etymology implies. This idea is now out of date. Until our time, it was considered to be the unavoidable auxiliary to all formalized knowledge. The meaning we give to education today, and thereby to pedagogy, is infinitely more vast and complex. It includes the cultural process of bringing forth and developing all an individual's potentialities.[1] Until very recently, education—confused with in-

1. This concept could lead to the following interesting conclusions: 'Education does not merely involve the implementation of certain intentions, the realization of certain ideals or forming the man of tomorrow that we imagine today. It is a cluster of difficult *trades*, an aggregate of processes based on specific *techniques* (the effectiveness of which can be gauged) and action with individuals and groups, that is organized, planned, controlled and evaluated. This search for a science of education demands first that practitioners of the trade be professional. But the combination of education as a science and teachers as professionals can degenerate into a so-called applied science, merely a rationalized improvisation. Pedagogy can no longer be only a philosophy of education that clarifies objectives, but provides no concrete means of action. Nor can pedagogy confine itself to dreaming up useful techniques. Pedagogy must therefore strive for its own scientific autonomy, which presupposes that it is *an organized whole with a specific aim*. I propose that universities recognize *a science for the training of man* to be known as "andragogy", as some universities have already done. This science should be called andragogy and not pedagogy because its purpose is no longer to train children and adolescents, but *man throughout his life*' (Pierre Furter, *Grandeur et Misère de la Pédagogie*, University of Neuchâtel, 1971).

116

struction—was supposed to give people their 'start in life'. Now, prospects for pedagogic action are radically changed; it must anticipate lifelong education.

The transition from the idea of initial training to that of continual education is the mark of modern pedagogy.

In contrast with traditional school forms of initial education, continual education is becoming a complex cybernetic system, based on a 'response-sensitive' situation comprising the following elements: a learner whose behaviour may be evaluated and modified; a teacher, functionally speaking the educator; sources of structured knowledge, to be presented to the student or else explored by the student himself; an environment designed specifically for the learner to have access to necessary data; arrangements for evaluating and checking modified behaviour, that is to say for recording reaction and the new behaviour which it stimulates.[1]

From initial to continual education

Traditional pedagogy failed to differentiate sufficiently between educational methods and content in relation to the age of pupils and their intellectual levels. It frequently treated the child as if he or she were merely a kind of undergrown adult. It even failed to discern that adolescence was a specific psychological phase.

Psychopedagogic phases

Contemporary psychology, particularly genetic psychology, is concerned with distinguishing between the characteristics of people of different ages. Specialists in child development generally agree in distinguishing several stages of mental development. Up to the age of 2, causal relations are established through sensory-motor exploration. Between the ages of 2 and 7, the symbolic function develops, through games, drawing and language, with a trend to interiorizing action and 'de-centration'. At the age of 7 or 8 a third period develops for mastering two-way reversible operations. Towards 11, a fourth phase appears, characterized by the mastery of a new form of reasoning based on hypotheses (propositional operations: implying, deducing, discerning incompatibilities). Near the age of 14 or 15, the mind becomes truly experimental (factors may be dissociated, elements may be varied or placed in systematic combinations). Finally, between the ages of 15 and 20, professional specialization begins, with the construction of life programmes reflecting individual aptitudes.[2]

1. See C. Saury and M. Scholl, *Education and the Computer*, p. 1, Paris, Unesco, 1971, document of the International Commission on the Development of Education, Innovations Series, 8.
2. 'But studying young adults is unfortunately far more difficult than studying children, for they are less creative and already belong to an organized society which channels

A number of specialists in psychopedagogy, notably in the Soviet Union, criticize this chronological classification on the grounds that it considers mental development as a spontaneous process independent of instruction.

Psychology of early childhood

During the first half of the twentieth century psychology and psychoanalysis emphasized the importance of harmonious emotional development. Contemporary educators accept this almost unanimously. Recent research in intellectual development and early learning of cognitive concepts is, on the other hand, running into opposition, as usually happens when entrenched ideas are questioned, especially when this concerns man himself.

The present state of knowledge would, however, appear to indicate that:

Development quotients (not to be confused with intelligence quotients) are roughly the same for all children up to the age of 3 years.

Influences affecting children between 0 and 4 years old differ from those determining behaviour as from the age of 5 to 6, although this does not mean the latter are 'new'. They may have taken root in very early childhood, and have had a kind of delayed action. Other influences—really new ones—modify behaviour during school and adolescence, and nothing is finally fixed until death.

Little correlation exists between the intelligence quotient calculated during the first year of life and the IQ found one, three, six or twelve years later. Recent work has shown that IQ varies in relation to the emotional environment and the attention which educators devote to the child.[1]

During the last ten years, pedagogic research, especially in mathematics and linguistics, has shown that, under certain conditions, children who are very young indeed may develop a precocious capacity for conceptualization regardless of their socio-cultural background.

Current research appears to confirm the close relationship between socio-cultural handicaps and basic family attitudes. In-depth analysis of the causes of failure in school highlights the importance of parental behaviour, not necessarily of the kind linked to social

---

them, applies brakes or arouses them to rebellion' (Jean Piaget, 'Intellectual Evolution from Adolescence to Adulthood', *Proceedings of the IIIrd FONEME International Convention on Human Formation from Adolescence to Maturity*, Milan, 9–10 May 1970).
1. cf. M. Boulanger Balleyguier, 'L'Évolution du Q.I.', *Enfance*.

environment, but personal factors such as rigidity, permissiveness, authority, comprehension, dialogue, etc.

Traditional educators (who base their system on the laws of biological maturation and who accordingly recommend letting the child develop according to his 'natural trajectory') are currently clashing with certain research workers who claim that an individual's evolution depends largely on what he acquires before the age of 4. But others are arguing that both groups are too sweeping. They stress—backed by a solid body of supporting research—that little is ever final in a human being's life.

Psychopedagogic research hardly goes beyond adolescence. The possibilities of adult learning—a crucial question for the practical application of the concept of lifelong education—are far from having been studied in such a systematic fashion as the aptitudes of children and adolescents. The results of research carried out so far do not in the least seem to corroborate the widely accepted postulate that education must be concentrated on the second phase of childhood and adolescence and that within these limits it must not be. interrupted. Two new notions of education are being substituted for this: that of education spread throughout an individual's lifetime, and that of recurrent education, in successive but discontinuous periods.[1] *Psychopedagogy in adulthood*

Modern pedagogy takes into account the individual, his capacities, his mental structures, his interests, motivations and needs— even when he is a member of a group.[2] In this view, the schoolmaster, the teacher, the instructor is not the only active agent, however great a part he may still play. The pupil himself, the individual being educated plays an increasingly active role in his own education. *Group pedagogy and personalization*

We now have technologies derived from the psychosociology of 'intervention' and from a psychology of human relations based on the essential idea that the group is distinct from the sum of the individuals composing it, while at the same time being dependent on the relations arising among those individuals.

This approach lead to modifying authoritarian constraints in the traditional type of school and to helping pupils to acquire knowledge significant to them. By comparing groups of children learning *Group techniques*

1. H. Janne and M. L. Roggemans, *Educational Systems and the New Demands*, p. 19–22, Paris, Unesco, 1971, document of the International Commission on the Development of Education, Opinions Series, 3.
2. The technique of group pedagogy is not in the least incompatible with a personalized educational process. For in fact, a well-oriented and well-run learning group should not have a stifling effect on the individual.

in the different contexts of authoritarianism, democracy and *laisser-faire*, researchers have shown that a permissive and self-directive atmosphere tends to produce the best results for development.[1] They have also shown that such an atmosphere helps members of the group to become conscious of the interior phenomena of emotion, sympathy and antipathy arising within it, and to release resulting tensions. Such techniques also facilitate relations between pupils and teachers, favour the development of reciprocal, multi-lateral communication, institutionalize feedback and stimulate aptitude for sharing in community life. Contacts become more natural and easier. Self-mastery is accompanied by a decrease in aggressivity and inhibition. Personal judgement becomes finer and critical spirit develops. Members of the group tend to assume functions (observation, analysis, diagnosis, evaluation) initially vested in the group leader.

Institutional pedagogy

Other interesting experiments concern so-called institutional pedagogy. Its starting-point for investigation is analysis of the sociology of institutions, with particular reference to recent studies of bureaucracy[2] and the alienation affecting pupils, teachers and administrators. Institutional pedagogy aims to change 'instituted combinations' in school—that is, imposed from without—into 'instituting combinations', based on free exchange between individuals and leading to self-management. It operates by 'replacing permanent action and the school-master's intervention by a system of activities, of varying intermediaries and of institutions which continually ensure both the obligation to carry on, and the reciprocity of, exchanges with and outside the group'.[3] These ideas are even more important in adult training, especially in teacher-training colleges, reconversion centres, residential seminaries and long-term courses. Adults demand different teacher–learner relationships from those traditionally prevailing in school. Use must be made of adults' specific motivations, each of whom brings into the learning process structured professional and cultural content. The instructor seeks to be an 'inducer of change' (like the psychologist with his patient), while members of the group take responsibility for research written into the study programme and for finding solutions to problems arising in daily collective life.[4]

1. Research by Kurt Lewin.
2. Mainly Lukacs, Weber, Merton and Crozier.
3. A. Vasquez and F. Oury, *Vers une Pédagogie Institutionnelle*, p. 248, Paris, Maspero, 1971.
4. cf. for example the CUCES experiments in Nancy, France and the Workers' University in Zagreb, Yugoslavia.

Whereas the 'institutionalists' stress the fabric of power and responsibility, non-directive pedagogy[1] proposes that daily pedagogic practice be based on psychotherapeutic data 'centred on the client'. The psychotherapist remains neutral, 'transparent'. He does not interpret. He encourages the individual to express himself. Concepts such as 'congruence', 'positive unconditional consideration' and 'understanding empathy' are being used today to build up a pedagogy of individual self-development, especially in secondary education.

In many countries, communications technologies are classified according to the nature of the distribution networks they serve and which to a large extent determine their use. They are divided essentially into inertia and non-inertia networks. Inertia methods include films and video tapes and channel production into widely distributed, lasting programmes which potentially may be incorporated into modules. Non-inertia networks include radio and television and help develop better integrated, more diversified programmes, easily evolving and renewing themselves. They favour decentralization of production and distribution, due to the low cost of programmes.[2] The cost structure of inertia networks tends to restrict decentralization, since investment and high fixed costs lead to a concentration of distribution systems.

Theory and technology of communication

Inertia networks, slides, cassettes and other equipment—affording educators maximum freedom in their choice of programmes and the way these are used—have interesting applications as pedagogical instruments in audio-visual language and science teaching, closed-circuit teacher training, etc. However, programmes of this kind rarely reach an audience sufficiently large to produce radical changes in teaching systems.

Development of communications technologies is currently moving in two opposite directions: towards the individualization and towards the mass distribution of educational messages.

Direct-wire television

One of the most interesting communications techniques promoting individualization is 'wired' or 'piped' television,[3] which

1. Inspired by the psychotherapist Carl Rogers and his work.
2. Such as in the Ivory Coast, where television is being used to reorient primary education towards rural development, and El Salvador, where television has gone into action under the Plan Básico (secondary level) to extend the quality and increase the quantity of education dispensed. In adult education, attempts have been made (e.g. Canada's Tevec programme) to bring systematic programmes of instruction to large audiences through television.
3. In the United States, private wire television went out over 2,400 subscriber networks

makes it possible to relay more than twenty programmes simultaneously to the entire subscriber network, or to serve one subscriber with a single programme selected from a range of several dozen. The wire-transmission system means that educational programmes may be delivered to groups with specific needs, particularly for professional training. Self-contained networks with a limited coverage, serving a district, a town or a rural county, afford groups linked by language or cultural affinities an opportunity to express themselves. They replace mass communication with a differentiated action.

Other aids to selective, individual education include video-tape cassettes and cartridges which may be plugged into a television receiver, and the video disc, which is used in conjunction with a video player. These comparatively low-priced aids offer rapid random access and possibility of programme repetition, factors which promise a wealth of didactic possibilities for the future.

Mass transmission techniques capable of making educational messages available to millions of children and adults include two of great importance for developing countries: radio and communications satellite relays. (They are more interesting to developing countries than to many industrialized nations, since the latter are tending to refine techniques favouring the individualization of educational programmes and have all the appropriate technical resources at their disposal.)

Radio

Radio is the only advanced communication technique which has found its proper place in developing countries. Where conditions have permitted, it has become well established and widespread. Yet, it seems to us that insufficient educational use is made of this virtually universal method of distribution. People often seem to have been deterred by the reputedly greater efficiency of other media which, however, have the major defect, compared with radio, of being unable to hope for such widespread distribution—or anything like it—for a long time to come. The very low cost and adequate reliability in all climates of miniature transistor radios mean that radio broadcasting should more and more be recognized as a particularly suitable medium for educational purposes.

Space communications

Meanwhile, space communications have developed at a staggering

---

in 1970, delivering programmes to some 5 million receivers, or one-tenth of the total in the country; the growth rate was 25 per cent per annum. Subscriber television by wire also exists in Belgium, Canada, Japan, Switzerland and the United Kingdom.

speed.[1] Five years after the first sputnik was launched in 1957, Telstar was orbited, in 1962; the first operational satellites, Early Bird (United States) and Molnya (U.S.S.R.), were placed in orbit three years later. More than eighty nations participate in Intelsat, which recently orbited the first of the Intelsat IV series, capable of relaying 6,000 telephone calls simultaneously.

Certain countries facing serious educational difficulties may be tempted to put satellites into orbit for widespread diffusion of education programmes before precise objectives have been clearly defined and content carefully prepared. Outside the enormous expense of such projects, this would mean taking the risk—calculated or not—of a failure that would so break the budget and so shake the faith that it would block any other possibility for large-scale technological innovation. At the present time, considering the fact that audio-visual means—particularly local television and radio networks—have not yet been sufficiently developed and utilized, projects of this kind may well appear to be incompatible with the commonly prevailing situation in which resources are scarce and serious, balanced educational plans are necessary.

National spatial telecommunications systems are only of interest to linguistically homogeneous regions, to very large countries such as India,[2] Brazil and Canada or to a few with very unusual

1. There are two main techniques in communications relays by satellite which concern us here: indirect and direct relays. Communications satellites handling indirect relays are low-powered and their antennae are only moderately directive. They relay low-intensity signals from a transmitting station to a receiving centre on earth which amplifies them for retransmission to subscribers. It has now become possible to orbit direct-relay satellites, expected to have a power of several hundred watts, and a highly directive antenna, relaying from a transmitting centre to subscribers' stations across the territory. This technique will make a central receiving station unnecessary but will require individual television receivers to be modified. There is also a hybrid system combining reception of a space-relay communication by central stations, which rediffuse to the usual individual receivers through the usual channels, while these same space-relay programmes could be picked up directly in isolated rural regions by specially equipped receivers.
2. Studies of the Indian model, scheduled for 1974, bring out two obvious advantages of space communication. First, time is saved. In India, the ground network as originally envisaged will still cover only 17 per cent of the territory and reach 25 per cent of the population by 1980, whereas a satellite can cover the entire country immediately it goes into service. Second, coverage is extensive. Conventional systems restricted reception to zones covered by transmitting stations, usually set up in big cities. A satellite makes it possible to plan a system according to socio-educational criteria instead of technical and geographical ones. A high-powered transmitter can cover a radius of a hundred kilometres, that is, an area of more than 30,000 square kilometres. A 500-watt stationary satellite covers a zone contained within an angle of about nine degrees, which in practice means about 12 million square kilometres. Furthermore, communications satellites enable low-cost programmes to reach sparsely populated zones and migratory groups such as pastoral tribes, migrant workers and waterway populations.

geographical outlines such as Indonesia and Japan. Economically and technically, it would not be feasible to justify or to carry out nationally organized programmes virtually anywhere else. Satellite-relayed broadcasting will therefore have to be handled on a multi-national scale.[1] Broadcasting messages from one and the same source and from nation to nation means that over and above existing economic communities there will have to be 'pedagogic communities', harmonizing joint resources to be used for preparing and producing televised programmes. These must be based on agreements respecting national sovereignty and the specific traits of each country's educational system, accompanied by firm common desire for pedagogical renovation. Various possible ways of doing this include: national programmes decided on and produced jointly; national modular elements produced for insertion in programmes for international use; international modular elements to be combined with national ones; national programmes which may be readapted, pedagogically or linguistically, at local level. There would be various methods of preparing international programmes. Sometimes these would be based on common core subjects (geography, mathematics); sometimes elements of a national character would be added (history); sometimes polyvalent material that could be adapted to local conditions would be used (science, rural development). One might even envisage setting up international bodies to decide on programme production policy, manage time-tables and, if necessary, arbitrate among differences of opinion. Taking institutional measures of this kind could provide a guarantee against possible risk of educational levelling or systematic westernization, or even against outside pressure which might be brought to bear under cover of technical aid.

These immense prospects certainly justify hope, but they should not lead us to neglect current communications systems, which form a complex organic whole. Educational strategy must take advantage of all these elements, and act on both structure and content. Public authorities often have many ways of bringing their influence to bear on these problems. But if this is to be effective, *subsequent planning and preparation must be combined with action in the target environment to pave the way for reception, including thorough study and adaptation of programme content and analysis of any potential audience resistance.*

1. On the lines of the Latin American cultural integration scheme (SERLA) or the Franco-German 'Symphony—Socrates' project for Africa south of the Sahara.

The development of data processing also opens new paths for *Data* education. Computers, particularly, render multiple services, *processing* ranging from aid to management and research to their strictly didactic uses.[1]

In educational systems and establishments, computers are widely used for solving administrative problems such as payment of salaries, control of funds, invoicing and accounting. They have also been found useful in organizing school transport networks with maximum efficiency, solving complex problems of organization, and in planning and building, etc. Especially when the volume of data involved is massive, computers can identify, evaluate, collect and classify information in all its complexity and detail, and supply it when required.

Computers made available to students help in developing self-educational practices, by devising library classification systems, by data selection and by career guidance (providing selective information on educational and employment possibilities).

They are also very useful in pedagogic research, especially in evaluating and checking school work. They can store large quantities of information about the entire school-going population. This mass of data may be organized and interpreted so as to provide a complete profile of each pupil during his entire school career, a profile which may conceivably be substituted, in the end, for a final examination. Information accumulated in the course of studies may also be used to perfect methods and develop individualized teaching.[2]

But the most important and innovative functions of the com- *Computer-* puter emerge in the teaching process itself. Dialogue between *assisted* pupil and computer creates conditions for efficient, rapid learning. *teaching* Researchers have explored many possibilities in recent years ranging from elementary tasks such as repetitive exercises and

1. Universities and other educational establishments in the United States contain an estimated 3,000 computers, or about 6 per cent of all computers operating in that country. In the Soviet Union, theoretical cybernetic research is very active and systematic use is made of computers at Sverdlosk University and in technological institutes at Minsk, Kiev and Lvov, where the Alpha 5 teaching machine and tester was developed. Computers are used for experimental purposes in the German Democratic Republic (at the Dresden data-processing institute) and in Prague, Czechoslovakia. Of about 4,000 computers in Japan, some 200 are used for teaching in universities. In the United Kingdom, almost all teaching computers are in the universities, while many universities in the Federal Republic of Germany have also acquired computers.
2. This is the theory of 'individually prescribed instruction' (IPI), practised in the United States.

intensive practical work[1] to higher education in complex disciplines[2] and the training of teachers.[3]

The computer will also assuredly be called on to play an important part in lifelong education.[4] Pedagogic experience has shown that the didactic functions of the computer are by no means limited to simple presentation of information, enabling students to acquire and understand a body of knowledge. It can also help them to learn to manipulate concepts and techniques, and develop intellectual aptitudes. The computer enables a learner to explore at will possible solutions to a problem, to study the reactions of a representative model according to variables which he introduces, and to develop his decision-making faculties. It sets up conditions for a dialogue between pupil and system.

Intellectual revolution

But this is not the limit of the computer's educational scope. Data processing is bringing about a veritable intellectual revolution. It contributes both a logic and a grammar which, while not supplanting earlier forms of logic and grammar, will complete and influence them.

The paramount virtue of the computer is that it releases man from the routine of mental labour, freeing the human mind to specialize in operations where it remains irreplaceable, such as posing problems and taking decisions.

It would be premature to try to draw general conclusions from our fragmentary experience in this domain. It is undeniable, however, that the computer enables learning to be accelerated in many subjects and that at the same time it stimulates and broadens

1. The Stanford University computer has 500 terminals in primary schools in California, Kentucky and Mississippi, working with 20,000 pupils; more than 170 teachers devise the exercises.
2. A total of 910 different programmes were developed in various universities in the United States for computer courses covering the 1969/70 university year, according to the 1970 catalogue. Programming methods were extremely varied; the subjects most often prepared for computers included astronomy, biology, chemistry, demography, economics, geography, history, languages (Russian and Chinese), management, mathematics, mechanics, medicine, music, philosophy, psychology and statistics.
3. The Spanish Government, working with Unesco and the International Bank for Reconstruction and Development, is developing a project to train 200,000 secondary-level teachers by 1980 and give reconversion courses to 150,000 existing personnel.
4. 'In former times we used to reckon on several generations to an epoch, but now we reckon on several epochs to a generation. We believe that through computer-assisted teaching it will be possible to achieve the lifelong education which is necessary to effect a continual adjustment in our knowledge. This form of teaching allows elements of knowledge to be permanently available and up to date; furthermore, the attendant logic brought into play enables pedagogy to be selective in a way to which traditional teaching was only a crude approximation' (Maurice Peuchot, *La Stratégie Modulaire en Enseignement Assisté par Ordinateur*).

126

understanding. We may very reasonably expect more and more positive results as the teaching of data processing itself develops, beginning at the elementary level and related to the study of modern mathematics.

It would be a mistake to regard the use of advanced techniques like the computer to be excessively expensive. Electronic equipment is among those rare industrial products the cost of which is continually decreasing, while at the same time they are becoming more reliable.[1] The cost of a data-processing operation on a computer is 600 times less than it was twenty years ago. Lowering software costs is not such a simple matter. It does however seem possible to have the computer itself programme certain educational material using basic algorithms (so-called computer-generated programmed materials).

In addition, terminals will be more flexible, more human and better adapted to dialogue. Computer terminals devised by adults for adults are generally ill-adapted to the activity and dimensions of young people. We are admittedly far from being able to set up a practical spoken dialogue between learner and teaching machine, due to the quantity and complexity of the minimum necessary verbal structures,[2] but this is by no means a merely utopian prospect.

Another question arises here. To what extent can pedagogic and didactic techniques benefit from the experience acquired and the tools used in other sectors, especially in industry which is naturally the most 'modernistic'?

In this respect, the principles of ergonomy[3] would appear to have many beneficial applications to education: analyses of working conditions by specialized teams from many disciplines, including architects, engineers, doctors, physiologists and psychologists; measurement of tasks involving perception; distribution of functions; research on the role of environment in tasks and performances;

Ergonomy

1. A transistor worth $10 ten years ago is replaced today by an integrated circuit which does the work fifty transistors did ten years ago and only costs $1.
2. Teaching first-year arithmetic in elementary school would require more than 2,000 words.
3. The term ergonomics was devised at Oxford in 1949 and denotes the 'law' or science of work, the study of a specific kind of behaviour: that of a man making a programmed physical or mental effort in return for some remuneration. In the broad sense, ergonomics covers the psychology of work; in its restricted sense, the technology of communications within a man–machine system. A terminological problem has arisen in this domain: French-language authors prefer the term *ergonomie*, or ergonomics, while American authors speak of 'human engineering', 'engineering psychology' or 'system engineering' (cf. *Encyclopaedia Universalis*).

study of mental behaviour, etc.[1] Ergonomic studies (e. g. the modes and conditions of communication between work cells, the effects of checks and inspections, the causes of deficiencies and work accidents as an indication of malfunction in the system) also appear capable of providing us with a number of elements enabling the functioning of school and out-of-school institutions to be improved.

Operational research

We may expect similar results for education from the procedures denoted by the generic term 'operational research', comprising the totality of theoretical and experimental methods of applying mathematical analysis to the organization and optimal development of industrial enterprises (linear programming, simulations, models, etc.). In human activities other than education, this body of methods does in fact enable us to detect weak points in an organization, to propose a choice of remedies, to envisage combining its components differently or modifying them.

Systems analysis

Systems analysis[2] endeavours to decide on an optimal structure for any organization, in a state of mobile equilibrium resulting from successive adjustments prompted by the environment. Many people admittedly believe these processes are too complex to be analysed except in terms of probability, education being theoretically an open system. But it is precisely a characteristic of systems analysis to integrate uncertainty into daily action. Be this as it may, to the extent that it enables us to orchestrate many agents into a unified process leading to the greatest possible efficiency, *systems analysis would appear to be an intellectual instrument which may be applied to an over-all critical study of existing educational systems and is likely to suggest new scientifically calculated pedagogic patterns.*

Educational activities may be modernized at various levels: management, adaptation to needs, pedagogic options, operational structures, finance, etc.[3]

1. As developed over the past ten years in the United States and the Soviet Union, ergonomy aims at a concrete evolution of industrial work—focused first on the machine and then on man—towards a system-centred activity conceived as a totality in which elements of all categories interact.
2. By 'system' the analysts understand the sum of separate parts acting both independently and in relation to each other in order to achieve previously declared goals. The system is not therefore to be defined only as the elements composing it but by the organization enabling it to function; analysis aims at exactly measuring the goals to be achieved in terms of performance, at locating levels of application and integrating limiting factors so as to arrive at rational operational models.
3. For example, certain countries have adopted general or partial budget-programmes. This method involves discarding the traditional idea of budgetary divisions. The tasks

Various recent experiments lend credit to the idea that a quantity of industrial systems' new management procedures[1] may have practical application to education, not only on the national level—in supervising the way the entire educational system operates[2]—but also on that of the internal organization of educational institutions.

It cannot be denied that applying methods which need abundant and reliable quantitative data and require specialized personnel may raise difficulties in developing countries. But the spirit of such methods counts for more than the letter and, while we would not claim they are panaceas, their use might clarify many problems. Some techniques would seem to be easier to apply at micro-level (that of the school institution and group) than at macro-level (that of total systems), particularly in enabling individual rates of progress to be charted and efficient techniques for diagnoses and orientation to be introduced.

––––––

of the State and its objectives, that is to say its measurable functions, are defined for several years. This technique helps decision-making, especially in the event of a budgetary squeeze, since the authorities know to what extent each reduction in credit will affect the ultimate objective of each programme. Its advantage is that the budget is no longer classified by government ministries or agencies, or according to its functions, which are not in general measurable objectives, but according to the products to which various administrations contribute (for example, the production over a certain number of years of university graduates with clearly defined qualifications, in relation to known employment possibilities). The cost of public action may accordingly be compared with its utility, and a number of agencies may participate in a single programme, or one single agency may promote several programmes. Budget-programmes therefore permit of strategic choices linking expenditure, spread out in time, to partial objectives and to constant factors in programmes.

1. In addition to the routine processes of operational research, industry uses certain more advanced methods today. These include the Planning, Programming, Budgeting System (PPBS), for determining explicit objectives and performance criteria for an entire programme. It proposes machinery for harmonizing long-term plans and defining tactics for using resources, at regular intervals. The method helps, among other things, to reduce the effects of the so-called 'Parkinson's Law', in this respect preventing institutions from 'swelling'. PERT (Programme Evaluation and Review Techniques) is designed to organize a series of activities by identifying and ordering both favourable and unfavourable events before they occur. The Delphi method proceeds by systematically consulting groups of experts who are asked—while remaining anonymous—to list probable events and trends. One particularly advanced technique is known as the interaction matrix, by means of which probable interference from future events is evaluated, allowing for the fact that they interact as a function of three factors: fashion, strength and time. We may also mention the scenario method, which consists in simulating the future by describing events following on a choice or decision, in detail. Various game theories are also widely applied.

2. There can be no doubt that at least at this level there will be little delay in putting methods inspired by operational research into practice. For example, one experiment undertaken with Unesco assistance is currently under way in Indonesia; it involves drafting a plan on the basis of systems analyses, a reading of input-output charts, 'reference trees' and PPBS.

There is hardly an important contemporary scientific or techno-logical discipline not capable of making a new contribution to the understanding of the educational phenomenon and to improved mastery of techniques for transmitting knowledge and training personality. To those already mentioned, we may add: ecology, which helps us understand the relationship between education and the environment, and to place it in the context of development; medicine, which has helped reduce dyslexia and develop audio-oral learning; psychometry, with new measurement formulae, inquiry scales and tests, and many others.

Interdisciplinary links

But these contributions too often seem to be dispersed. It is probably desirable for more organic interdisciplinary links to be forged among them rather than the simple forms of juxtaposition currently grouped under the 'education sciences'. Machinery should be set up, both national and international, to bring about new correlations between parallel branches of learning.

This kind of co-ordination has become a necessary condition for developing educational theory, which itself is indispensable.

Scientific and technical progress has three major consequences for education.

Changing educational action

We are now entitled to talk of a change in the learning process, which is tending to displace the teaching process. New theories of learning[1] highlight the principle of contiguity and the importance of needs and motivations, of choice of content, of the hierarchic nature of learning, the interrelationship between educational content and environment, etc.[2] Learning practices are affected at present by the disorderly and sometimes competing relations between the various vehicles for transmitting knowledge. Hence the need for multi-media systems to co-ordinate their utilization and effectiveness.

Integrating technology into the system

The second major consequence of advances in educational technology is that it is impossible really to derive advantage from it without overhauling the entire educational edifice. The problem is

1. The term 'mathetic' is coming into use to denote the transition from teaching to learning. Certain researchers in the United States (Gilbert) and the Soviet Union (Lev Landa) are now using it and so is the European Education Centre in Frascati, Italy, where a first, small-scale 'mathetics laboratory' has been set up. The term is derived from the Greek *mathesis* (from *mathein*, to learn), and *mathet* means pupil—he who learns. Mathetics is accordingly the science of the pupil's behaviour while learning, just as pedagogy is the discipline in which attention is focused on the school-master's behaviour while teaching. The mathetic processes and their study are assuming increasing importance.
2. cf. J. L. Laroche, 'A Propos des Theories de l'Apprentissage', *Education Permanente* (Paris), No. 8, 1970.

130

not merely to modernize education from the outside (although this is often what people try to do), 'simply solving equipment problems, preparing programmes for using that equipment and inserting them into traditional pedagogic activities, but to make systematic use of available resources to develop a scientific awareness in the individual of methods of acquiring and using knowledge. The aim is to avoid economic and financial wastage by co-ordinating those educational techniques which are at present available to us, as completely as possible'.[1] Educational technology is not just apparatus to be clamped on to a conventional system, adding to or multiplying traditional procedures. It can only be of value if it is really integrated into the entire system and if it leads us to rethink and renovate it.

For technological innovations to be meaningful and effective, the implications of its use must be considered in relation to the total education system.

Many 'poor techniques' require neither complex equipment nor large numbers of highly qualified staff. Slow-scan television for example, utilized in the developed countries for industrial purposes only, could serve educational purposes, broadcasting successive sequences of still pictures instantaneously on a large scale. These possibilities have been little explored in industrialized countries because other, more elaborate techniques are available. However, their application to development would be worth examining.

Intermediate technologies

Moreover, research in industrialized countries appears to be aimed irreversibly at the most sophisticated techniques and therefore ill-adapted to a reorientation towards research on 'poor' or 'stripped' techniques. Work on these should be undertaken in developing countries which have mastered modern technologies (India or Brazil, for example), to encourage the production of new models for communication or technological organization.

The question arises whether education has given the development of intermediate technologies all the attention they deserve. Specialists in educational technology are generally content to oppose the individual master craftsman concept by recommending advanced pedagogic industrialization, based on the massive production of equipment and messages. This is no doubt due to the fact that educational advances in developing countries—still deeply influenced by colonial patterns in structure, organization and content—have

1. Third Regional Conference of Ministers of Education and Economic Planning in Asia, Singapore, May–June 1971.

not yet reached an adequate stage of critical awareness and technological invention. Also, programmes for introducing use of intermediate technologies (still sometimes referred to as 'adapted technologies') are too often presented merely as an attempt to provide work for more people, while the first problem in education is to raise the effectiveness and output of existing staff just as much as to set up new educational systems.

The ultimate objective of intermediate technology is to promote a spirit of technological invention and creation oriented towards development. This endeavour therefore involves an ultimate pedagogic aim of importance to all educators.

For practical purposes, this would entail systematically developing organized patterns of specific methods and techniques meeting the needs of a region, a State or even a racial, cultural or linguistic group. These patterns would range from standardized national or international mass production (as perfected in industrialized nations for textbook publishing, manufacture of audio-visual aids, use of radio and television networks) to craft work organized by the village school-master.

Finally, scientific and technological progress has an intrinsic value, which may be independent of the quantity of material resources deployed, for the spirit inherent in that progress can influence educational systems even before the vast range of modern equipment becomes available. This is not in fact indispensable to taking advantage of the findings of recent research.

'Unless these theoretical principles are developed and applied to education, intermediate technology runs the risk of becoming a blind alley in development instead of a necessary stage. Technological creativity which, as it outlines new methods, will ensure the indispensable standardization of intermediate technology, and consequently its universalization.'[1] We therefore consider that it would be useful, at the same time as advanced technology is developed, to *use simplified technologies, adapted to a country's particular needs and possibilities. We would encourage use of new technologies which do not require massive investment, and intermediate technologies able to help the regeneration of education in developing countries. We should not delay moving ahead while waiting for new principles to be deduced from advanced educational technology, the significance of which is far greater than that of mere techniques.*

1. Henri Dieuzeide, *Educational Technology*, p. 13, Paris, Unesco, 1971, document of the International Commission on the Development of Education, Opinions Series, 30.

In many countries, the infrastructure needed to introduce modern technology does not exist. The cost of the investments required is prohibitive and it is impossible to train professional personnel and develop the facilities required in a short time. These constitute such serious obstacles to applying the most advanced techniques that the dazzling prospects opened up to developing countries, especially in education, risk being nothing more than a mirage, for a long while to come, generating possibly dangerous illusions.

Using the people's energies

Yet certain countries which are technologically retarded have made some original experiments which show there is another way out: that of using everyone's creative ability through mobilizing and organizing the people in new ways. To do this means calling on all their energy and intelligence, so that they join in promoting a new type of technological and scientific development answering to the nation's needs.

The promotion of new techniques in no way implies dismissal of the most vital component of the fundamental educational reforms required by our age: the massive development of latent human resources.

In the years to come, progress in educational technologies will permit a large measure of individual fulfilment for those in the advantageous position to benefit from it. And increasing use of new technologies will not be limited to formal education. It will spread beyond this sector and lead to considerable advances, in the fairly near future, in other fields of educational activity—promotion of literacy, basic education and public information—through the deployment of modern mass-communication media.

But prospects for mobilizing the human potential—at present scarcely tapped—are far from being dependent on technological means alone.

There are immense possibilities for mass participation in the social and educational enterprise. Peoples until now submerged by the tides of history are becoming aware of their will and their power. The size and strength of the potential to be unleashed through mobilizing the people, through volunteer movements and spontaneous popular organizations, is clear from examples in many countries over the past fifty years.

Liberating the energies of the people, unleashing their creative power, heads the list of future prospects for the development of education in the world of tomorrow.

133

New inventions
from practical applications

*Innovating
from practice*

Polyvalent classes, integrated schools, non-graded schools, transition courses, *scuola senza muri*, comprehensive schools, multivalent schools, *classes passerelles*, unstreamed classes, *shramek vidyapeeth*, Harambee schools, community colleges, *universidad libre a distancia*, drop-in high schools, workers' universities, *universités invisibles*, *enseñanza en equipo*, open universities, *radnicki universiteti*, open schools, *scuola nel campo*, parallel schools, modular scheduling, free studies, individually prescribed instruction . . . This far from exhaustive list shows the dimensions of the wave of innovation which has emerged in developed and developing countries alike over the past ten years, with varying strength and success, according to resources available and political policies.

These innovations, which all aim at evolving more effective and more flexible forms of education, are too recent for their merits and impact to be assessed, but their focus is significant.

*Individualized
teaching*

Many forms of individualized teaching stress personal diagnosis and extending the practice of self-education. According to requirements and abilities, each student is assigned a programme of studies comprising data to be assimilated and research and practical work to be carried out, sometimes in a group, sometimes alone. He is also given the means of checking his own work.

New learning methods multiply independent learning procedures and equipment[1]—surveys and research, documentation centres, equipment banks—and promote development of adaptive techniques, such as collective examination stations and teaching machines.[2]

1. Self-service education systems are based on the concept that efficacious study does not depend on the scientific rigour of the teaching, the value of which is in any case partly illusory since it becomes outdated, but on the quality of the learner's relation to the source of knowledge. The individual can be advised as to his choice of aims, but it is for him to select the means of attaining them. These means generally consist of more or less modular components or groups of systems (packages), to be consulted on the spot (documentation centres), borrowed, hired or purchased.
2. It should be noted, however, that certain original experiments are conceived in a very different spirit, such as the intensive system used in Japan and the United States, especially for staff of large firms. The student is placed in 'teaching clinics', where he is treated for relatively short periods of time (three weeks to three months), for a specific purpose: professional retraining, to learn a language or specialized technique. Following an entry diagnosis, he is subjected to rigorous and repetitive mechanisms making massive use of conditioning processes (audio-visual presentations, language laboratories), organized so as to keep time and energy wastage to a minimum.

Concepts in the organization and structure of knowledge are changing. School programmes are often no longer a continuous discourse divided into chapters of equal importance. They are becoming modular systems allowing for the creation of packages, which can themselves be divided into interchangeable blocks. Paths imposed on pupils are no longer linear; diversions enable optimal paths to be proposed, according to levels of knowledge. Learning resources are diversified, particularly by multi-media approaches developed through school radio and television programmes.

School time is ceasing to be cut into uniform slices. Its pace varies, diversified work replaces lock-step, uniform advancement for all. A certain amount of time can be set aside for individual study at the learner's own pace (up to 40 per cent of school time in some American and Swedish secondary schools). In the time devoted to study, there is a tendency to draw a more or less empirical distinction between periods of instruction (individual or in large groups), periods of work in small groups, periods of individual assimilation, periods of transference and periods of checking (individual or collective).

Education is drawing closer to sections of the population usually *New clients* excluded from educational circuits, providing the system with new clients. The need is felt throughout the world for institutions aimed at special categories of adults, workers wanting qualifications, professional men, executives and technicians on whom political or social changes suddenly impose responsibilities for which they were not trained or which technological changes have superseded. In this respect, certain systems providing broader access to higher education are of special interest.[1] They generally demand no formal entrance criteria and offer access to a central stock of resources which can be individualized: computer-stored or taped data and subscriptions to distribution networks (radio, television, correspondence courses, etc.).

The reappraisal of the authoritarian transmission of learning in traditional schools entails a reduction in the constraints imposed on pupils' behaviour (discipline, exercises, examinations). Knowledge can be acquired in groups and considerable time devoted to

1. Examples: TeleKolleg (Federal Republic of Germany) or the secondary correspondence and radio school of NHK Radio (Japan). The most highly developed current system is that of the Open University in the United Kingdom, which combines radio and television broadcasts, the use of special manuals and learning kits, correspondence courses, consultation of video cassettes, group seminars and summer schools.

discussion and seminars. This can lead to sometimes violently rebellious forms of co-operative management unrelated to any of the established structures, as in the case of the 'anti-universities'. Elsewhere, however, these forms may be determined by economic or pedagogic factors such as the search for a better use of resources, attempts to achieve more authentic, individualized teaching or to practice mutual education.[1]

Modification of the teacher's role

In general, the teacher's role is changing, in that the authoritative delivery of knowledge is being supplemented by spending more time diagnosing the learner's needs, motivating and encouraging study, and checking the knowledge acquired. Teaching teams, set up on the pattern of hospital teams, are beginning to appear and there are more supplementary teachers and assistants, mainly responsible for non-teaching duties, such as supervising and evaluating pupils, and administrative tasks. At the extreme, the possibility is being voiced of reconsidering the very idea of the permanent educational specialist in certain areas of education.

Changing school architecture

School space is no longer necessarily a cell containing thirty or forty individuals. There are many schools where the interior architecture is novel and original. Multi-purpose areas with mobile partitions and separate booths can be adapted at will to large or small groups or to individual study. Large areas may be used for debating. Documentation points have increased. The educational establishment is becoming at once a club, a workshop, a documentation centre, a laboratory and a place of assembly.[2] Student-space arrangements, time-tables, staff distribution, allocation of equipment all tend to be more mobile, and the institution more flexible and better adapted to social and technical developments.

The typical school building has lost much of its importance in countries with limited resources. Although a modern style of architecture incorporating advanced technical innovations does theoretically have advantages, experience has shown that shortcomings in school installations, equipment and buildings can be largely

1. An experiment in 'free reception' by Tele-Niger, in 1970–71, led to the pupils, whose average age was 10–11, managing the broadcasts themselves.
2. Access to documents by a telephone dialling system or by an alpha-numerical keyboard, and widespread distribution of data by television or headphone, change 'traffic' patterns. Adaptable paths and student mobility, on the other hand, require constantly available sources of knowledge, through libraries, research centres and methods such as micro-index systems, information centres, equipment centres, tape libraries, memory banks, in order to offset the temporary, fleeting quality of radio, telephone and television, which they share with learning from masters.

compensated for by new relationships between teachers and learners, by the introduction of creative pedagogy and, in general, by setting up a new kind of educational atmosphere. In this respect, results obtained in the open countryside by applying novel educational methods to classes held in tents or using the most rudimentary means have often been far more convincing[1] than those obtained from expensively equipped schools lacking appropriate professional teachers or a creative atmosphere, which accordingly fail to live up to expectations. When we consider the often exorbitant cost of building schools calculated to rival the best of their kind elsewhere, it would appear that developing countries would be better advised to focus most of their attention on the non-material aspects of schooling. Above all, competition with other countries in this field in order to enhance 'national prestige' should be avoided. Succumbing to temptations of this kind not only leads to imposing an unjustifiable burden on the educational economy; it can also send general educational development in an unhealthy direction. Besides, methods diametrically opposed to these may be used to forge far more satisfactory links between schools and the surrounding environment.

For on the whole, in fact, progress within schools themselves goes hand in hand with improved practical links between schools and society. In the last resort, it is through his natural environment that man has educated himself down the ages. Everything seems to show that this natural education, through the combined effects of the biological and social environment, has been the major instrument in the growth of man's awareness and intelligence.

School and society linked

Close correlation between society and education would seem to be especially important now that possibilities of improving one's mind and acquiring knowledge and culture are increasing.

Under these conditions, learning at school, based on the concept of effort, discipline and competition, is often rivalled by more lively, easier and less coercive forms of educating young people and adults. At the same time, conflict is sharpening in many countries between the values represented by school and the patterns of life depicted by mass media, which often glorify violence, eroticism and luck, as well as poetry, spontaneity and pleasure. The need to harmonize

---

1. Bahmanbegui, of Iran, has experimented with a system of 'schools without buildings' for nomad tribes in the Fars region, especially the Qachqaï tribe. Results obtained by participants in these schemes are often superior to those of pupils in near-by regions attending regular classes.

school and out-of-school aims and methods in their broadest sense is felt more and more keenly.[1]

The opening of the school on to the world works both ways. The former tends to see itself as a multi-purpose cultural centre. The school library serves as public library; the assembly hall is the local theatre; the science laboratories, workshops, sports facilities, audio-visual studios and documentation centres are made available to the community, at least after school hours and during the holidays. An attempt is thus being made to give the school roots in the surrounding social context, to draw it out of isolation and fit it into the community, not only in rural districts, but in the towns and urban centres too (although it is difficult to set up good schools in bad cities). In the same way at family level an attempt is being made to integrate parents directly into the school structure, to associate them with the design of education, especially in 'community schools'[2] or 'schools for parents'. Similarly, efforts are being made to bring the school closer to the working world, despite the fact that these are often superficial attempts to overcome the rigid dividing-line between intellectual and manual work. However, contacts of this kind often help to give children a taste and respect for physical work and to set up a climate of mutual understanding between schools and neighbouring factory or farm workers.[3]

Freedom from constraint

Progress in the biological, psychological and social sciences has given the great traditional humanist movement a new scientific foundation. All in all it indicates that man, freed from socio-economic and historical enslavement, is indeed very different from man living under a dominating or poverty-stricken society. Whatever the almost pathological state to which a past of poverty and violence may have reduced him, we are becoming more and more convinced that man is not necessarily a ravening wolf to other men, that his bio-mental structures predispose him to love and to creative work, and that if his deeper drives may have found expression

1. In the socialist countries, for instance, an attempt is being made to co-ordinate certain peak-listening-time television programmes with school activities. Many television projects in various countries are aimed at catching up cultural lag and at discouraging school drop-outs.
2. Developed in Laos, Liberia, the Philippines and Sierra Leone, among other countries.
3. There are many instances of schools closely linked to the agricultural environment and of workshops set up in schools, with the help of local craftsmen, carpenters, printers, etc. It is interesting to note in this connexion that in some African rural areas such attempts sometimes meet with strong resistance from craftsmen. They believe that the blacksmith's or fisherman's secrets should not be revealed to the young outside tribal initiation rituals.

138

in negative forms of violence and irrational aggressivity, this has been because throughout his history he has lived in what may be called the vicious circle of human underdevelopment. For the first time in history he is facing a real way out. He has an increasingly clear picture of the material realities surrounding him, of his own condition and being, and he is beginning to acquire hitherto undreamed-of powers.

In this way reality coincides with the creative intuition of all those teachers and educators of the past who, individually or collectively, drew their inspiration from the idea that education can and must be a liberation.[1] More and more are inspired by that idea today. Examples abound: A. Ferrière (Switzerland) and his 'active school'; Maria Montessori's 'self education' (Italy); John Dewey's 'team work' (United States); Pavel Petrovich Blonsky, who opened the first 'working schools' in the Soviet Union immediately after the October Revolution; O. Decroly's 'active method' (Belgium); Célestin Freinet's 'new school' movement (France); P. Petersen's 'Lebensgemeinschaftschulen' in Germany; schools such as A. S. Neill's Summerhill (United Kingdom); Tai Solarin's 'Mayflower' school (Nigeria); the literacy and education campaigns modelled after Paulo Freire's 'conscientization' method,[2] in north-east Brazil and later in Chile; the functional literacy projects launched in various regions of the world in the framework of the World Literacy Programme, in co-operation with Unesco; measures in the People's Republic of China to overhaul the entire educational system, in close contact with an environment in a state of profound change; the Bac-ly pilot rural school and 'green laboratory' in the

Education as liberation

1. 'Contrary to education for domestication, education for liberation, utopian, prophetic and hopeful, is an act of knowing and a means of action for transforming the reality which is to be known. . . . While in education for domestication one cannot speak of a knowable object but only of knowledge which is complete, which the educator possesses and transfers to the educatee, in education for liberation there is no complete knowledge possessed by the educator, but a knowable object which mediates educator and educatee as subjects in the knowing process. . . . While in the domesticating practice the educator is always the educator of the educatee, in the liberating practice the educator must "die" as exclusive educator of the educatee in order to be "born" again as educatee of the educatee. At the same time, he must propose to the educatee that he "die" as exclusive educatee of the educator in order to be "born" again as educator of the educator. This is a continual passage back and forth, a humble, creative movement, which both have to make' (Paulo Freire, *Unusual Ideas about Education*, p. 7, Paris, Unesco, 1971, document of the International Commission on the Development of Education, Opinions Series, 36).
2. The term 'conscientization' comes from the Brazilian, *conscientização*, which corresponds to 'learning to perceive social, political and economic contradictions, and to take action against the oppressive elements of reality' (Paulo Freire, *Pedagogy of the Oppressed*, p. 19, translator's note, New York, N.Y., Herder & Herder, 1970).

Democratic Republic of Viet-Nam; experiments in Tanzania under the 'education for self-reliance' programme; the Angolan women who have managed to integrate the literacy movement into the Angolan people's struggle for liberation; experiments in 'Schools without Buildings' in Arab States; current endeavours to reform education, based on a philosophy of creative participation by the people, currently under way in Peru, Chile and Cuba. . . .[1]

These and many other experiments are concrete evidence of the immense possibilities of liberating actions in education. Many have indicated, as well, the limitations and even the setbacks with which all enterprises of this kind are faced, when they fail to insert themselves in the surrounding socio-cultural structures, which tend to reject them as if they were foreign bodies.

Yet this liberating power of education does not only depend, under present circumstances, on pedagogues' innovative will, generosity and courage. Modern technologies do not necessarily need to be used by educators imbued with the idea of progress, or in a context of political innovation, in order to yield their advantages. They do this by their very nature. Mass-communication media, especially intensive use of radio, enable knowledge to penetrate deeply into environments inaccessible to earlier forms of communication. One of the great merits inherent in mass media is that they relieve the teacher of exclusive concern with the transmission of knowledge and thereby enable him to pay greater attention to his mission as educator.[2] Because of this, the media help considerably to develop the qualitative and quantitative possibilities for learning available to individuals and societies.

1. 'Education is not the work of specialists alone, but of all the people, organized . . . (it requires) the broadest participation by, and resolution on the part of all sectors concerned . . . (it is) the fruit of a great struggle which will only be won if we are able to consider it as a problem affecting ourselves, and not only teachers and students . . .' (extract from a report presented to the National Congress of Education, Chile, December 1971). 'The people are not only the object of massive, continuous and integral education but also the protagonists, an important fact possible only in a revolutionary process; the popular educational organizations are the ideal device to co-ordinate and organize popular action aimed at giving a boost to education and solving its problems' (declaration by the first National Congress on Education and Culture, Cuba, April 1971).
2. 'Modern technologies have a liberating power to the highest degree, for they widen cognitive fields and possibilities, enabling larger and larger social groups to insert themselves into the "depot" of culture and knowledge; they allow the individual's intellectual potential to be used on a hitherto unimaginable scale; they allow an ever-greater "recuperation" of intellectual activity; and finally, they permit any and every individual to master an unceasingly growing cognitive field with an ever-greater critical awareness of social situations' (G. Gozzer, 'L'Educazione Intellettuale et le Nuove Tecnologie Metodologiche dell'Apprendimento', *Pedagogia e Vita*, June–July, 1971).

140

The experimental functional-literacy programme, under which experiments are being carried out in twelve countries[1] with Unesco aid, is an original undertaking whose doctrine and methodology have their place among attempts to renew educational systems and their relationships with development. Obviously, when illiteracy is an aspect of underdevelopment, literacy training should form an integral part of any development undertaking to help man to become a conscious agent and master of himself. This correlation gave rise to the principles of functional literacy, as an educational, social and economic activity in areas regarded as priorities for development and where illiteracy is a major drawback. Individual motivations were taken as a starting-point to ensure that teaching-content was really functional, that is to say favouring socio-economic and cultural activity. The means were diversified programmes, 'made to measure', based on an ecological approach and the learning of directly usable knowledge. The objective was to train individuals and groups who would be called on to carry out given social and economic tasks. Learning to read and write was no longer an end in itself; it was a means of personal liberation and development and of extending individuals' educational efforts. Learning content is no longer the usual educational subject-matter, but involves overall interdisciplinary responses to concrete problems. Functional literacy aims at developing individuals' mental equipment and communicative powers, as well as their technical and vocational capacities. It offers educative functions to broad sectors of society, promotes the formative part which the major economic activities may play, defines the principles and practical methods of education, objective by objective and problem by problem, and invites all concerned, not just illiterate adults, to participate in educational activity.

Functional literacy

Educational action, so conceived, necessarily runs into all kinds of difficulty. This may arise equally from conservative, traditionalist resistance and from the tendency among technocrats to underestimate the importance of the educational factor in development enterprises.

The functional-literacy campaign has many innovative aspects and has produced positive results, and therefore deserves to be

1. The experimental world literacy programme is being carried out in Afghanistan, Algeria, Ecuador, Ethiopia, India, Iran, Mali, Niger, Sudan, Syria, Tanzania, Venezuela. Some idea of the proportions of this scheme, undertaken by national governments in an international framework, may be gained from the fact that at least 400,000 adults took part in literacy courses and more than 8,000 literacy teachers gave lessons in 1971.

*Developing
the concept
of lifelong
education*

*considered as a very constructive contribution to the reform of
educational systems.*

The idea of lifelong education has gathered great strength over
the past ten years, although it is an illusion to think it a discovery of
our time. There is nothing new in the idea of the continuity of the
educational process. Whether they do so consciously or not, human
beings keep on learning and training themselves throughout their
lives, above all through the influence of the surrounding environment and through the experiences which mould their behaviour,
their conceptions of life and the content of their knowledge. However, until the present day, there were few structures in which this
natural dynamic could find support, so as to transcend chance and
become a deliberate project. Especially, preconceived ideas about
instruction—it was for the young and took place in schools—prevented people generally from conceiving of lifelong education in
normal educational terms. Yet it is true that in the space of only a
few years the same obvious fact has come home to people from one
end of the world to the other: most men are not sufficiently equipped to face the conditions and vicissitudes of life as lived in the
second half of the twentieth century. Hundreds of millions of
adults need education, not only for the pleasure of perfecting their
capacities or contributing to their own development, as before, but
because the demands for over-all social, economic and cultural
development of twentieth-century societies require the maximum
potential of an educated citizenry.

As has been noted, the educational enterprise will only become
efficient, just and human by undergoing radical changes affecting
the essence of educational action, as well as the time and place for
education, in short, by adopting the concept of lifelong education.

Now that this idea has spread around the world, lifelong education has also become a historical problem, that of civilization itself.[1]

At the outset, lifelong education was scarcely more than a new

---

1. 'Life is bringing pedagogics face to face with new problems, placing before it tasks
immeasurably more complicated and difficult than those which it had solved in the
recent past. . . . How can the school keep up with science, with life? How can two
irregular, unequal processes be co-ordinated: on one hand the avalanche of scientific
information, the ever intensifying differentiation and integration of modern knowledge, the growing enrichment of science, technology and art with values of great
significance, and on the other, the process of school instruction in which everything is
limited by the bounds of the textbook, the bounds of time which cannot be extended
at will, just as the possibilities of a developing man cannot be extended to infinity. We
already today fully comprehend this discrepancy. Its disappearance in the future cannot
be counted on; on the contrary its tendency to become ever more acute is evident'
(P. Korovlev, *Soviet Schools: Their Present and Future*).

term applied to a relatively old practice: adult education, not to say evening courses. Then, progressively, the idea was applied to professional training, following which it came to cover the multiple aspects of personality—intellectual, emotional, aesthetic, social and political—within an integrated vision of educative activity. Now, finally, the concept of lifelong education covers the entire educational process, from the point of view of the individual and of society. It first concerns the education of children and, while helping the child to live his own life as he deserves to do, its essential mission is to prepare the future adult for various forms of autonomy and self-learning. This later learning requires many wide-ranging educational structures and cultural activities to be developed for adults. These, while existing for their own purposes, are also a pre-condition for reforming initial education.

Over-all educational process

Lifelong education thereby becomes the instrument and expression of a circular relationship comprising all the forms, expressions and moments of the educative act.

Education from now on can no longer be defined in relation to a fixed content which has to be assimilated, but must be conceived of as a process in the human being, who thereby learns to express himself, to communicate and to question the world, through his various experiences, and increasingly—all the time—to fulfil himself. It has strong roots, not only in economics and sociology, but also in findings from psychological research which indicate that man is an unfinished being and can only fulfil himself through constant learning. If this is so, then education takes place at all ages of life, in all situations and circumstances of existence. It returns to its true nature, which is to be total and lifelong, and transcends the limits of institutions, programmes and methods imposed on it down the centuries.

The conditions required for strengthening the scientific foundations of education have been established. The task now is to improve relations between interdisciplinary research and educational development, translate scientific achievement into pedagogic reality and make educative institutions rational entities which fully exploit technological achievement. New ecological and cybernetic models are available. They are sturdy, self-adjusting, self-balancing and self-renovating. Thus, we have reached the point where we foresee methods of organizing education which are based on the principles of dialogue between man and machine, providing the possibility for widespread individualized learning.

These scientific aims seem to be contradicted, in many countries, by educational thought and practices endeavouring to make education an instrument for individual reintegration into society and for social liberation, and by young people's protest, in many cases, when they demand the right to emotional expression and proclaim their rejection of constraints.

This opposition finds justification in the indifference displayed by educational systems towards social phenomena surrounding them: war or peace, the legitimacy of governments, population control, economic and social injustice or racial discrimination. Science— focused on defining objectives, modernizing methods, on cybernetic organization and efficiency—and government authorities—anxious to prescribe rationally organized educational systems for their citizens—are confronted by demands for the right to initiative, to individual inventiveness, to creativity, to be different. The aversion which people feel towards the rationalization of educational procedures must lead us to expound new concepts and these tend to go against the laws of scientific development. People react to the process of mechanized integration by proclaiming rights to individual originality.

Is this a hopeless situation?

Not at all, in so far as we are capable of taking the contradiction— between those who want to programme, regulate and supervise educational functions and objectives, and those who see the problem as one of perpetual negation of society's real goals—to its logical conclusion.

The future of education lies in devising educational institutions which combine industrial or technological efficiency, centred on the acquisition of knowledge, with the vitality of creative groups whose action will enable human relations to evolve.

Are these two propositions incompatible?

Rationalization of types and methods of pedagogic action, utilization of mass-communication technologies and introduction of cybernetic principles would seem to be conducive to stimulating individualization and awakening consciousness. They might also lead to increasing sociability, strengthening learners' independence and providing them with better weapons to seek more just social patterns, new conceptions of power and authority, and more effective means of communication and participation.

The future belongs to those able to unite criticism, democratic participation and imagination with the power residing in operational, scientific and rational organization, so as to evoke the latent resources and potential energies dwelling deep within the peoples.

144

CHAPTER 6

Goals

Every educational act is part of a process directed towards an end. These ends are dictated by general, ultimate aims which are themselves essentially laid down by society.

This is the pattern followed in the contemporary world. The objective reality of a given situation necessarily conditions present aims for education in each particular national context. But these also result from acts of will and subjective choice on the part of those participating in educational activity, as well as the general aims of the community.[1] Assigning some ultimate end to education does not mean investing it with this or that function, it means that those functions which devolve on it must be exercised in relation to aims which go above and beyond it.[2]

This series of determinants should not be regarded as merely mechanical. Just as the forms of society usually lag behind economic and social realities, so for a long time education may reproduce former social states. Or, on the contrary, it may anticipate new ones and hasten their evolution.

1. 'The purposes of education cannot be deduced from cosmic principles, nor are they established as a body of absolute values laid up eternally in some platonic heaven. Those purposes are not irrelevant to metaphysical considerations, and they certainly are intimately involved with, and in some instances identical with, elements of moral philosophy and value theory. But attempts to derive them from philosophical theory will fail to produce anything genuinely viable and relevant as a body of principles unless that theory is brought into some meaningful relationship with the facts of personal and social experience; with the needs, interests, and aspirations of individuals; with the failures, successes, and goals of society; with the established personal and social values and the criticism of those values' (Sterling M. McMurrin, 'Innovation and the Purposes of Education', in: *The Schools and the Challenge of Innovation*, New York, N.Y., McGraw-Hill, 1969).
2. 'There is a radical difference between aims and objectives. You can measure objectives but you cannot measure aims. An ultimate aim is philosophic *élan*, it is the transcendental essence of our action. To train free men, creative minds, to develop each person's potentialities to the maximum, these are ultimate aims. An objective is independent of individuals' (A. Biancheri, op. cit.).

Nor should these determining conditions be conceived of in over-simplified fashion. When we say that education reflects society, we mean that it reflects a complex reality. It is a mistake to try to see education, or even its schools and systems, solely as the expression of dominant social forces, the State, or the régime in power, to the exclusion of other complementary, independent or hostile social factors. In fact, the educational world and particularly the school are the scene of ceaseless controversy and strife, all of which affect its aims.

These conditions are not exclusive; social factors are not the only ones affecting educational objectives. Individuals—learners present and potential, teachers, parents—exert a conscious or unconscious influence on the way the ultimate aims of education are determined or modified. Pedagogic thought, philosophy, the theory and science of education and general ideologies, each with their particular emphasis and effect, also contribute to the expression of goals.

There are as many options for education as there are societies, historical phases, dominant ideologies. There are as many choices to be made as there are futures imagined and wanted.

Yet—convincing proof of a consensus—emerging from the many objectives pursued, *there are a number of common orientations which indicate that certain of the modern world's major ultimate aims coincide.*

Towards a scientific humanism

The search for a new educational order is based on scientific and technological training, one of the essential components of scientific humanism.

Scientific thought and language

However, we could also say real humanism, in the sense that scientific humanism rejects any preconceived, subjective or abstract idea of man. The kind of person it concerns is a concrete being, set in a historical context, in a set period. He depends on objective knowledge, but that which is essentially and resolutely directed towards action and primarily in the service of man himself.

146

The content of man's universe has changed. Whether he likes it or not, the individual is precipitated into a world steeped in science. This applies as much to the Indian peasant, caught up in the green revolution, as to the automated factory-worker or the technician in a nuclear-physics laboratory.

In modern civilization man can only participate in production if he is capable of understanding a certain number of scientific methods, rather than merely applying them. What is more, he can only properly perceive and understand the universe in which he finds himself to the extent that he possesses the keys to scientific knowledge.

Command of scientific thought and language has become as indispensable to the average man as command of other means of thought and expression.

This must be understood less as an accumulation of knowledge than as a basic grasp of scientific method.

In educational terms, we have not yet fully understood that science, substantially, is a decisive factor in training all parts of the personality and in meeting its demands. Science is not an agglomeration of 'bits of learning' and intellectual instruments to be fastened on to an individual who otherwise persists in all his traditional attitudes and behaviour. From this point of view, objectivity is the decisive value, overshadowing subjectivity, which quits a field where it has no place but flourishes all the more spontaneously in its own particular domain. Human relations have everything to gain when the common quest for a truth, which involves willing acceptance of reality and facts, prevails over clashes between emotions dressed up as reasons. *Rules of objectivity*

We must realize that access to knowledge results from a battle won against routine and inertia, against ready-made ideas and categories, against the complexity or obscurity of the object we are trying to understand. We must be aware that all knowledge[1] is the starting-point for a new search; acknowledge the labour of generations in the portion of truth we may have acquired; make decisions and act if necessary, but make no judgement before verifying it. These axioms for the scientific spirit run contrary to both dogmatic and metaphysical minds.

It seems indispensable that each individual be trained to grasp the relativity and interdependence of the various moments of *Relativity and dialectical thought*

1. The question of revelations of a religious nature, situated mainly outside of time and beyond critical study, does not arise here.

147

existence, whether from the individual's own point of view or that of the community. Dialectical thought is the usual instrument for apprehending reality in this way, since it introduces time and movement into concepts and operations. Relativity and dialectical thought would appear to be a fertile ground in which to cultivate the seeds of tolerance; this does not imply indulging evil or cruelty, but rather, accepting differences among men. Accordingly, an individual should avoid *systematically setting up his beliefs and convictions, his ideologies and visions of the world, his behaviour and customs as models or rules valid for all time, all civilizations and all ways of life.*

*Training
scientific minds*

The never-ending evolution in science makes traditional methods of teaching it less and less acceptable. We cannot hope to absorb the knowledge explosion by cramming brains with more scientific facts and by removing outdated subjects from the curriculum. Science must not be turned into a mere scholastic exercise. On the contrary, science teaching should be based on a pragmatic search for solutions to problems arising out of the environment, either directly from reality or derived from models.

For all these extremely diverse and powerful reasons—ranging from present labour needs and the need to control reality, to the need for self-control, scientific method and ethical training—training in science and in the scientific spirit appears as one of the major goals of any contemporary educational system.

For creativity

*Security
and adventure*

By nature, man seems torn between two longings: security and adventure. Because of the first, he seeks shelter. Because of the second, he has a taste for risk and accepts it; all forms of risk—the risk of being wrong or led astray as much as the risk involved in discovering, in being discovered and in facing life's great experiences. There is a price to be paid for each of these contrasting feelings. The price of being creative is admittedly incomparably higher, since all of a human being's capacities must be devoted to it, whereas the price of security is the relatively modest one of discipline. But creativity does not mean leaving the field free to every expression of human nature. The ways of invention and discovery also follow the course of freely accepted discipline, of imitating chosen models and, even more, of opposing contradictory models. Denying the role of disciplines and rejecting all the rules is out of the question, although in the long run the disciplines and rules most compatible with the inventive faculties are those which an individual has perfected for his own use.

This creative, nonconformist, seeking spirit is particularly apparent in many countries among young people. The young—although this may not be true of all, or of all in the same way, or even always of the young alone—are aware of the realities of a world whose ethical values, even before they themselves begin protesting against them, have already been daily flouted by their own elders. They realize that the dialogue they are often invited to share stems more from the self-preservation instinct in dominating societies and from paternalistic attitudes, than from the desire to seek out new truths. The *malaise* of the young is due mainly to the gulf between the profound transformations taking place in the real world and the manner—uneven, chaotic and often inadequate—in which institutions are adapting to them. So, in countries where this phenomenon has taken on the form of a cultural and even a political fact, youth becomes a unified, self-sufficient group in quest of new values for a new world which may finally arise from 'the culture of silence' and oppression, freeing itself from all the machinery of socio-economic and intellectual dominance. *Quest for new values*

Exploiting a few superficial aspects of the life of certain youth groups, so as to avoid having to take explosive truths seriously, is too easy.

No long-term educational policy can do without an analysis of the profound reasons for the challenge young people are flinging down.

Education is increasingly called on to liberate all the creative potentialities of human consciousness. Hundreds of millions of men today are finding that the two components of their creative praxis—action and thought—are paralysed. A distorted vision of man and the universe, ignorance, violence and collective psychoses causing it, powerlessness, domination suffered and repressed, and fear of freedom—all converge in such a way that action and critical thought destroy each other. *Thought and action*

Man fulfils himself in and through creation. His creative faculties are those which are most susceptible to culture, the most capable of flourishing and transcending their achievements and also the most vulnerable to repression and frustration.

149

Education has the dual power to cultivate and to stifle creativity. Recognition of its complex tasks in this domain is one of the most fruitful intellectual achievements of modern psychopedagogical research. These tasks may be described as preserving each individual's originality and creative ingenuity without giving up the need to place him in real life; transmitting culture without overwhelming him with ready-made models; encouraging him to make use of his gifts, aptitudes and personal forms of expression without cultivating his egotism; paying keen attention to each person's specific traits without overlooking the fact that creation is also a collective activity.

Towards social commitment

Education has always played an important part in preparing men for life in society and moulding them accordingly, whether directly or indirectly, overtly or covertly. No socio-political system can forgo securing its foundations by winning over minds and hearts to the principles, ideas, common references and, beyond these, the myths which bind a nation together.

Schools exert a strong unifying action. Education moves children into a coherent moral, intellectual and affective universe composed of sets of values, interpretations of the past and conceptions of the future. At the same time it provides a fundamental store of ideas and information, a common inheritance, and the more heterogeneous the society or national community, the more significant this will be. While adult educational activity may have a less unifying effect (since it may be independent of and opposed to public education), it does contribute to awakening civic spirit and a sense of social commitment, to arousing interest in others and assisting people to escape isolation—whether chosen or imposed.

Political education

Politics, however, does not have the place it deserves in education, just as democracy is not given its proper importance in political education. People talk of political education instead of giving education in politics. They confuse political or ideological indoctrination with preparation for broad, free reflection on the nature of power and its components, on the forces working in and through insti-

150

tutions. The awakening of political consciousness and the development of democratic virtues are replaced by the idea of training docile and uniform citizens. People are content to inculcate political ideas instead of training men to understand the structures of the world they have to live in and to carry out their real tasks in life, so that they will not go feeling their way blindly through an indecipherable universe.

The essential thing in political education is not the more or less subtle or more or less excessive form it may assume, but for educational action to be linked to the just, efficient and democratic exercise of power. It is not enough to teach people about political machinery.

The practice of democracy

An individual comes to a full realization of his own social dimensions through an apprenticeship of active participation in the functioning of social structures and, where necessary, through a personal commitment in the struggle to reform them.

Whatever rules, forms and customs through which this or that country may apply the principles of democracy, democratic life necessarily presupposes debate of ideas and confrontation of opinions. People are willing to see the principle of debate practised in out-of-school institutions and even become an element in teaching and other activities, but they often take fright when they see discussion making its way into schools and universities. But to exclude politics from the school is to deny and contradict (as a principle and in practice) what people in general usually profess: that schools are a constituent of the *Polis*, the City, and that relationships between the two should be as close as possible.

Politics in school

Education, through its instruction, practice and commitment, should contribute to a project which is very typical of our time, that of replacing a mechanical, administrative type of authority by a lively, democratic process of decision-making. Participation of the greatest number exercising the highest responsibilities is not merely a guarantee of collective efficiency, it is also a pre-condition for individual happiness, a daily assumption of power in society and over things, a way of freely influencing fate. The citizen's job is no longer to delegate his power but to wield it, at all levels of society and stages of life.

Participation

Political and civic aims—opposed to the abuse or dogmatic, narrow use of the political and ideological element in education—are an essential component of the educational enterprise in any democratically oriented society.

151

*Education
in economics*

In the same way, development will not be served simply by raising the qualifications of the labour force. Each individual must be helped to become a conscious consumer and enlightened agent of development, for which he requires basic knowledge of the laws, machinery and intricate workings of the economic life of the nation, the local community and business enterprises. He must understand the inherent conflicts and their internal and external operative forces. He must appreciate the means available to the various economic classes for influencing the distribution of the social output, productivity, the choice of investment and the planning process. Economics is no longer the private preserve of specialists and initiates.

Knowledge of economic life has now become a field where continuing education is being applied; schools are far from being the only institutions involved. Trade unions, professional associations, political parties, producers' and consumers' co-operatives and employees' associations all participate. It is also among the most important educational activities for the press, advertising, radio and television.

Education in economics must become an essential element in everyone's consciousness and culture, beginning at school and continued through all out-of-school media.

*International
education*

The development of democracy is required for peace. It encourages tolerance, friendship and co-operation between nations. These are platitudes but, in the complicated and complex play of politics and diplomacy, the attitudes of the peoples concerned weigh more than might appear, particularly when they have a realistic and unsentimental idea of peace.[1] When State authorities have to deal with majorities of really adult citizens or with powerful, active

1. '. . . It is extremely important to have an exact idea of peace, and to strip it of pseudo-ideas which all too often mask it, distort it and make a travesty of it. We shall begin by telling young people that peace is not a static condition of life, which may find in such a peace both its perfection and its death. For life is movement, growth, work, effort, conquest. . . . Is the same true of peace? Yes, for the very reason that it coincides with the supreme good of man, ever a traveller in this world, and that good is never fully conquered, but always being possessed anew, never completed; peace is therefore the central driving idea behind the most active dynamism.

'But there is no question of peace coinciding with force. And we may say this especially to the leaders among men, who have an interest in—and the duty of—maintaining a system of relationships among the members of a given group (family, school, business, community, social class, city, State) since they have to face the constant temptation to use force to impose such a system of relationships, which assumes the appearance of peace. But then the ambiguity in the living community turns into a torment and corruption of minds' (message from Pope Paul VI in celebration of Peace Day, 1 January 1972).

152

minorities, they cannot sweep the people they govern into whatever dangerous designs they may have devised as easily as when they are handling malleable, ill-informed populations who have been tricked as to their real interests.

In educational activities, anything designed to help man live at peace with himself, anything which draws him out of unhappy isolation and loneliness, also helps towards harmony among the peoples. For hostility towards others, the desire to destroy, are closely linked to frustration, failure and diverse feelings of inferiority. A person frustrated by inferiority exults in nationalism, hides behind a provincial culture and refuses to recognize or understand the life, the concepts or the values of persons outside his own limited sphere. He looks for any opportunity, with the support of his fellow citizens, to bolster his own image, with the sure conviction of his superiority to foreigners.

Educational action must dissipate such self-defeating attitudes, by contributing to a full development of the individual and his personal integrity. Then, by logical extension, it will be able to develop in all human beings a profound aspiration for peace—for everyone, everywhere; to form people ready to refuse wars of aggression and conquest and to respect the independence of their neighbours.

One mission of education is to help men see foreigners not as abstractions but as concrete beings, with their own reasons, sufferings and joys, and to discern a common humanity among the various nations.

Towards the complete man

A new man for a new world! Some may protest that this is an abuse of the term 'man', cherishing an idea of a timeless Being. They will argue that the 'cynerbopoid' of the future will always act according to the same instincts and motivations as the anthropoid of the past; that his anguish, despair, finite condition and need to live, love and surpass himself—in short, his human condition—will remain the same. So it is false, fallacious, to speak of a new man.

The man now emerging is one whose knowledge and means of action have grown to such an extent that the frontiers of what he

Man's powers

153

thinks is possible are infinite. And it is a fact that man today is beginning to be able to control the processes of nature and take responsibility for them, thanks to his knowledge and mastery of scientific laws.[1]

His knowledge of his own powers spreads to knowledge of his own consciousness. Never until now has he stretched to such limits his attempts to elucidate the mystery of his inner world. Knowledge of the mechanisms of his brain, and of the conscious and unconscious sources of his own behaviour, enable him to give an account of his own and others' irrational conduct.

Yesterday, ignorance and incapacity condemned men to respond to outside influences—whether from nature, other people or society in general—with resignation or neurotic reactions. Today's new man apprehends, knows and understands[2] the world; he also has the necessary techniques for acting on the world, intelligently and in his own interest. Finally, he enriches the world with material goods and technological structures. All these elements mean that man is the potential master of his fate. But only potentially because, for this to become reality, the conditions which make men the victims of violence and tyranny must be eliminated.

If there are permanent traits in the human psyche, perhaps the most prominent are man's rejection of agonizing contradictions, his intolerance of excessive tension, the individual's striving for intellectual consistency, his search for happiness identified not with the mechanical satisfaction of appetite but with the concrete realization of his potentialities and with his idea of himself as one reconciled to his fate—that of the complete man.

Man divided It would certainly be unrealistic to aim at such a fulfilment of man in most modern societies. He is exposed to division, tension and discord on all sides. Social structures which defy all rules of justice and harmony cannot fail to affect the various realms of his being. All that surrounds him seems to encourage dissociation of the elements in his personality: the division of society into classes, alienation from work and its fragmented nature, the artificial opposition between manual and intellectual labour, the crises of ideologies, the disintegration of accepted myths and the dichotomies between body and mind or material and spiritual values.

1. 'His (man's) role, whether he wants it or not, is to be the leader of the evolutionary process on the Earth, and his job is to guide and direct it in the general direction of improvement' (Sir Julian Huxley).
2. 'The most incomprehensible thing about the world is that it is comprehensible' (Albert Einstein).

The way in which education functions and is distributed to adolescents, the training given to the young and the mass information which no one can avoid—all contribute to this dissociation of the personality. For training purposes, one of man's dimensions—that of intellectual cognition—has been arbitrarily chopped into pieces, while others have been forgotten or overlooked and have been either reduced to an embryonic state or left to develop in anarchic fashion. For the supposed needs of scientific research or high-level specialization, the full, general formation of many young people has been mutilated.[1] Training for certain kinds of highly subdivided or otherwise stultifying work has led to over-estimating the importance of improving technical aptitudes to the detriment of other, more human qualities.

This does not mean that acquiring the tools of knowledge, re-search and expression is not all-important in a man's development. Man's capacity for wonder is at the source of these and other activities, such as his ability to observe, experiment and classify experience and information; to express himself and to listen, in the course of a discussion; to train his faculty for systematic doubt; to read—a never-ending exercise; to question the world in ways combining the scientific and poetical frames of mind.[2]

Dimensions of the complete man

Respect for the many-sidedness of personality is essential in education, especially in schools, if the individual is to develop as he should, both for himself and his associates. Complex attitudes, indispensable for balanced development of all personality components, must be stimulated and given form in the course of the individual's education.[3]

1. A noted scholar has warned universities against narrow specialization: 'If the specialists have received a sufficiently broad education, they can if need be prepare themselves for the new spheres of science without having to follow new courses. The universities should, therefore, be opposed to tendencies which aim at too narrow a specialization, which is characteristic in fact of the development of contemporary science as a whole' (Dr Piotr Leonidovitch Kapitsa).
2. Speaking of imagination, necessary in both science and the arts, Lenin said: 'This is an extremely precious faculty. To think that it is only indispensable to poets is a mistake and a foolish prejudice. It is even needed in mathematics, for without imagination neither differential or integral calculus would have been invented' (V. I. Lenin, *Complete Works*, Vol. 45, 5th ed.).
3. There are many ways of expressing the simultaneous existence of several people within one and the same personality, and their possibly antagonistic relationships to each other. For example: 'While the "Homo Faber" will always search for concretization, "Homo Sapiens" will try to seek abstraction. While the "Homo Sapiens" searches for goals, the "Homo Ludens" enjoys the process without goals. While the "Homo Politicus" will search for freedom (his own and that of his society) and for ways to burst frontiers, the "Homo Religiosus" will believe in determination, will give in to fate. While the "Homo Sapiens" and "Ludens" will try to dare to reach out for the unknown, the abstract, the "Homo Faber" and "Religiosus" will be afraid of the

155

One specific aim of education is to develop affective qualities, especially in an individual's relationships with others. Systematic training helps people learn to communicate with each other, to co-operate in common tasks. Education, strengthened by discoveries in the human sciences, also has the responsibility for eliminating mental blocks due to ignorance or to traumatic experiences following an insufficient or poorly managed early training.

Another essential area of personal expression is aesthetic activity. However, interest in beauty and the ability to discern it and integrate it into one's personality, together with other components of artistic experience, should be inseparable from the exercise of one or several artistic activities.

Today's cultural values happily incorporate a natural esteem for physical well-being: a renewed appreciation of the body as the primary source of vitality and physical harmony, aesthetic enjoyment, self-confidence, personal expression and emotional experience. Mastery of the body, of its powers and qualities, requires knowledge, training and exercise. Due regard must be given to sex education, and strengthening the body, its skills and capacities, and to training the muscles and nerves. Cultivation of the senses, hygienic and dietary habits, the struggle against depravity and self-destructive tendencies caused by stimulants of all kinds, should from now on be a prominent concern for every educator who takes his responsibilities seriously.

The physical, intellectual, emotional and ethical integration of the individual into a complete man is a broad definition of the fundamental aim for education.

We find this pedagogic ideal throughout history, in almost all countries, among philosophers and moralists, and among most theoreticians and visionaries of education. It has been one of the fundamental themes for humanist thought in all times. It may have been applied imperfectly, but it has been fruitful and helped to inspire many of the noblest educational enterprises.

Abstract man and concrete man

Man considered as the subject of education is, in large measure, the universal man—the same, at all times and in every place. However, the particular individual who becomes the object of a particular educational process is an eminently concrete being, able to reconcile dialectically the two aspects of human nature in the course

unknown, of the abstract, feeling assured only in the known, concrete and present' (Erika Landau, *Toward a New Technology of Education*, paper presented at the International Future Research Conference, Kyoto, Japan, 1970).

156

of his limited existence in time and space. The truer he is to himself, the more closely he follows the laws of his nature and his own calling, the nearer he comes to humanity's common calling and, in addition, the better able he is to communicate with other people. For in fact we communicate both through our participation in the general, abstract world of ideas and through making an eminently original contribution of our own individualized feelings, thoughts and existence.

Every learner is indeed a remarkably concrete being. He has his own history which cannot be confused with any other. His personality is determined, more and more so with age, by a complex of biological, physiological, geographical, sociological, economic, cultural and professional data, which are different for each individual. How can we fail to allow for this in determining the ultimate aims, the content and the methods of education? Entering the educational process is a child with a cultural heritage, with particular psychological traits, bearing within him the effects of his family environment and surrounding economic conditions.[1] And, involved in continual education, we have the adult—producer, consumer, citizen, parent—and a happy or unhappy creature.

Recognizing this evidence must lead to a radical change in educational practices, wherever this has not already taken place. The machinery and even the spirit of most educational systems prevent consideration of individuals as differentiated persons. Inevitably, a centralized bureaucratic administration turns human beings into things. We shall manage neither to affect nor obtain the commitment of concrete man, the living man, in his real dimensions and with his many needs, unless we reform educational management, modify educational procedures and personalize educational activity.

Contemporary science has made a singular contribution to our knowledge of man by showing that he is biologically unfinished. One might say that he never does become an adult, that his existence is an unending process of completion and learning. It is essentially his incompleteness that sets him apart from other living beings, the fact that he must draw from his surroundings the techniques for living which nature and instinct fail to give him. He is obliged to learn unceasingly in order to survive and evolve.

Unfinished man

1. 'Children are different, much more different than we have up to now recognized. . . . Children are downright ornery. They refuse to grow up all of a piece' (John Goodlad, 'Meeting Children Where They Are', *Saturday Review*, March 1965).

As one contemporary psychologist put it,[1] the human being is born 'prematurely'. He comes into the world with a batch of potentialities which may miscarry, or take their form from the favourable or unfavourable circumstances in which the individual is compelled to evolve. Essentially, therefore, he can be educated. In fact, he never ceases to 'enter life', to be born in human form.[2] This is the major argument in favour of lifelong education.

Societies in our time have the experience and the existing or potential resources required (but we do not underestimate the difficulties involved) to help man fulfil himself in every possible way—as agent of development and change, promoter of democracy, citizen of the world, author of his own fulfilment—and to help him find his path through reality towards the ideal of the complete man.

Two questions arise when we turn to analyse the ultimate aims of an educational system: the first is, what is their real substance, beyond the language in which they are formulated; and the second, who defined them?

They must necessarily be both specific and general. To the extent that they are dictated by history, traditions and customs, by social patterns, economic and political systems and circumstances, they must arise out of specific situations. But, equally necessarily, they have a general character. For in our time, education is an enterprise of universal dimensions, huge and far-reaching, implicit in which are aims which have universal application. And these aims may be translated into the same explicit terms as certain of the great ideals typical of mankind today.

We see these universally valid aims in scientific humanism; in the development of reason; in creativity; in the spirit of social responsibility; in the search for balance among the various intellectual, ethical, emotional and physical components of personality[4] and in a positive perception of mankind's historic fate.

The choice of aims is not, however, the only problem. It is important that they be based on a broad consensus. Without disputing the part which political choices and pedagogic, scientific and technological achievements play in defining aims for education, it remains a task which cannot be left entirely to politicians' discretionary desires

1. Georges Lapassade, *L'Entrée dans la Vie*, Paris, Éditions de Minuit, 1963 (essay on man's unfinished state).
2. 'The individual's entire life is nothing but a process of giving birth to himself; in truth we are only fully born when we die' (E. Fromm, *Le Drame Fondamental de l'Homme: Naître à l'Humain*).

or to scientists' knowledge. For men of these professions are not the only ones from whom a joint contribution is required. There must be active participation by those concerned: the learners, parents and communities.

The role which education is called on to play depends on this kind of choice and consensus, which may turn it towards the past or the future, towards paralysis or development, towards a search for false security by resisting change or towards the discovery of true security by taking part in progress.

A learning society: today and tomorrow[1]

Normal man is designed to be a success and the universe is designed to support that success.

Educational activities, at first scattered, fragmentary and élitist, appear across the ages and the infinity of historical contrasts to have been moving irrevocably towards one and the same conclusion: the establishment of solidly structured and centralized school systems with a universal vocation. Yet when these constructions appeared to be approaching completion, more and more out-of-school activities and institutions emerged or re-emerged, most often without any organic attachment to formal, official education, which was too narrow and rigid to contain them. Then, enlightened people endeavoured to remedy this lack of harmony by amalgamating school and out-of-school systems. But just as they appeared to be winning the theoretical—if not the practical—battle, other horizons were unveiled. New realities and potentialities have enriched life. For present-day societies—and still less for those of tomorrow—the prospect is already not limited to setting up systems capable of grouping and adding up all kinds of education by multiplying and diversifying at will the educational edifice. Another scheme of things must be envisaged, going beyond a purely systemic conception.

'It is out of the question for education to be confined, as in the past, to training the leaders of tomorrow's society in accordance with some predetermined scheme of structures, needs and ideas or to preparing the young, once and for all, for a given type of existence. Education is no longer the privilege of an elite or the concomitant of a particular age: to an increasing extent, it is

1. The quoted texts have been borrowed in particular from the following authors: R. Buckminster Fuller, René Maheu, George Z. F. Bereday, Radovan Richta, Giovanni Gozzer, Robert Hutchins, Edouard Lizop, Henri Janne, Pierre Furter, Anthony Lewis.

reaching out to embrace the whole of society and the entire life-span of the individual.'

But there are those who, starting from similar premises, end with a radical conclusion, inverting the system into a non-system:

'It seems that what is needed in an age of unprecedented demands for education is not a system but an "un-system".'

Education is overreaching the frontiers which confined it in centuries-old tradition. Little by little, it is spreading, in time and space, to enter its true domain—that of the entire human being in all his dimensions, which are far too vast and complex to be contained within the limits of any 'system', in the static, non-evolutional meaning of the word. In this domain, the act of teaching gives way to the act of learning. While not ceasing to be taught, the individual becomes less of an object and more of a subject. He does not receive education as if it were a gift or a social service handed out to him by his guardians, the powers-that-be. He assimilates it by conquering knowledge and himself, which makes him supreme master and not the recipient of acquired knowledge.

'The school of the future must make the object of education the subject of his own education. The man submitting to education must become the man educating himself; education of others must become the education of oneself. This fundamental change in the individual's relationship to himself is the most difficult problem facing education for the future decades of scientific and technical revolution.'

Education, although based on an objective knowledge of the world drawn from the latest scientific data, is no longer focused *on* the learner, nor anyone, nor anything else. It must necessarily proceed *from* the learner.

'The stress today is on the "mathetic" principle of instruction and learning rather than on the traditional pedagogic principle of teaching.'

Society cannot exercise broad, efficient action on all its components —in any domain—through one single institution, however extensive it may be. If we admit that education is and will be more and more a primordial need for each individual, then not only must we develop, enrich and multiply the school and the university, we

161

must also transcend it by broadening the educational function to the dimensions of society as a whole. The school has its own role to play and will have to develop it even further. But it will be less and less in a position to claim the education functions in society as its special prerogative. All sectors—public administration, industry, communications, transport—must take part in promoting education. Local and national communities are in themselves eminently educative institutions. As Plutarch said, 'the City is the best teacher'. And especially when the city is capable of remaining within human proportions, it does indeed contain immense educational potential—with its social and administrative structures and its cultural networks—not only because of the vitality of the exchanges that go on, but also because it constitutes a school for civic sentiment and fellow-feeling.

> 'In Athens, education was not a segregated activity, conducted for certain hours, in certain places, at a certain time of life. It was the aim of the society. The city educated the man. The Athenian was educated by the culture, by *paideia*. This was made possible by slavery. . . . Machines can do for every modern man what slavery did for the fortunate few in Athens.'

Certainly machines can accomplish this if employed in suitable social conditions. It is also certain that society as a whole has a more important educational role to play. But this vision, increasingly widespread, will have many consequences. Every single institution will have to change in order to respond more effectively to man's new needs. New types of organizations will arise. The study of indirect methods of acquiring knowledge must be intensified, their efficiency improved and the value of their results objectively appraised. Need and demand are forcing existing institutions to consider an increasing variety of choices and streams, and points of entry, exit and transfer—the first stage of a powerful drive towards real democratization of education. Societies have successively consolidated or transformed their structures—the necessary foundation for man's 'right to be'. They have created material wealth, required for man's 'right to have more'. These, throughout history, have been societies' fundamental objectives. Now, should they not establish as their primordial priority the 'learning of fulfilment', that is, the education of mankind?

162

'Instead of delegating educative power to one, single, vertical, hierarchical structure constituting a distinct body within society, all groups, associations, unions, local communities and intermediary organizations must take over their share of educative responsibility. . . . Apparently self-evident ideas are losing their meaning. Such, for example, as the distinction between active and inactive life or the present conception of public and State authorities' statutes; from now on it will be possible for people other than specialized officials to teach; vertical compartmentalization is tending to fade away; the border-relations between the domains of school and what is known as the parallel school, between State and private enterprise, between the official or contracted teaching profession and those performing particular or occasional educative tasks no longer have any meaning.'

This carries us well beyond simple systematic change, however radical. The very nature of the relationship between society and education is changing. A social configuration which accorded such a place to education and conferred such a status on it deserves a name of its own—the learning society. Its advent can only be conceived as a process of close interweaving between education and the social, political and economic fabric, which covers the family unit and civic life. It implies that every citizen should have the means of learning, training and cultivating himself freely available to him, under all circumstances, so that he will be in a fundamentally different position in relation to his own education. Responsibility will replace obligation.

'In this light, tomorrow's education must form a co-ordinated totality in which all sectors of society are structurally integrated. It will be universalized and continual. From the point of view of individual people, it will be total and creative, and consequently individualized and self-directed. It will be the bulwark and the driving force in culture, as well as in promoting professional activity. This movement is irresistible and irreversible. It is the cultural revolution of our time.'

Is this a utopian vision? Yes, to the extent that any undertaking which aims at changing the fundamental conditions of man's fate necessarily contains a utopian element. Or to the extent that even if a powerful movement in this direction were to emerge in the near future, and if the means for such a change happened to be

163

available, it could still not take place from one day to the next. But it is not utopian when this prospect seems to conform not only to the present-day world's fundamental needs and major evolutionary direction, but also fits many phenomena emerging almost everywhere and in countries whose socio-economic structures and economic development levels are very different. Moreover, it is not so paradoxical as one might think to say there is no good strategy without a utopian forecast, in the sense that every far-reaching vision may be accused of utopianism. For if we wish to act resolutely and wisely, we must aim far.

> 'At the extreme, we might even dare claim that firstly, the more a philosopher allows for a utopian dimension in his thought, the more he acknowledges the importance of education; and that secondly, the more conscious of that dimension he is, the more he will stress the liberating aspect of training.'

Any innovative concept in education will, of course, face difficulties and lack resources. Drastic measures are often required, which involve the discipline, austerity and uniformity needed to build development infrastructures. To associate creativity with freely accepted discipline, to prepare the wealth of personal happiness amid the restrictions imposed by penury—this may be the right morality, particularly in developing countries. It is also true that any innovation in education admittedly runs into strong resistance, conscious and unconscious, practical and metaphysical. From the traditionalists, whom their opponents label outdated, and from speculators over the future, whom the former call utopian. From the inside, among educational structures, and from the outside, among political reactions. In the name of legitimate fears inspired by the frailty of children's psychological mechanisms, and in the name of unjustified horror at the idea of alleged disorders following real reforms. It is vain to claim to be 'fighting' for a learning society which will spring up one fine day, fully formed and equipped, shiny as a new toy, under the effect of ringing phrases. At the most, it may be one of the slogans on the banners in a rough political, social and cultural battle, leading to the creation of objective conditions, a call for effort, imagination, daring ideas and actions.

> 'Can it conceivably be done? . . . The first step is for politicians to take the issue seriously—the whole problem, the philosophical challenge. Who will begin?'

164

Yes, indeed! Who—and how?

It is not for us to answer the first question. It will be answered in practice by nations and governments. In the following pages, we shall try to give a partial answer to the second question.

PART THREE

Towards
a learning society

CHAPTER 7

Role and function
of educational strategies

It has been said that one cannot predict the future; one can invent futures. We might also say, 'we can predict a plurality of futures; we must choose and want one future'. That would be more in line with these pages, and a better indication that those called to play a part in developing education need a broad vision of the future, regarded not as some obscure fatality but as a defined aim. They need to discern the paths leading to it, through all the crossroads and alternative routes they may find. In short, they must have as clear a view as possible of the way to carry intentions through to reality.

Policy, strategy, planning

Terminological discussions are usually somewhat forbidding. But it would seem useful to define certain terms related to our argument which correspond to the various phases of drafting an educational plan and putting it into effect.

It is obviously impossible to ask all education authorities and users of educational systems to comply with the demands of a rigorous terminology. The essential thing is for them not to lose sight of certain basic aspects of the problem.

Policies occupy the initial phase during which fundamental *Choices* choices, formulated in the name of the community, are made by organs or individuals designated for this responsibility, with the people participating to a greater or lesser extent or giving implicit approval of certain postulates (if they are sufficiently integrated, socially and culturally, into the management of their public affairs).

169

Any educational policy reflects a country's political options, its traditions and values and its conception of its future. Clearly, in the first place, it is a function pertaining to each State's national sovereignty.

Expounding an educational policy is the end result of a process of thought which consists in:

Ensuring that educational objectives comply with over-all objectives.

Deducing educational objectives—in fact—from aims approved in over-all political policy.

Harmonizing educational objectives with those adopted in other sectors of national activity.

Educational policy cannot be reduced to the proclamation of a few over-all guiding principles. It must comprise a close-knit, unified structure of specific objectives, including: general objectives of a spiritual, philosophic and cultural nature reflecting a certain idea of mankind; political objectives corresponding to the national community's major options; socio-economic objectives fixing goals to be reached in terms of a certain idea of society and development; broad educational objectives defining the main guidelines which the educational system requires in order to achieve whatever objectives are assigned to it that go beyond education; finally, the strictly educational objectives, expressing orientations approved for different types and levels of institution or action within the system.

Once objectives have been determined, it is not enough merely to list them. They must be arranged according to priority and given their place in a co-ordinated whole which only then deserves the name of educational policy.

Orientations   We may then move from the policy phase to the strategic phase.

The concept of strategy covers three ideas:

1. The organization of elements into a coherent whole.
2. Allowance for chance in the way events unfold.
3. The will to confront that chance and control it.

To summarize: the combining element, the probability element, the element of will.

The object of strategy is to transcribe policy into a body of conditional decisions, determining action to be taken in relation to different situations which may arise in the future.

The translation of policy objectives into operational terms brings out: concrete goals, resources likely to be allocated, decision-making criteria and models forming the range of possibilities.

170

We then reach the stage of laying down combinations of paths calculated to lead us to the chosen objectives and, with as much exactitude as possible, allowing for uncertain contingencies and the time factor.

Transcribing policies into operational terms (which, by a kind of reverse reasoning, also throws further light on the policies in question) is not the only purpose of strategy. In addition, it provides planners with elements enabling them to envisage different possible ways to serve policy goals. Strategy is therefore the central link in a chain, from which depend, on the one hand, the detailing of policy and, on the other, the methodology of planning.

The foregoing remarks on strategies in general are applicable to educational strategies.

If educational strategy is to meet policy requirements—which is its primary function—it must be:

Global, that is to say, it must cover all educational forms and levels.

Integrated into other systems of policy objectives, both social and economic, in which education is either a constituent or subordinate element.

Reasonably long-term, reasonable being understood here as related to the pace at which political choices will probably evolve.

If strategy is to meet planning requirements—its second function—it must be both specific, so as to meet the technical demands of planning, which must be able to rely on fixed elements; and dynamic, so as to take fully into account the creative process of evolution and innovation, which during operations modifies the basic information known at the outset.

Evolution in education is so closely linked to that of social and economic factors that educational strategy can only play its part efficiently if it is constantly related to the totality of national aspirations, needs and resources.

The object of planning is to make decisions easier at the various *Methods* levels where strategical directives must be applied. It does this by making the calculations required to quantify the terms of technical choices, and by taking care that all necessary factors are brought together when the time comes to take action.

Planning cannot therefore be reduced, as too often believed, to a set of projections of desirable objectives. It is mainly a combination of ways and means for implementing policy. Social reality being in a state of perpetual change, and analytical tools being constantly improved, planning must be a continuous operation.

171

There has been a growing tendency to make educational planning (up to now nearly always synonymous with the planning of school systems) the privileged, even the only, instrument for co-ordinating the components and controlling the development of action affecting educational systems.

But the role of planning will grow to the extent that it goes beyond school education and takes in the entire educational enterprise—without becoming dictatorial and without confusing over-all planning with total planning.

The links in this chain of operations must all interlock in harmonious fashion. This is an essential condition if an educational system is to function properly and make progress, whatever its nature, degree of development or underlying doctrine. And the more all-embracing a system is, the truer this becomes. Rarely are all phases suitably structured. Policies may fail to end in decisions, or lack a clear view of ways and means of putting them into effect. Discrepancies at strategic levels occur more often than elsewhere, due to the confusion of strategy with the preceding, policy phase, or with the succeeding, planning phase, while planning may not be based on clear previews of targets.

The principle of methodically applying the associated concepts of policy, strategy and planning to education has only emerged slowly, after a long period of development.

Failure to adhere to the logical process, moving from policy to strategy and from strategy to planning, ensuring the continuity and relevance of decisions made from one level to the next, is responsible for education having been too often oriented by chance, guided blindly and developed in anarchic fashion.

Characteristics
of educational strategies

We may now pass from these preliminary remarks to a closer analysis of the particular problem at hand: strategies for education.

Quantitative expansion

From an examination of national educational strategies applied in the course of the 1960s, especially in countries where school enrolment has made comparatively little progress, it emerges that their guiding principle was linear expansion[1] of systems and the numbers of people involved. This method is now out of date. No mechanical extrapolation can now yield valid forecasts of developments in such a dynamic and living enterprise as education.

This old system programmed educational needs as a direct function of the probable evolution of student flows and of the potential for expansion of the different elements of the school system: teaching staff, equipment, buildings, classrooms, etc. Objectives were established in the light of these various forecasts.

These exclusively quantitative methods are now only valid for a stable education system making normal, regular progress. But when a system organized to handle a specific quantity of children has to take in far more, extrapolation becomes unsatisfactory.

Applying the method we are criticizing has, of course, led to undeniable quantitative progress. But status reports on the past decade make it clear that growth conceived and expressed in terms of global indicators conceals both the appearance and the exacerbation of a certain number of defects and points of imbalance.

Many countries have found that quantitative expansion of their educational systems did not go hand in hand with efficient educational action. Enormous financial and human resources were laid out to develop costly school models, the results of which often fell far short of expectations.[2]

Linear expansion strategies can no longer be justified, either from the point of view of results obtained or their methodology. When an education system has to absorb a huge number of children, strategies must be modified, must move from the quantitative to the qualitative,

1. 'Linear expansion' in the present context is understood to mean the development of an educational system's activity and capacity according to the lines of its earlier evolution, without modifying its qualitative aspects, such as: the configuration of types, levels and structures in the system, the professional teaching personnel employed, the kinds of programmes offered and technologies used. That is to say, it involves quantitative growth at the various levels of schooling, measured by global indicators and proceeding mainly by simple extrapolation of the system's past trends.
2. 'It is no exaggeration to say that the lessons of the past decade show the frailty of some of the postulates current ten years ago. This is the first paradox of expansion, but it is not the only one. It may, in fact, be claimed that the virtually absolute priority given to developing one particular educational instrument—the school and university systems—has the effect, in a by no means negligible number of cases, of working against that right to education which it is reputed to translate into concrete fact. Indeed, many education ministers, crushed by the problems arising out of management of the expanding conventional system, have thereby become ministers for schooling, thrusting out of sight, and disclaiming responsibility for, the problem related to the section of the population, whether children, young people or adults, which is not integrated into the system' (R. Hennion, Unesco).

173

from imitation and reproduction to a search for innovations, from a uniform procedure to diverse alternatives.

This means we must rethink our approach to the problem.

Specificity

We must clarify our ideas concerning the objectives appropriate to each given society, the way its structures and environment will probably evolve, and the type of man to be trained. Conclusions on these questions will be closely linked, in each particular situation, to the society's cultural traditions, its ways of life, its prevailing philosophies and its ideological aims. Naturally, the choice is not the same for all countries. In some, it seems difficult to lay down long-term political, social, economic and cultural objectives. For others, on the contrary, forecasting is the order of the day; anticipating the future of the entire society is a favourable condition in which to define an educational policy and to deduce strategies from it.[1]

Inter-relationships

The search for non-linear strategies must not be based on extrapolation of past trends, but on an up-to-date, concrete analysis of individuals' and groups' needs and aspirations, that is to say on objectives devised for them not only in education but in related sectors such as employment, industrial output, agricultural productivity; and they must also be based on other factors such as conditions of life and work, urban development, relations within society, individual aspirations, progress in communications media and techniques, standards of living and development projects.[2]

Integrated educational objectives

We may accordingly arrive at a definition of integrated educational objectives, arranged in their appropriate hierarchy and phrased in operational terms, adapted to specific environmental conditions, selected population groups and local communities.

1. '. . . the big problem in methodology will be to find the right balance between the results of a series of quantitative and qualitative predictions concerning education, outlining a possible, plausible or desirable future and the results of analyses of the various futures which might confront society and education following present and future decisions' ('Goals and Targets of Educational Policy', discussion paper submitted to the Conference on Policies for Educational Growth, Paris, OECD, May 1970).

2. '. . . it is essential to re-examine the compatibility between proclaimed educational objectives and those actually being attained, and thus derive new objectives. The re-defined objectives may themselves be implicitly influenced by the goals or targets corresponding to other sectors, such as agriculture, development of mineral resources, industry, services, etc. Educational objectives, however, cannot be limited by definition to quantifiable targets linked specifically to employment or self-employment objectives. By definition, educational objectives must also correspond to the development of individuals within their own community and within their wider society, which may well be the nation itself or the different regions making up the nation. Such objectives must also include the attainment of solutions to problems affecting community organization, inter-communal, inter-ethnic and linguistic relations, etc.' ('In the Field of Education, What should Determine the Optimum Contribution of UNDP?', p. 4, Paris, Unesco, November 1971, Secretariat document).

This concept is valid in many educational spheres—in school and especially out of school—and may be defined as an ecological approach, since every school or out-of-school system is a component of the environment in which both individuals and groups evolve. That environment therefore determines not only the range of the learning society and the content of programmes, but also pedagogic methods. It follows that educational effort should be diversified according to the environment and aim at making such action authentic in relation to each particular environment and especially to the values inherent in the civilization of the various groups in the population.

New educational strategies must proceed from an over-all vision of educational systems and resources according to their capacity to meet the needs of societies in continual change.[1] They must conceive of education as an enterprise transcending the framework of schools and universities, overflowing its constituent institutions. Under no circumstances should strategies be bound by the confines of one single medium, one form of institution or one so-called 'systemic' structure.

Over-all vision

Once we acknowledge that it is time to enlarge present systems and even to adopt alternatives or replacements, we quickly become aware of the educational wealth to be found in the daily life of the community: in economic and administrative structures, in the mass media, at work and in the home. In order to realize this potential, *strategies of a new type must be adopted and applied. The introduction of alternative educational strategies should be a feature of the present decade.*

Today, it is no longer desirable to undertake educational reforms in piecemeal fashion, without a concept of the totality of the goals and modes of the educational process. To find out how to reshape its component parts, one must have a vision of the whole.

Today, whether reforms are partial or more general, we cannot dismiss the need to conceive of both one and the other in relation to the over-all situation, and to envisage their consequences.

The reasons for this are that the effects of education are ranging

1. 'Many educational problems can be successfully understood and approached only in the context of the larger societal system of which the educational portion is but a part. Such educational problems cannot be resolved through strategies which are restricted to the educational system alone. Broad, comprehensive strategies are requires, involving various interacting sectors of society' (W. W. Harman and M. E. Rosenberg, *Methodology of Educational Futurology*, p. 15, Paris, Unesco, 1971, document of the International Commission on the Development of Education, Opinions Series, 44).

further and further and that we now have the necessary tools to make short- and medium-term forecasting a very different thing from intuitive speculation.

We therefore no longer have the right either to improvise or to limit ourselves to narrow pragmatism.

This does not mean we should dare nothing, fail to grasp new possibilities or commit ourselves to tomorrow. It means on the contrary that we must think clearly in exploring new paths for the future. When developing and reforming educational institutions and methods, we must not overlook the means and techniques in the present-day world which not only enable us to improve existing modes, institutions and systems, but also to find fresh alternatives to them. This search for practical alternatives as part of a genuine strategy of innovation seems to us to be one of the primary tasks of any educational undertaking.

CHAPTER 8

Elements for contemporary strategies

If we accept the idea of a permanent, over-all educational system, of a 'learning society', not as a dream for the future, but as an objective fact and social project in our time (to which educators, pedagogues, scientists, politicians and learners are already contributing, whether consciously or not), then we must take action in two directions at once:

Dual measures

Internal reform and continual improvement of existing educational systems.

Search for innovative forms, for alternatives and fresh resources. Educational systems are the highest expression of each people's national consciousness, culture and traditions. Since no one nation is identical to another, there are as many definitions of educational problems as there are countries in the world. In education, possibly more than in any other field, *decisive action takes place at national strategy level.*

National characteristics

Moreover, each country has distinct geographical, cultural and socio-professional environments, not to mention possible linguistic divisions. Many countries are therefore *decentralizing and diversifying their national strategies*, leaving local communities with a fairly broad freedom of action.

We do not in the least gainsay each nation's specific sovereignty over its political and strategic choices, by recognizing that any endeavour to renew education, in whatever society, must necessarily draw its inspiration from a certain number of common ideas, considerations and orientations; and these have to be discerned and formulated. This does not presuppose (nor does it exclude) similarities among various countries, which may or may not belong to the same region, leading them at times to apply very similar reforms and envisage similar solutions.

International inspiration

177

While educational strategies are substantially national, involving a nation's own sovereign choices, they may at the same time draw ideas from the international context and benefit from useful examples contained in the wealth of educational experience in all countries.

Possible courses of action are numerous and in many respects convergent. But action must be taken and progress made step by step—not just through ministerial decision or administrative decrees, but by the community at large—so that all those involved in the future of education—users, practitioners and promoters—are brought together and carried along with the movement. The development and application of over-all national strategies, whether of a reforming or innovative kind, require a powerful mobilization of mind and will, uniting the efforts of many people. This is all the more necessary in that it is probably true that 'only the person who has helped prepare for change will be able to accept it'.

Improvements and reforms

It is a characteristic of contemporary educational systems that they undergo a continual process of adaptation, improvement and modification, amounting to partial reform. While such reform does not fundamentally modify existing institutions or practices, it generally precedes more far-reaching, innovative changes, often accompanies them and at times replaces them.[1]

Motivations

Three distinct kinds of situation may trigger reforms.

First, reforms may be introduced out of concern to remedy certain defects and inadequacies in the way an educational system functions, and which experience necessarily brings to light. Present-day demands can hardly fail to prompt awareness of these. Many of these defects may surely be regarded as 'growth problems'. Others may be seen as a consequence of objective socio-economic disorders. Education, not being in a position to eliminate the causes of

1. 'Innovation', as this term is used in this report, is taken to mean a change in which invention, research, application of new techniques and modification of educational practices, related to increase in productivity of the educational process, etc., all play a part. Consequently, any improvement in practice is not necessarily an innovation, nor is any change in educational activity. Thus, the transfer of well-tried practices (and still less the return to earlier practices), propagation of elementary techniques, partial overhauls of administrative procedures, progressive adaptation of certain teaching contents and methods may not, short of an abuse or confusion of terms, be accorded the status of innovation.

the trouble, can only try to alleviate its harmful effects. However, it would be a mistake to overlook certain disquieting phenomena which are neither passing disorders nor accidents of circumstance. They are, rather, symptoms of internal malfunctioning within educational systems themselves, which must be identified and properly analysed, and which can then be corrected. This view, shared by many educators and education officials, leads to severe self-criticism and helps reformers work out new ideas.

But internal disorders in an education system are not the only reason underlying corrective reforms and improvements. Exterior factors are also influential: scientific discoveries and research findings continually suggest and provide new ways to perfect educational practice or to make it more rational.

Finally, despite the often-criticized inertia and conservatism of educational systems, stimuli from within may contribute to their renewal, modernization and improvement. Education is a living thing, a social undertaking, a building inhabited by men of good will. It is wide open to new ideas, whatever some people may say. As such, it is necessarily driven by the desire for self-improvement.

It would be futile to try and draft a complete catalogue of all the reforms, major or minor, which researchers and educationists, administrators and governments have introduced—or would like to introduce—into school systems. We shall therefore confine ourselves to trying to give some idea of their range:

Infinite range of internal modifications

From the desire to bring education closer to community life and needs, to the concern to fulfil individual aspirations more effectively.

From the determination to integrate educational establishments into the community, to the definition of business and industry's obligations to train workers and technicians.

From projects to create tighter bonds between local communities and primary education, to the establishment of closer relations between industry, research institutes and universities.

From the restructuring of education systems (eliminating dead ends, bottlenecks, etc.), to modernization of educational methods.

From action to eliminate the complex causes of school wastage, to mechanisms for rehabilitating 'failures'.

From harmonious development of all elements in the educational process—knowledge, understanding, mental attitudes, motivations, practical aptitudes—to greater consideration of emotional and personality problems.

179

From increased attention to physical education, to underscoring of moral elements in education.

From the introduction of sciences of life into all kinds of education, to the insertion of basic technology courses into primary- and secondary-school curricula and adult-education programmes.

From lightening curricula, to reducing pressure of tests and examinations.

From improving textbooks, to increasing sources of learning.

From the introduction of subject-centred and polyvalent education, to improvement of specific scientific disciplines.

From greater attention paid to mother tongues, to the development of instruction through other media, especially mathematics (both conventional and modern).

From the development of activities aimed at stimulating the pre-school mind, to measures intended to prepare adults for senior citizenship; etc.

Nationally and internationally, the almost endless range of these internal reforms has been considered, studied and argued over *ad infinitum*. No useful purpose would appear to be served here by discussing them further or attempting to establish some order of preference among them.

We shall deal here with only one aspect of internal reform: its place in the over-all strategy of educational development. In this respect, the following points should be made:

Encouragement from the top

1. Internal reforms cannot be separated from the search for alternatives to existing educational practice. These reforms may be effective enough in some cases to make it possible to postpone applying more radical measures. At the same time, they may also help to prepare for fundamental change later on. The capacity to effect partial reforms is a sign of vitality in an educational system and proof that it may be able to undergo even more sweeping changes. For this reason and even if they regard such measures as inadequate, education authorities should encourage modification of educational methods and content.

2. Research in pedagogy and related sciences is insufficiently developed in many countries. Many questions in psychology, pedagogy and educational technology remain unanswered. Seen in this light, reforms play the part of experiments.

Initiative from below

3. Experience shows that when internal reforms are ineffective, or lead to great wastage of talent and energy, it is generally because of poor communication and co-ordination between man-

180

agement at the top and action below. This leaves the creative, imaginative reformers isolated. The propagation of ideas and experiments is slowed down. Educational authorities in all countries should set up special machinery for promoting innovations; this should include information and application campaigns for tested reforms.

4. Success or failure in the concrete application of reforms depends on teachers' attitudes. In most schemes devised by innovative theorists, however, the aim appears to be to act *on* teachers—for them possibly, but rarely with them. This technocratic paternalism is based on distrust and evokes distrust in return. Teachers, on the whole, are not against reforms as much as they are offended at the way they are presented to them, not to mention imposed on them; thus, the major importance for educators to be actively associated with any educational reform project.

Innovations and search for alternatives

In present circumstances, taking the increased possibilities for future action into account as well as experience already gained, partial reforms will not in general be adequate, even if they are major ones. We must innovate and envisage fundamental alternatives to the very concepts and structures of education.

1

Principle

Every individual must be in a position to keep learning throughout his life. The idea of lifelong education is the keystone of the learning society.

Guiding principle for educational policies

Considerata

The lifelong concept covers all aspects of education, embracing everything in it, with the whole being more than the sum of its

181

parts. There is no such thing as a separate 'permanent' part of education which is not lifelong. In other words, lifelong education is not an educational system but the principle on which the over-all organization of a system is founded, and which should accordingly underlie the development of each of its component parts.

Recommendation

We propose lifelong education as the master concept for educational policies in the years to come for both developed and developing countries.

Comment

The various applications of this idea will of course differ greatly. We may even say—to remain true to the spirit of this report—that it could be applied in as many different ways as there are countries in the world. And neither, of course, will the extent of its introduction and progress be the same in all countries; this will vary from one to another. But we remain convinced that the question of lifelong education, the decisions to take and the paths to follow in order to achieve it are the crucial issues of our time, in all countries of the world, even in those which have yet to become fully aware of this idea.

Illustration

The educational reforms drafted recently in Peru propose a thorough overhaul of the system based on the principles of lifelong education. The reforms bear on all educational institutions and activities in the country, both in school and out of school. They extend well beyond the framework of a pedagogic reform and are conceived in relation to radical structural changes in Peruvian society. They proclaim that all the people have the right to education and guarantee each individual's right freely to choose the form his education shall take. It thereby goes beyond ideas of school and State monopolies. In the words of the Draft Law No. 19326 in question, the reforms are intended to 'make a final break with the two equally pernicious vices inherent in traditional education: authoritarian State control and discriminatory "privatism"', by replacing these with 'a community education based on an educational community involving responsible dialogue and participation'. The law derives inspiration from a philosophy of education which makes a break with traditional educational schemes 'reduced to a formal teaching operation linking pupil and master through a one-way relationship limited in time on both sides' and supersedes the 'exclusive and rigid' concept of a 'formalized system excluding and refusing to recognize activity which the community and its members may themselves develop independently'. The law provides for three broad educational levels: initial education, basic education and higher education. One of its interesting innovations involves splitting all the country's educational services and programmes into 'nuclei' or cells. Thus, communal educational cells are derived directly from the local community, while schools, colleges and universities, like all other institutions which carry on educational activity, directly or indirectly, are interdependent and form a network.

2

Principle

The dimensions of living experience must be restored to education by redistributing teaching in space and time.

Over-all perspective

Considerata

Education must be carried on at all ages of man, according to each individual's needs and convenience. He must therefore be oriented from the outset and from phase to phase, keeping the real purpose of all education in mind: personal learning, self-teaching and self-training. Education must cease being confined within schoolhouse walls. All kinds of existing institution, whether designed for teaching or not, and many forms of social and economic activity, must be used for educational purposes.

Recommendation

Educational institutions and means must be multiplied, made more accessible, offer the individual a far more diversified choice. Education must assume the proportions of a true mass movement.

Comment

So great is the demand for education, training and instruction today, and so great will it be in the years to come, that present institutionalized systems are and will be incapable of absorbing it. If they are to do so, they must abandon their rigid interior divisions and become more open to the outside world. This presupposes an over-all reorganization of educational structures and teaching-content on the following general lines:

Education in early childhood should set up the most favourable conditions possible for physical and mental development.

Basic education must be many-sided, designed not only for children and adolescents but also for adults who, at any age, may have need of it. While dispensing fundamental knowledge, such education aims at learning how to perceive and comprehend the world. It must endeavour to instil, especially in children, a taste for self-learning that will last a lifetime; to arouse their desire to know, to ask questions and to question themselves, while developing the faculties of observation and judgement and the critical spirit. Finally, it should try to awaken the feeling in an individual that he belongs to a community and that each person has a creative responsibility towards himself and others.

The object of post-basic education should be not so much to provide adolescents with access to university as to prepare them for active life, and to keep alive in those who, for the time being, go no further, the hope of undertaking at one time or another some post-secondary education and/or professional or vocational training at a higher level, whether in school or out of school.

Higher education should be accessible through many different paths and at any age, in many forms, especially with a view to continual self-improvement and development.

Occasional education should be available at all ages to suit each person's momentary or permanent needs.

Illustrations

1. The Educational Planning Commission in Alberta Province, Canada, spearheaded the very interesting educational reform policy in that province with a provisional report recommending that reforms be centred on the idea of life-long education. Education, said the report, should 'develop ability in the learner to learn under a variety of circumstances and conditions, on a part-time basis, at home using a variety of media, and in informal settings. . . .

'. . . we believe that the school-dominated, classroom centred, full-time teacher-oriented, eight-hours, eight- or ten-month system is an expensive one, and apart from the demands of further population increases, very little additional investment should be placed in this form of education,' the report said.

The commission was in favour of conceiving of lifelong education—within the over-all educational enterprise—as 'a process and a system which begins at the beginning of life, takes in what are now conventionally thought of as school years, and continues throughout life. It is an integration of learning into our work and our leisure. Learning we see as a process of man's growth toward fulfilment as an individual as well as a member of many groups in societies.

184

We are concerned, therefore, with the total man, not just man as a product; with creative living, not just materially productive living'.

The commission said that 'society requires the acceptance of the belief that education is life and life is education; the belief that people will spend periods throughout their lives in some structured learning experience, that they can leave and return as they see fit and as they can meet certain pedagogical demands. Under such assumptions, our early years of schooling can concentrate on learning how to learn, and should be oriented towards social and emotional as well as intellectual development. This will include the appropriate use of educational technology for independent learning. The content of the various disciplines should come later. The early period would deal primarily with the basic language of learning; speech, numbers, writing, visual arts, etc.'.

This system, the Alberta commission added, would also have the advantage of making the elementary and secondary school systems 'more open and welcoming' to people of various ages who needed the skills associated with these educational levels.

It noted three basic principles: the close relationship between lifelong education and 'assumptions of future trends in a given society'; the use of 'a variety of ways to meet needs' ranging from formal to informal programmes and including the use of modern technologies, and the concept of education 'as a part of all we do'.

2. Educational activities in the Democratic Republic of Viet-Nam are organized very much on the lines of a people's movement. Noteworthy features include: rapid large-scale development of one single kind of general education for children, using a teaching-content drawn directly from social, economic and political activities; a simultaneous widespread lieteracy programme affecting millions of people in the thick of war; development of complementary education for adults; combination of studies and productive work, especially in rural regions, where it is easier to graft pupils' productive activities on to those of co-operative farms, the principle underlying this being not to allow young people to 'plunge themselves into purely book-learning without ever doing anything with their hands, until a late age'; involvement of production centres and various services and branches of the society in education, especially complementary education, thereby underlining the mass-movement aspect of education. Some idea of its extent may be gained from the example of Cam Binh, a small village where 95 per cent of 3- to 6-year-olds attend kindergartens, 100 per cent of school-age children attend general education classes, 90 per cent of adults have completed primary-school studies and a growing number of adults are attending complementary education courses. All in all, six out of ten inhabitants are studying in one way or another.

3

Principle

Education should be dispensed and acquired through a multiplicity of means. The important thing is not the path an individual has followed, but what he has learned or acquired.

Less formalism in institutions

185

Considerata

Two current trends are emerging. First, educational institutions are growing in number and becoming more diversified. Second, traditional structures are becoming less formal. These developments are in no way incompatible. The fact that certain school institutions are losing their sacrosanct character may go hand in hand with the maintenance and development of well-knit school structures. Teaching circuits may be extended by increasing the quantity of schools of the existing kind, by setting up schools of a different kind, by part-time teaching and by out-of-school methods, all of which may take place at the same time.

From now on, all these paths, whether formal or informal, institutionalized or not, will be acknowledged—on principle—as equally valid. This is the sense in which the terms 'deformalization' and 'de-institutionalization' should be understood.

Recommendation

Each person should be able to choose his path more freely, in a more flexible framework, without being compelled to give up using educational services for life if he leaves the system.

Comment

There must be freedom of choice as to means and methods. These include full-time education, part-time education and education by correspondence, as well as all the many forms of self-education making direct use of information sources (with or without the aid of modern communication media). All of these must be regarded as equally valid, and interchangeable at the learner's will. The final result is all that counts.

Basic education should in general be more uniform than education later on. Possibilities for varying the content of teaching (according to environment or individual requirements) should preferably be made available from the beginning, while the method and pace of learning should to some extent be individualized. As a student grows up and his judgement matures, he should have greater latitude in choosing and organizing his study programme. Pupils' individual capacities will accordingly become easier to assess, in the various disciplines, and it will also be easier to group them in terms of their real interests.

Illustrations

1. Many possibilities for education and learning are available in virtually all countries. Education usually has a broad range of facilities and activities at its disposal. Furthermore, the composition of the student body and its effect on participants vary greatly. While the over-all picture differs from country to country, the organizational 'spectrum' of available educational programmes and resources ranges, as a rule, from closed and lightly prescriptive systems to open, non-prescriptive ones.

The closed systems tend to be selective and competitive, depending primarily on standards set within the system to determine those who will and those who will not be allowed to study, and at what ages.

The open systems tend to be non-selective, non-competitive and non-prescriptive. Choice of lectures and subjects listened to, read or otherwise studied depends mainly on the participants' own interests.

Many very varied educational activities and institutions, of course, fall between these two extremes. At the closed, selective and competitive end of the scale is traditionally structured, formal education. At a slight remove in the other direction are 'alternative' schools, multi-unit schools and individually prescribed instruction (IPI) involving some degree of flexibility in structures and programmes. Facilities such as self-learning centres, work-study schemes and 'open university' organizations are less structured, but remain directed towards prescriptive learning goals.

Towards the other end of the spectrum are loosely structured educational programmes: on-the-job training schemes, agricultural extension services, community development services, clubs, co-operatives, labour and political organizations, etc. And right at the other end is a wide range of media for information and education, including information centres, radio, television, libraries and newspapers, from which individuals select programmes according to personal needs and interests.

Many countries are currently endeavouring to make fuller use of the entire range of educational facilities, with lifelong education in mind. Total educational reform inevitably affects all these activities, as well as possible linkages between them.

The problem nowadays is less to develop them (many are developed already) than to correlate them, so that different learners may use them to best educational advantage in a non-traditional way. The problem is how to offer educational services of a similar kind at various points along the spectrum, depending on this or that learner's convenience; also, how to ensure that students are evaluated 'in action', according to results achieved, rather than in terms of the educational method they have used. The aim is to enable each student to combine available activities, programmes and facilities in the way that suits him best. Many countries, at varying levels of development, have already taken steps in these different directions.

2. One interesting attempt to broaden access to higher education and offer greater freedom of choice is that of the 'university-without-walls' (UWW) in the United States (several other countries have staged more or less similar experiments). Participating institutions at present include Antioch, Bard, Hofstra,

187

Loretto, Heights, Monteith, Nasson New College (Sarasota), Northern Illinois State, Sarah Lawrence, Shimer and Stephens. Essentially, UWW features: admission for anyone aged between 16 and 60 wanting to continue their studies; programmes designed to meet individual students' needs and interests; inventories of sources for whatever information may be required (such as tapes, texts, laboratories, personal contacts, etc.); the possibility for each student or group of students to organize his or their own studies; the obligation for each student to spend at least half the university year in a campus experimental centre; and a continual dialogue between student and tutor. UWW teaching staff includes a certain number of professors and teachers attached to a particular campus, visiting experts from agriculture or business, scientists, artists and politicians. If a student wants to obtain a university degree, he merely registers to sit an examination when he feels ready to do so.

3. Many other kinds of educational establishment designed to provide a considerable choice of educational activities and programmes exist in most parts of the world. Among these, the following deserve mention: community schools welcoming adults and children in turn; 'collegial' centres grouping a variety of different educational establishments in one place, making it easier for students to move from one discipline to another within the selfsame complex; centres for cultural and other activities where buildings and equipment may be used round the clock by different groups whose organizers are both producers and consumers of educational messages; technical-training centres offering study programmes at various consecutive levels (specialized workers, skilled workers, masters of trades, etc.); people's universities; workers' universities; free universities and other similar establishments easily accessible to the public.

4

Principle

Mobility and choice

An over-all open education system helps learners to move within it, both horizontally and vertically, and widens the range of choice available to them.

Considerata

Mobility and diversification of choice are complementary, each presupposing the other. There is no real freedom of choice unless the individual is able to follow any path leading to his goal without being hindered by formalized criteria; his progress should depend only on his capacities and aspirations. Mobility has no meaning unless it is accompanied by sufficiently varied possibilities.

188

Recommendation

Artificial or outmoded barriers between different educational disciplines, courses and levels, and between formal and non-formal education should be abolished; recurrent education should be gradually introduced and made available in the first place to certain categories of the active population.

Comment

This presupposes that more students will be able to move more freely from one level to the next throughout the establishment and from one establishment to another. Students will be able to enter freely at various stages and leave at many different points. At the end of compulsory schooling, each individual will be able to choose between continuing his studies or embarking on active life (without excluding the prospect of studies later on) or even remedying an earlier period of schooling, the results of which may have been unsatisfactory. Students may undertake higher studies without having previously completed the traditionally necessary period of formal schooling. There must be plenty of opportunity to move from one branch of education to another and to enter and leave this or that walk of productive and community life. Young people and adults must have many practical opportunities for combining work and education.

Individuals must be able to leave and rejoin the educational circuit as it suits them. Education and labour law must be made more flexible. Unnecessary barriers between various types of educational institution must be brought down, material aid for young people must be gradually extended to adults (so far as financial possibilities allow) and those wanting to begin or resume studies must be able to take leave more easily, which implies that employers' obligations to employees absent for part-time study, or apprenticeship courses or research, must be clearly defined.

Uninterrupted study is certainly not the only conceivable method, especially at the university level. It will become increasingly acceptable to interrupt studies between one cycle and another or even during one course. It may even be psychologically and culturally beneficial.

This conception—recurrent education—may resolve the contradiction between institutionalized and non-institutionalized edu-

189

cation by integrating them into a coherent system in which they complement and supplement each other harmoniously. It may help to refute the traditional idea according to which all education is provided during the first years of life, before entry into 'active life'. The application of the idea of recurrent education as a consequence of this would lead, in particular, to recognition of every worker's right to re-enter the educational circuit in the course of his active life.

Illustration

One developing country, Ceylon, has envisaged adopting a recurrent educational system. This would provide: (a) the award of an end-of-study certificate to the large majority of pupils completing initial education; (b) immediate admission of a very small number only of these certificate holders to pre-university studies; (c) orientation of all the others towards active life or technical or professional education; (d) recognition to all of the right to request admission to pre-university studies after two or three years, with selection based not on the results indicated by the initial certificate but following aptitude tests reserved for those who have received a certain professional training or acquired certain working skills.

5

Principle

The education of pre-school-age children is an essential pre-condition to any educational and cultural policy.

Considerata

Pre-school education

The importance of early childhood in the later development of aptitudes and personality is beyond doubt, as modern psychophysiology and ordinary observation testify. None the less current educational systems very frequently operate as if this phase of life were of no concern to them. Their shortcomings in this respect may obviously be explained in many countries by the inadequacy of resources available to meet the demand for education, but they do also result from a failure to recognize the importance to individual development of educational conditions in early childhood.

190

Recommendation

The development of education for pre-school-age children must become one of the major objectives for educational strategies in the 1970s.

Comment

An excessive proportion of available resources can obviously not be allocated to the education of pre-school-age children to the detriment of school-age children. It is difficult, if not impossible, to set up kindergartens in rural areas where the population is scattered, and the cost of such institutions in these and other areas too, together with staff problems, administrative, psychological and various other kinds of resistance often combine to prevent these institutional models and methods being used.

Education for pre-school-age children (as from 2 or 3 years old) must then be organized on a free, flexible pattern, finding the best ways of getting families and local communities to work together and share expenses. (This implies training relatively few staff for the job of organizing informal pre-school education in their sector and educating the parents themselves in special schools and other organizations formed for that purpose.) Mass communication media are also useful in this work when pre-school education has to be brought quickly to a large number of children, especially those living in environments where the cultural background is limited.

Illustrations

1. There is extensive pre-school education in the People's Republic of China. Kindergartens are imaginatively organized, some daily, some weekly, to take care of children aged from 3 to 7. In some areas, kindergartens are attached to primary schools, in others they may be provided by factories or village or district authorities, or organized and staffed by street committees, local grass-roots bodies and welfare groups. Assistance comes from many non-professional people, especially grandparents.

2. In the U.S.S.R., more than 9,500,000 children are currently enrolled in crèches and kindergartens. In addition, the kolkhoz pre-school educational establishments, functioning either permanently or seasonally, handle some 3 million children. Education given to children in these various institutions is designed to encourage harmonious physical, intellectual, moral and aesthetic development. It follows a uniform programme based on pedagogic experience and the results of scientific research. Research in recent years at the pre-school

191

Education Institute of the Soviet Pedagogic Sciences Academy and in other institutions shows that the psychophysiological faculties in very young children and children of pre-school age are more developed than hitherto believed, and that in specific pedagogic circumstances these children are capable of acquiring knowledge, intellectual aptitudes and moral qualities thought in earlier times to be accessible only to much older children.

3. The most important audio-visual educational experiment aimed at pre-school-age children so far is the *Sesame Street* programme, in the United States, and which has now spread to Latin America. It is an attempt to prepare pre-school-age children from underprivileged environments to enter school in circumstances similar to those of the average child. The programme is aimed especially at the working population in poor districts without kindergartens but where nine families out of ten have a television receiver.

4. Villagers in the Casamanca region of Senegal have organized, financed and are now operating some thirty day-care centres under the guidance of social services. They function during the seasons of the year when men and women of the villages are entirely occupied with work on the land. The centres take care of all children aged from 1 to 7, and also school-age children before and after school hours. The children receive breakfast and lunch based on local products, the dietary balance of which is supervised by the social service. Staff are recruited on the spot, receive minimum necessary short-term training and are remunerated in kind or by having their fields cultivated for them. In one way or another, everyone in the village helps the centres.

6

Principle

Basic education

All children must be guaranteed the practical possibility of receiving basic education, full-time if possible, in other forms if necessary.

Considerata

The initial precept of virtually all educational systems is that each child must receive full-time instruction in school. It follows that those unable to benefit from this precept are in fact condemned to do without instruction. Millions of children and young people are in this situation. This is therefore one of the fundamental issues for educational strategy.

Recommendation

Universal basic education, in a variety of forms depending on possibilities and needs, should be the top priority for educational policies in the 1970s.

Comment

Considerable progress towards giving all people in the world a primary education has already been made. This is a long-range effort, and it must, of course, be continued. However, it would also seem possible to find a remedy for many of the harmful effects of this situation on the present generation by judiciously balancing several solutions: complete, full-time primary education; complete, part-time or 'appropriate rhythm' primary education; incomplete elementary education for children and adults; and special teaching programmes for young people aged between 12 and 16, especially for those who have not previously attended school.[1]

Solutions of this kind cannot be applied in the same way in all countries and are obviously of especial economic, financial and social significance to developing countries, although some are not devoid of interest for developed nations as well. Education in alternating periods, for example, can yield very positive results, while appropriate rhythm instruction, the effect of which is usually to spread primary and post-primary studies over a longer period, may help to solve the delicate problem of the age at which a student enters active life, a problem causing concern to educators and governments virtually everywhere.

1. A working document prepared in 1970 for the International Bureau of Education, Geneva, contains a passage in which the authors record a similar concern: 'It may be that many of the countries with the most severe wastage problem might not be able to continue to increase the proportion of children enrolled in school if they were successful in retaining at school the large number of pupils who are present leaving prematurely. A difficult choice of policy may be forced upon such countries, between fully educating the present proportion of children enrolled in school, and partly educating a larger proportion' (*Wastage in Education: a World Problem*, p.115, Geneva, Unesco: International Bureau of Education, 1971).

Illustrations

1. In India, Intensive Educational District Development Projects are a distinctive kind of experiment with a comprehensive approach to educational needs in selected areas. (For the time being, these projects are under way in four districts, affecting a total of some 9·5 million people in the States of Punjab, Bihar, Maharashtra and Mysore.) The idea is to cover the entire population in the 3 to 45 age group under one programme or other in the project. It combines full-time and part-time teaching and programmes broadcast over radio for those enrolled at various levels of education, for those who have dropped out of school at various stages, and those—adolescents and adults—who have never attended school at all. Efforts are directed towards evolving an integrated approach which would combine a variety of educational inputs and means, cutting across the different levels and areas of education, developing formal and informal institutions for the benefit of the entire community. In order to develop elementary education, unorthodox methods are also used, such as double-shifts, i.e. reducing, by about half, the time the first two or three primary classes spend in school, thus making wider use of teachers' services; introducing part-time and continuation courses for children who may not be available all the time; adopting an ungraded system, under which pupils are not held back during the first three to four years of primary school, and using the existing school plant uninterruptedly for several different branches of instruction during the same day.

2. Integrated primary schools in Tanzania are regarded as centres for the development of human resources, serving the whole community. Structurally, the schools contain adjustable classroom space which is also used for adult education, a day-care centre and kindergarten and a large multi-purpose room for teaching practical skills to children and a training centre for small village industries.

3. In Kenya, there are some 400 self-help secondary schools (Harambee schools) additional to the government system, financed by the local community through voluntary contributions and fees paid by parents. Also, the Kenyan Red Cross operates a network of centres for village women who during a four-week training period live in the centres with their children and receive instruction in hygiene, nutrition, child and home care, small animal husbandry, etc.

7

Principle

Broadening
general
education

The concept of general education must be markedly broadened, so that it definitely includes general socio-economic, technical and practical knowledge.

194

Considerata

For a long while, the idea of general education was a limited one. It bore on a certain number of traditional subjects. But the distinction between general and special subjects is fading away. Many fields of knowledge which until recently were the preserve of specialists have now become open to general culture. They include knowledge of economics and sociology, the importance of which is growing as economic and social factors exercise increasing influence over individuals, and—above all—technological knowledge; as technology affects more and more people, compelling them to understand and master the technical world, so education in theoretical and practical technology becomes necessary to everyone.

Recommendation

Rigid distinctions between different types of teaching—general, scientific, technical and professional—must be dropped, and education, as from primary and secondary levels, must become theoretical, technological, practical and manual at the same time.

Comment

If so-called general education is to become truly general, technological education must be developed, and if the teaching of general subjects is to have its full educational value, care must be taken to harmonize intellectual and manual training and constantly to correlate studies and work.

However, technological education is not limited to the study of scientific laws and their applications, or to the study of technical procedures already in use. Two changes must be made in the usual forms of technological education if it is to take on its full significance. Firstly, technological instruction must be given its due place together with instruction in languages, history, geography, sociology and community life. Secondly, technological problems must be dealt with in relation to many aspects of life: technology and work, technology and leisure, technology and social machinery, technology and communications, technology and the environment, etc.

Illustrations

1. In the German Democratic Republic, polytechnic education is integrated into (and throughout) the ten-year basic educational cycle. Polytechnic education is founded on an intimate interaction between pedagogy and technology. Teams of research workers including educationists, pedagogues, professional scientists and technologists have been active in developing new and dynamic concepts. Results of experience and practice are used as feedback to act on present research and thinking.

Polytechnic education involves practical, manual activities from the earliest grades, and from the seventh grade on, four hours weekly of pre-vocational training in industrial and agricultural enterprises or polytechnical institutions, where the students do practical, productive work. The emphasis is not on skill-training for specific jobs but on familiarizing all students with technological methods and their applications, and with industrial processes. The intrinsic value and importance of manual work is also stressed.

2. 'Family hostels', established mainly in France and Italy, have carried out interesting educational experiments based on alternative schedules and appropriate rhythm teaching. The method was devised and developed in rural, Catholic regions with strong traditions, and its objectives are: to avoid uprooting children, at least at an over-early stage in education; to help children coming from a family background which offers only minimum cultural support to gain knowledge under the best possible psychological circumstances; to develop an education in which individuals are strongly motivated and closely linked to the surrounding environment; to overcome mental resistance to intellectual effort and, ideally, to provide those in whom such resistance cannot be entirely overcome with some less ambitious cultural satisfaction. The alternating schedule enables a pupil to spend one-third of his time at school and two-thirds in a family environment in the course of a three-year period.

8

Principle

Maximum vocational mobility

Educational action to prepare for work and active life should aim less at training young people to practise a given trade or profession than at equipping them to adapt themselves to a variety of jobs, at developing their capacities continously, in order to keep pace with developing production methods and working conditions. It should help achieve optimum mobility in employment and facilitate conversion from one profession or branch of a profession to another.

196

Considerata

While the essential aims in education are of an individual and social nature, it plays an extremely important part in professional training and consequently in the economy.

Continually developing production techniques mean that there is less justification today than there ever has been for expecting the traditional type of educational system to dispense training which keeps up with job requirements. Critics in economic circles have complained that many branches of education are over-theoretical and out of touch with the realities of life in industry. They may be right. The fact remains that schools have a task of a general nature. They must provide learners with a solid grounding of knowledge designed to back up a multiplicity of different skills. They have to cultivate the mental faculties and stimulate a creative state of mind, develop some understanding of scientific principles and a degree of ability to apply them technically, help develop general skills and encourage positive attitudes towards work and the morale of work.

Recommendation

Professional and technical training colleges must be developed in conjunction with the secondary education system. The instruction they give must be followed by practical training at places of work, all of which must, above all, be completed by recurrent education and vocational training courses.

Illustration

In the U.S.S.R., one of the most fruitful means of achieving universal secondary level education—while leaving general school education to continue in its leading role—is to develop professional and technical schools which provide secondary education running parallel to professional specialization and its corresponding qualification. Directives laid down at the twenty-fourth Communist Party Congress of the Soviet Union for the 1971–75 development plan for the Soviet economy, which determine the country's development for a period of five years, provide for training 9 million specialists having had special or secondary training; in addition, special attention is paid to training specialists in new branches of science and technology. Directives approved during the preceding, twenty-third Soviet Communist Party Congress on training 7 million specialists with special higher or secondary instruction have been totally fulfilled. The figure scheduled for the new five-year period would therefore appear to be entirely achievable.

197

9

Principle

Lifelong education, in the full sense of the term, means that business, industrial and agricultural firms will have extensive educational functions.

Considerata

The responsibility for technical training should not reside solely, or even basically, in the school system. It should be shared by schools, businesses and other enterprises, and out-of-school activities, with educators, leaders in commerce and industry, workers and governments all co-operating actively for this purpose.

To fulfil its growing obligations, education needs the help of other institutions, especially of establishments which have to employ workers trained by it. The kinds of participation and the ways in which tasks are shared vary considerably from country to country, ranging from those where schools give most of the training available to others where it is provided mainly on the job. But in general, close co-operation of this kind is increasing. Economic circles in industrialized countries have realized the need for improved training and generally agree that expenditure on it is a worthwhile investment. Many developing countries, however, still tend to underestimate the importance of 'training-within-industry'.

Recommendation

Efforts must be made to bridge the gap, still found in all too many cases, between educational establishments and business companies, whether privately or publicly owned, for the latter constitute a key element in the over-all education system. Their role should not be limited to training workers, but extended so far as possible to training technicians and researchers.

Comment

In fact, even in countries where basic training is considered one of the prime functions of the school system, businesses retain or

198

acquire important responsibilities in training and in this way contribute towards the nation's educational effort.

Young workers with a professional or technical education still need complementary training, and also have to learn to adapt to the conditions and rhythm of work in industry. They can only do so on the job.

It would also appear logical for business companies to take responsibility for various types of subsequent training, such as specialization, improvement of qualifications, courses preparatory to promotion, retraining, training of professional, executive, managerial and other highly skilled personnel, etc.

In so far as education is to be carefully shaped to meet the needs of the economy, it is imperative for educational institutions to work hand in hand with industry.

In many countries both privately and publicly owned enterprises allocate a portion of their profits to educating and training their employees and managerial personnel. This practice should be more widely adopted.

Illustration

Japan has a highly organized system of technical and vocational training supported by commerce and industry. At the beginning of this century, the larger companies established their own apprentice training facilities. These activities were expanded as from 1948 under two government programmes: TWI (Training Within Industry) and MTP (Management Training Programme).

Enterprises participate in the public vocational-training programme authorized by the Ministry of Labour. This comprises 407 training centres with an enrolment of more than 100,000 trainees.

In addition, most large firms have within-industry training programmes to provide initial training for new employees, upgrading and retraining of skilled workers, supervisory training and management-development courses. The Yawata Iron & Steel Company, employing 50,000 persons, is a typical example, with a deliberate policy of encouraging all employees to develop themselves and daily on-the-job coaching by their immediate supervisor. The company has an education council directly under the president which establishes training programmes and policies to be carried out by the education sectors in each of the company's plants. The programmes cover the training of workers and foremen, clerical and engineering staff and top management personnel.

10

Principle

*Expansion of higher education should lead to broad development of
many institutions capable of meeting more and more individual and
community needs.*

Considerata

Many economic, social and political factors combine to make change
in post-secondary education necessary. But they cannot be achieved
merely by adding or superimposing elements on to the existing
system. Really suitable education for increasingly numerous and
differentiated learners calls for a thoroughgoing diversification in
post-secondary institutions. But this presupposes a change in traditional attitudes towards universities. If the public feels that institutions of a new kind lack prestige, these institutions will fail to
fulfil their function, while the traditionally organized universities
will continue to be overloaded and inevitably apply discriminatory
procedures.

Recommendation

*Throughout the post-secondary educational system, structures, sub-
ject-matter and student categories must be very broadly diversified.*

Comment

This involves multiplying the number of programmes, introducing
short study-cycles running parallel to longer ones and setting up
small-scale establishments to meet specific or local aims and needs:
colleges, technical institutes, 'free' universities, etc. Other institutions should give para-professional and middle-level technical training carefully adapted to labour market requirements. Criteria for
admission should be liberal, non-formal; they should be devised
with an eye to candidates' motives and their professional future,
rather than to their official school credits and diplomas.

This means that far greater attention will have to be paid to
training professional and executive personnel at all levels than in
the past. The 'centres of excellence' method would appear to be an
interesting solution to this problem, particularly in developing

200

countries, on condition such centres do in fact maintain standards complying with international norms. Inserting institutions of this kind into the educational system—multidisciplinary centres and schools, colleges and institutes for professional training in technology, agronomy, medicine, management, etc.—is one possible way to answer the nation's economic needs without excessive expenditure. It would further enhance the educational system's prospects for the future, more so than other 'prestige' institutions of low calibre and ill-adapted to real conditions.

This implies, finally, opening higher education establishments to a far greater variety of people than the usual 'regular' students: former, returning graduates, workers and professional people of all kinds requiring advanced training or retraining, etc.

These principles may of course be differently applied according to the degrees of development and industrialization in different countries. It will probably become increasingly necessary, therefore, to examine various possible models in terms of which developing countries, and especially the least developed among them, may improve, diversify or in certain cases, institute their post-secondary systems.

Illustrations

1. The Vincennes university centre (France) currently includes twenty-six departments employing 400 full-time teachers and many other lecturers, handling some 12,000 students. Its guiding principles are to admit as many workers and students who have not passed the usual French school-leaving examination (the *baccalauréat*) as possible, to apply innovative pedagogic methods, based mainly on contact between various disciplines, and to orient teaching and research towards a study of the contemporary world.

About two-thirds of all students at the Vincennes centre are wage-earners and about half do not have the *baccalauréat*.

A number of innovations first tested at Vincennes have been adopted by other French universities, in particular those of organizing studies into 'unit values' (ten per year for a full-time student), and of allowing students the freedom to select a large number of courses from disciplines outside their major subjects.

Within the French university system, certain features remain, for the moment, peculiar to Vincennes; in particular, the replacement of formal teaching and examinations by various forms of team-work, in which the teacher's role is mainly that of an adviser who catalyses and co-ordinates activities carried out by small semi-independent groups. Much of their work comprises research on themes selected by the students themselves.

The Vincennes experiment has developed from the following ideas:
1. Opening the university to those who do not necessarily have the *baccalauréat* enables working people to continue their studies.

2. The confrontation between young students just out of secondary school, with no professional experience, and adults closely acquainted with the concrete problems of a profession does away with the disembodied, abstract atmosphere in education.
3. Subjects are presented so as to fit students' capacities to grasp them; a student's interest, aptitudes and performance are more crucial to his progress than the static order of lectures. The path he follows therefore becomes a process of research, rather than an accumulation of knowledge.
4. Running initial training and retraining courses simultaneously stimulates a ferment of ideas and exchange of knowledge not to be found in traditional universities.

2. In the Arab Republic of Egypt, reforms leading to changes in higher institutes of technology and to their fusion into a university of technology illustrate some interesting research into alternative paths for higher education. These institutes, having played an active part in training skilled technical-executive personnel during a certain development period, are now being given the task of setting up centres to initiate and renew relationships between certain educational sectors and the continually developing national industry.

3. The Parkway Program, Philadelphia (United States) is a high school which utilizes community activities, and the skills of those who work in them, as an integral part of its curriculum. Pupils learn on location from the specialist on the spot: in factories, in motor-repair workshops, in law and newspaper offices, in museums and art galleries. This work is related to a more structured academic programme based on the school's own premises, although much of its content is organized following staff–student discussion. There are no entrance qualifications; pupils are chosen by ballot.

4. The Indian example shows that broad development of higher education in a developing country requires a small number of 'centres of advanced studies' which comply with the highest international standards. Those concerned believe that democratization without a properly organized core sector would seriously undermine the utility and quality of the whole system and retard its development.

An important component of the core sector in Indian higher education is the 'centres of advanced studies' begun by the University Grants Commission in consultation with the universities in 1963. So far there are thirty centres, seventeen in science subjects and thirteen in humanities and social sciences. The centres have received valuable support from Unesco, the U.S.S.R. and the United Kingdom. Apart from improving the general tone of academic work, they are expected to give rise to more 'centres of excellence', serving as 'breeders of excellence'.

Besides the centres of advanced studies, also in the core sector are six institutes of technology which have received considerable assistance from the developed countries. Enrolment—about 10,000—in the technology institutes is about 5 per cent of total enrolment in technology. Several special universities for agriculture have also been set up, in co-operation with the United States; and the All-India Institute for Medicine deserves mention.

5. Poland illustrates attempts by a number of universities to encourage people from widely varied walks of life to pursue their studies, with its extremely far-reaching correspondence-course network. It is available for virtually all specialized studies and is the main development in the process of opening up the post-secondary system. Many facilities are offered to students so enrolled—including special paid holidays—enabling them to continue studying while remaining in productive work. Higher education institutions operating through correspondence courses or evening classes are linked to a number of big factories, providing workers with an opportunity to study either while working as usual or in alternate periods of work and study.

11

Principle

Access to different types of education and professional employment should depend only on each individual's knowledge, capacities and aptitudes, and should not be a consequence of ranking knowledge acquired in school above or below experience gained during the practice of a profession or in private studies.

Selection criteria

Considerata

Few essential, widespread changes have so far been made to the traditional methods of selecting candidates, checking their knowledge and grading them. They can still only move from one level to the next along pre-established paths and by clearing a series of obstacles.

However, a number of new elements, including pupils' and students' origins, ages and destinations, the content of curricula and methods of teaching, are making modifications in selection, evaluation and orientation procedures necessary.

In general, the concept of lifelong education rules out any form of final, premature selection. It should radically change promotion and certification procedures, stressing the value of real competence, aptitude and motivation over and above marks, class ranking and list of credits obtained.

Recommendation

As educational systems become more diversified and as possibilities for entry, exit and re-entry increase, obtaining university degrees and diplomas should become less and less closely linked to completing a predetermined course of study. Examinations should serve essentially as a means of comparing skills acquired under varying conditions by individuals of different origins, a mark not of a conclusion but of a starting-point, helping each individual to assess the effectiveness of his own study methods. Evaluation procedures should measure an individual's progress as much as the extent to which he conforms to externally fixed standards.

Comment

Real evaluation of a pupil's or student's achievement should be based not on a single, summary examination, but on over-all observation of his work throughout a course of study. It should pay less attention to the volume of memorized knowledge and more to the development of his intellectual capacity: reasoning ability, critical judgement and proficiency in problem-solving. Modern learning methods, such as programmed or computer-assisted instruction, television courses, language laboratories and various other modes of self-education, allow examinations to be arranged differently.

Finally, it may be predicted that appointments to jobs will depend increasingly on a concrete evaluation of the candidate's aptitude for a particular function rather than on perusal of his school certificates or university degree. In this respect, employers themselves will shoulder most of the responsibility for selection. In short, if results obtained are evaluated and checked in new ways, examinations may then become an instrument for setting people free of time-honoured teaching habits and criteria for assessing professional qualifications.

Illustration

Sweden has abolished the comprehensive school-leaving examination at the end of the secondary cycle and requires no written or oral testing for university entrance. The replacement of traditional examinations as a measure of progress and ability by many other more diversified means of assessing capacities, skills, understanding and critical judgement is becoming commonplace: a film or tape recording, a book of poems or a painting or piece of sculpture, a model plan for an urban-renewal project.

12

Principle

The normal culmination of the educational process is adult edu-   *Adult education*
cation.

Considerata

There are many possible definitions of adult education. For a very large number of adults in the world today, it is a substitute for the basic education they missed. For the many individuals who received only a very incomplete education, it is the complement to elementary or professional education. For those whom it helps respond to new demands which their environment makes on them, it is the prolongation of education. It offers further education to those who have already received high-level training. And it is a means of individual development for everybody. One or other of these aspects may be more important in one country than in another, but they all have their validity. Adult education can no longer be limited to rudimentary levels, or confined to 'cultural' education for a minority.

Adult education assumes especial importance to the extent that it may be decisive in the success of non-adults' school activities. For children's primary education—a primordial objective—cannot be dissociated from their parents' educational levels. The rising generations cannot be properly trained in an illiterate environment. Since the development of education depends on using to the full the capacities of all people able to teach or help train others, the number of professional people engaged in working towards educational objectives can only be increased by intensifying adult education. We should never set adult education against the education of children and young people: the concept of global or over-all education goes beyond the semblance of contradiction, enabling the two extremes to be enlisted, parallel to each other and at the same time, in the service of common educational objectives, in the broadest sense.

It follows that adult education can no longer be a fringe sector of activity in any society and must be given its own proper place in educational policies and budgets. This means that school and out-of-school education must be linked firmly together.

Recommendation

Educational strategies in the coming decade should have rapid development of adult education, in school and out of school, as one of their priority objectives.

Comment

Given the fact that present facilities are lagging far behind the world adult-population's educational and cultural needs, step by step progress is not enough: what is required is a giant leap forward. This can only be achieved if private individuals and public bodies join in contributing both effort and resources. Action must be taken to:

Utilize all existing scholastic establishments (primary, secondary, technical schools) for adult-education activities, and to increase the number of adults admitted to higher education institutions.

Create special adult-education institutions or integrate out-of-school activities to assist adults to function better as citizens, producers, consumers and parents.

Promote the organization of individual and community educational activities, encourage self-education, develop spontaneous initiative and make all educational means available to the greatest number.

This three-point action can only be carried out with financial and technical support from State and government and co-operation from both the industrial and agricultural sectors of the economy. But much of the work to be done depends on individual and group initiative. This role of private initiative provides an essential guarantee that both freedom and diversity will be respected, and encourages pedagogic innovation.

Illustrations

1. Yugoslavia's 'workers' universities' are adult education institutions in which attempts are made to find answers to many questions arising in the field of education today. They provide both formal schooling and out-of-school education, and are open to all adults whatever their earlier training; the only criteria for admission concern each individual's aptitudes. Courses are offered at all levels, ranging from elementary education to instruction in extremely specialized subjects for highly qualified workers. Each learner may choose among many different possibilities in laying down his own study programme. For example, he may combine parts of different courses, or he may make parallel use of group

techniques, especially in working groups, and individual methods such as self-instruction and studies of 'case-histories'. His programmes may be adapted to the environment, diversified according to community and individual, established on the basis of a preliminary analysis of the learner's (and the environment's) educational and socio-economic needs. Functional education is equally important (serving professional, civic or social purposes), and so is the workers' general and cultural development.

2. Adult education has now reached extensive proportions in at least one, admittedly extreme case, as the following figures from Sweden show: the number of members of study circles in the budget year 1970/71 was about 1.6 million. Some 170,000 persons attended local and national government adult-education courses in the same year. There were about 30,000 students on folk high-school courses. More than 100,000 persons received labour-market training. Nearly 11,000 took courses arranged by employees' organizations. The total number of participants in publicly supported adult education was thus nearly 2 million (in a country where adults over the age of 20 number about 5.5 million).

13

Principle

Literacy training is only a 'moment', an element, in adult education.   *Literacy*

Considerata

For a long time, literacy training has been separated from, or even opposed to, adult education. It has also been considered as a rival to primary education. Learning to read and write was contrasted with other means of acquiring knowledge, aptitudes and skills. Literacy was long regarded as an end in itself.

Survival of folk prejudice and even political demagogy hampered the early adult-literacy programmes and their educational effects were generally short-lived. Links between literacy programmes and development objectives were very loose, while literacy was not integrated into the immediate environment.

Recommendation

In all areas where there is widespread illiteracy, programmes organized for the adult population must include a strong literacy campaign. Action must be taken in two ways: it must aim firstly at functional literacy among strongly motivated sections of the working population and secondly at mass literacy when conditions are appropriate and, above all, when social development conditions— political, economic and cultural—are suitable for active large-scale participation by the people.

Comment

All literacy action, motivated by and directed towards employment possibilities, must be integrated into the development objectives of the country or local environment. Its range must be proportionate to that of the over-all socio-economic development effort. The strategy behind this effort determines the strategy for literacy programmes, which must attempt not merely to propagate a means of communication but also to spread immediately useful information and knowledge.

Mass literacy campaigns are justified so long as they help the people participate in the changing of their environment. To avoid past disappointments, it is important for the literacy programmes now under way in many countries to be linked to basic education on civic life and the world of work. And these campaigns must be preceded, supported, accompanied and followed through by a large quantity of radio and television programmes.

Illustration

The principle behind the functional literacy project in Isfahan and Dez (Iran) is the following. Literacy, to be functional—that is, to meet exactly the specific difficulties which the illiterate must overcome—implies a prior sounding, an in-depth study, of the environment chosen for the project. In this way, a range of specific programmes can be established by singling out points of intervention determined by economic analysis and classification of the areas in question. Definition of this economic 'typology' is a function of the intermediate development objectives of the zones covered by the pilot project, in so far as these can be deduced from the general objectives of the third and fourth national plans. In each of these sectors, it seemed possible to identify socio-vocational groups of sufficient homogeneity, so far as their working situation was concerned, as to require similar job qualifications, and sufficiently numerous to enable working teams to be set up.

In this way, for the last two years' operation of the pilot project, fifteen specific programmes linked to the needs and motivations of illiterates from different environments were selected and planned. This diversification of programmes was an attempt to ensure that all elements required for literacy training were integrated into a simultaneous learning process in which emphasis was placed first and foremost on vocational training. The object of this was to integrate language learning into technical training; mathematics into technology, technical draughtsmanship into technical subject-matter. In this manner intellectual elements (reading, writing, symbols) are integrated into technical, vocational and socio-economic components.

While evaluation of this experimental project has not yet been completed, analysis of first results, following tests held in the course of 1971, shows that these were positive and significant in several branches of study: pedagogy (acquisition of knowledge), practical work (adoption of measures recommended for agricultural programmes), sociology (attitudes, open-mindedness towards modern life) and even economics, in which verification of results is continuing.

14

Principle

The new educational ethos makes the individual the master and creator of his own cultural progress. Self-learning, especially assisted self-learning, has irreplaceable value in any educational system.   *Self-learning*

Considerata

The diversification of educational paths, the increasing facilities available to anyone who undertakes to teach himself, all combine today to disseminate the practice and affirm the principle of self-education, of self-learning. With a few exceptions, this does not arise from the individual's spontaneous development. Learning to learn is not just another slogan. It denotes a specific pedagogic approach that teachers must themselves master if they want to be able to pass it on to others. It also involves the acquisition of work habits and the awakening of motivations which must be shaped in childhood and adolescence by the programmes and methods in schools and universities. Each individual's aspirations to self-learning must be realized by providing him—not only in school and university but elsewhere too, under conditions and circumstances of all kinds—with the means, tools and incentives for making his personal studies a fruitful activity. The effectiveness of solitary study is greatly enhanced by acquiring techniques for self-instruction and having many auxiliary aids available. One of the conditions for achieving this objective—if it is not to remain a mere declaration of intent—is that sufficient credits be allocated in education budgets to the development of self-learning.

Recommendation

Institutions and services of a new kind, intended to help people teach themselves—language laboratories, technical training laboratories, information centres, libraries and related services, data banks, programmed and personalized teaching aids, audio-visual aids, etc.— should be integrated into all education systems.

Comment

Far too often ignored as a goal, self-learning has no less a place in the educational strategies of every country, even those which are ill-equipped to undertake it. The important thing is to take concrete measures in this direction, even if they are limited at first to certain sections of the population regarded as having priority.

Illustration

In his investigation of several hundred young people and men and women who have developed serious and sustained self-learning projects, Professor Allen Tough and associates at the Ontario Institute for Studies in Education have found that 'self-directed learning' is carried out by very large numbers of people at all economic and social levels, and that children, youth and adults can be helped to develop capacities in managing their own learning. Self-directed learning is not the same as individualized learning; sometimes the learner chooses to enrol in a class or group for part of the process. But the learner himself initiates, selects the experiences and the persons who assist him in learning and evaluates the process. This research also indicates the wide range of persons, beyond teachers and librarians, whose help is sought in these learning episodes and shows clearly that many human beings are not only learners but 'teachers'. Research and experiences with self-directed learners have many implications for schools and colleges, for the organization of libraries and museums and for the form and content of media.

15

Principle

Educational technology

The accelerating and multiplying effect of new techniques of reproduction and communication is basic to the introduction of most educational innovations.

Considerata

Until now, school systems have usually only been able to make scattered and makeshift use of new possibilities offered by technological progress and scientific discoveries. The application of new equipment in education has mainly been confined to fringe jobs such as recording, rote repetition and distribution, within the old educational patterns. At the same time, because of failure to link them at the outset to the development of technological innovations, many structural reforms have become bogged down or have gone astray. However, systematic use of educational technology has in some cases made it possible to speed up work on earlier plans for educational development and so gain time. It has also helped to redistribute and make better use of qualified teaching personnel, and to improve the system's internal efficiency and yield by reducing the number of drop-outs and repeaters.

Recommendation

1. *In the conception and general planning of education systems, allowance must be made for the possible contribution of new techniques with a view to developing a unified process aimed at using available means and resources in the most efficient way.*
2. *When getting systems with technological support under way, strategies must be differentiated according to different levels of economic development.*

Comment

Strategy adopted in relation to educational technology must depend on the nature of the educational system in question, the resources available to it, the types of technological media applied and the educational sector into which they are introduced.

The integration of technology—at individual student or study group level, as well as at institutional or national community levels—into educational systems should help make them more open by introducing more and more networks for distributing information, larger data-storing facilities and increasingly efficient evaluation and guidance techniques. So far as the choice of technological media is concerned, the multi-media solution has many advantages, involving a combination of various media integrated into one complex approach.

Cheap and easily available means for disseminating information instantaneously, especially radio, should be used more widely for mass education, particularly for basic instruction in rural areas. More sophisticated communications systems using a variety of auxiliary methods could, however, usefully be introduced into certain countries and at certain levels where they can be financed and properly integrated into their educational context—higher technical education, for example. Finally, original technological adaptations (intermediate technologies) should be developed and used far more than hitherto. Those concerned must be encouraged to produce them on the spot, especially where over-all social and environmental development is a priority.

Educational technology should first be applied in sectors such as out-of-school activities and long-distance teaching, which are the least hide-bound by archaic structures that risk provoking its abrupt rejection. Other propitious areas are those requiring urgent overhaul because of heavy outside pressures, for example, technical and higher education. School systems based on integrated use of diverse technological means are an alternative solution where the expansion of traditional systems is seen to be impossible.

Illustrations

1. The general objective of the Tevec project in Quebec (Canada) was to bring the part of the adult population which had not completed nine years of schooling up to that level.

The training programme linked two components: first, so-called scholastic subjects (French, English, mathematics) and, second, a socio-economic-cultural theme chosen from a catalogue of topics: health, justice, participation, social welfare, government, etc. The aim was to develop understanding of living conditions, in a society undergoing rapid socio-economic change, and the skills needed to participate in it.

On the pedagogical level, the fundamental idea was to combine different ways of overcoming apathy among the people. So far, methods have included: 90-minute television programmes, five days a week; correspondence courses (an average of 15,000 reply cards per day); personal contact between participants and teachers (systematic house visits every three weeks); weekly tele-club meetings, with the central discussion topic arising from the programme viewed. Sampling surveys indicate that 35,000 persons viewed the programmes regularly, and 110,000 saw them more than once a week.

This experience seems innovative and exemplary; it covered an entire region, went further than exclusively scholastic training, combined several methods of transmitting and acting on subject-matter, and linked research to application.

212

2. In the U.S.S.R., special television programmes for pupils and teachers are broadcast daily for between five to eight hours. The broadcasts for teachers, the content of which is determined by the Soviet Academy of Pedagogic Sciences, bring eminent scientists to the television screen: pedagogues, psychologists, specialists in various problems arising out of school education. Pupils, for their part, have an opportunity to increase knowledge gained in school of the most difficult and important subjects in their school programme. Also worth mentioning are the many radio and television programmes for parents, intended to introduce them to the main principles of family education and to familiarize them with child and adolescent psychology.

16

Principle

Widespread and efficient use of new technologies in education is only possible if sufficient change takes place within the system itself.

Application of new techniques

Considerata

It is not enough to adapt educational structures for the introduction of new technologies. Teachers must be prepared and adequate resources must be available.

Recommendation

1. *Modify teacher-training programmes so that teachers are equipped for the different roles and functions imposed by new technologies.*
2. *Reserve a fixed part of the increase in education budgets for the rational development of sophisticated techniques.*

Comment

All possible resources of educational technology must be systematically introduced into teacher-training institutions. These must be gradually transformed into centres for permanent training and opened to persons engaged in other activities outside the education sector who are called upon to fulfil part-time or short-term teaching tasks. In the professional training of educators, particular attention must be paid to their preparation for supervisory and co-ordinating roles within the framework of teaching by new technologies. It is equally necessary to train specialists at all levels in designing and revising curricula and learning objectives, systems organization, guidance and evaluation, production of materials (printed, programmed, audio-visual), group dynamics, maintenance, etc.

At the same time, national authorities should set aside a predetermined portion of the annual increase in education budgets (one-half, for example, over a period of several years) to developing new ways of making the educational system more efficient.

Illustration

The Ivory Coast's scheme for giving primary education over television is a good example of over-all organization and of the way large-scale introduction of new technologies may lead to radical changes in education. Its aims, defined in that country's current five-year plan, are to provide basic education for all school-age children through systematic use of television, and to bring television to the entire population. This will also provide a means of communication contributing to the nation's political and cultural unity.

Under the programme, some 16,500 classes will be equipped with television by 1980. By then, education through televiewing will become available to first-grade classes, to young people between 13 and 17 pursuing their education, and to the entire adult population for cultural activities, lifelong education and information.

Meanwhile, the number of pupils receiving primary education is expected to rise to 830,000 in 1980 (from 406,000 in 1969). For State education alone, an increase to 720,000 is predicted (from the earlier figure of 371,000). By 1980, it is estimated that the increase in school enrolment will be running parallel to the demographic increase. Each year, 5,000 more children reach the age of 6. Total enrolment for the 6 to 11 age group is predicted for 1986, when all children will be receiving televised education.

The annual unit cost per pupil, including television expenses and qualified teachers, is expected to rise from 13,500 CFA francs in 1967, when this study was carried out, to 18,500 CFA francs. This increase will probably be virtually cancelled out, however, by adoption of the automatic promotion system and reduction of drop-outs. Even allowing for a certain percentage of repeaters and drop-outs, there will be a substantial saving. The World Bank has estimated that maintaining the traditional system would cost the Ivory Coast 44 per cent more than adopting the education-through-television system.

During the preparatory phase, technical pedagogy and socio-economic studies preceded over-all detailed planning. A new infrastructure for pedagogic experiment and programme production was set up to give the project a firm foundation. Content, methods and inevitable changes in school buildings were also the subject of research. Among the innovations following the use of television for a steadily increasing number of learners were automatic promotion for pupils and the training of better-qualified teachers. This required a new intensive programme of teacher training, which also had to be modified. Substituting television for traditional teaching procedures meant that methods had to be

214

changed, while teachers required training not only in new subject-matter but in the use of audio-visual techniques, communication psychology, group dynamics, after-school activities, new evaluation techniques, etc.

Class organization and the order of courses also had to be modified for the new programme.

This series of modifications will be carried over to secondary education, to meet the needs of children who have received a very different kind of education at primary school. The introduction of television will also influence out-of-school education and training; the ministries responsible for these activities will also be compelled to modify their procedures.

17

Principle

The teaching profession will not be in a position to fulfil its role in the future unless it is given, and develops itself, a structure better adapted to modern educational systems.

Status of teachers

Considerata

The multiplication and diversification of educational activities will necessarily lead to an increase in the number of educators. This increase seems inevitable and desirable. The important thing is for results to increase correspondingly to the increase in expenditure on teaching staff. Until now, the continual rise in expenditure on salaries has taken place to the detriment of spending on equipment and, of course, of spending on innovation and research. We must therefore seek out teaching methods which are as 'profitable' as possible, if we wish to avoid running expenses reaching such a level that they prevent educational systems being modernized. This is one pre-condition of enhancing the social status and imparting greater value generally to the role of teachers in contemporary societies.

Distinctions among school-teachers, technical-college teachers, secondary-school masters, university professors, etc., should imply no hierarchical difference. Neither salary scales nor promotion systems should depend on type of teaching. A teacher should be able to reach the highest level whatever his field in education; this should depend only on his personal worth. Ideally, the teaching function should be regarded in the same way, and as deserving of the same dignity, whatever the particular sphere in which it is carried on.

Recommendation

Legislative, professional, labour union and social action should gradually reduce and finally abolish hierarchical distinctions maintained for no valid reason among the various categories of teachers.

Comment

The teaching function should be regarded as one and the same thing everywhere, in nature, worth and calling. The same is true of its means and techniques. Each teacher should choose his speciality in terms of his preference for handling children, adolescents or adults, or according to his taste—which may change from one period to another of his own personal or family life—for living in the country, in a medium-sized town or in a big city. The desire for promotion, with its financial and social advantages, should not send him inexorably towards a bigger and bigger town, a larger and larger educational establishment, or towards the highest levels of education and the highest grades within those levels.

Illustration

In some countries, legislation is being considered to abolish differing levels of training and remuneration for teachers in primary and secondary education. Several other countries, including Czechoslovakia, Denmark, the United Kingdom and the United States, give training on identical levels to both these categories of teachers, in universities or equivalent post-secondary institutions. Many other countries, such as France, Poland and the Soviet Union, are following the same path by training teachers to university level. Furthermore, the fact that the teaching function is to all intents and purposes identical whether it is exercised at the primary, intermediary or secondary level is underlined by the widely recognized importance of giving secondary-school teachers training in pedagogy; meanwhile both content and method of this training are undergoing far-reaching reform.

18

Principle

Teacher training   *One of the essential tasks for educators at present is to change the mentalities and qualifications inherent in all professions; thus they should be the first to be ready to rethink and change the criteria and basic situation of the teaching profession, in which the job of educating and stimulating students is steadily superseding that of simply giving instruction.*

Considerata

Present-day divisions between formal and informal, school and out-of-school, child and adult education are steadily fading. Furthermore, teachers trained today will still be exercising their profession after the year 2000. Their training should be designed with these two facts in mind.

Recommendation

Conditions in which teachers are trained should be profoundly changed so that, essentially, they become educators rather than specialists in transmitting pre-established curricula; the principle of a first, accelerated training stage, followed by in-service training cycles, should be adopted.

Comment

Training tomorrow's educators should follow two paths. Specialization should be scheduled for a fixed number of future professionals in pre-school education, school pedagogy, technical education, backward child training, 'andragogues', etc. Others should be trained as organizer-educators, including the general body of teacher-trainees who, at least in theory, should be capable of practising their profession with both children and adults, in school and out of school.

But this is far from exhausting the range of skills which education will require in the future. It will need specialists in teaching materials, in self-learning equipment, in the use of educational techniques. It will need audio-visual assistants, 'animators' for community centres, specialists in tests and vocational guidance, psychologists, new kinds of administrators, systems analysts, etc.

But the fundamental change in educators' training will be required by their changing task, which in the future will be that of educating the personality, opening the way to the real world.

Illustrations

1. Secondary-school teachers in Ethiopia now take a four-year university course (separated in the middle by a year of field service); it is now proposed to restructure the course, substituting six summer vacation courses for the final two full years. By using facilities and staff during the vacation periods the university

will be able to double the intake of teachers, and students will be available for taking up posts two years earlier.

2. In England, the James Report on reorganization of teacher training placed great emphasis on the necessity of increased in-service education and training, recommending that all teachers be released with pay for one full term every seven years and, as soon as possible, every five years. These periods would be complemented by an expanded programme of short-term in-service activities.

3. In recently established Unesco-assisted teacher-training institutes in six African countries (Cameroon, Ethiopia, Ivory Coast, Liberia, Niger, Togo) the essential purpose is not simply to train classroom or subject specialists but to produce rural educators well adapted to the local conditions under which they will work and skilled at initiating and organizing a wide range of community-development activities. The institutes set up in these six countries have two main objectives:
1. To train teachers qualified to handle primary education in an essentially rural country, and skilled as 'animators' able to play an effective part in community development.
2. To give retraining and advanced training courses to personnel already at work: primary-school inspectors, pedagogic advisers, high-school teachers, headmasters and primary-school teachers at all levels, so as to keep them informed on current pedagogic reforms and initiate them into new methods and techniques.

19

Principle

Conventional and non-conventional educators

Education is developing continually to the point where it is becoming a function of the entire society: larger and larger sections of the population should therefore take part in it.

Considerata

Given the educational situation in many countries, adopting this principle would certainly be a powerful stimulant to socio-economic development and spark a no less powerful movement in favour of social justice.

Recommendation

Auxiliaries and specialists from other professions (workers, technicians, professional and executive personnel) should be called in to work beside professional teachers. Authorities should also enlist the co-operation of pupils and students, in such a way that they teach themselves while instructing others, and become imbued with the idea that acquiring an 'intellectual capital' involves its possessor in the duty of sharing it with others.

Comment

The concrete aim is to increase the number and diversity of volunteers and auxiliaries working with children in schools. These auxiliaries should assume as many non-instructional responsibilities as possible so as to 'free teachers to teach', and should assist teaching practice through contributing from their own experience. For this, they should receive the supplementary training required for the execution of educational tasks.

Illustrations

1. Their activities can range far wider than this, as examples drawn from the United States illustrate:

Volunteer Parent Aide. This position is usually held by a mother who may be asked to perform a variety of functions: correcting papers, checking for specific errors on written work such as stories or themes, reading to small groups of children, making instructional materials, supervising groups of children on the playground or during lunch, and assisting the teacher in other ways.

Volunteer Community Aide. These are individuals who possess special skills: handicraft workers, opticians, photographers, stamp collectors, politicians, salesmen, insurance experts, policemen, chefs, dairy farmers, members of minority groups—the possibilities are endless.

Volunteer Student Aide. On the assumption that helping someone to learn can be a significant learning experience for the one who teaches, many schools now provide opportunities for students to teach students. The usual plan is for an older child to come to the classroom of a younger one to hear him read or read to him, to drill him on arithmetic fundamentals, or to assist in some other skill area.

2. Starting in 1961, Cuba has built up a day-care system providing for 50,000 children up to the age of 5, which in the beginning was run almost entirely by community women with little or no formal schooling, much less any special training in early childhood education. These para-professionals were equipped only with their own experience and a willingness to undertake intensive in-service training. Parents also help maintenance teams for carpentry, painting, sewing, gardening, etc.

20

Principle

*Teaching, contrary to traditional ideas and practice, should adapt
itself to the learner; the learner should not have to bow to pre-
established rules for teaching.*

Considerata

The place and role of the learner are essential criteria of the nature,
worth and ultimate aims of any educational system. This place is
determined mainly be the degree of freedom he is allowed, the
standards applied in selecting him and by the nature and extent of
the responsibilities the learner is able to assume.

Recommendation

*It should be made a principle to centre educational activity on the
learner, to allow him greater and greater freedom, as he matures,
to decide for himself what he wants to learn, and how and where he
wants to learn it and take his training. Even if the learner has to
accept certain pedagogic and socio-cultural obligations as to subject-
matter and methods, these should still be defined more in terms of
free choice, of psychological propensities and drives among learners
than hitherto.*

Comment

Pupils' freedom of choice necessarily runs parallel to their acceptance of certain responsibilities towards themselves and the school
community. They must be encouraged from a very early age to
take part in organizing school life. They ought to be able to discuss
the regulations governing their rights and duties and these regulations should become gradually more flexible.

·The same reasoning may be applied to educational methods and
subject-matter. The learner, particularly when he is of adult age,
must be free to choose which establishment he wants to attend and
the type of training he wants to acquire. He must be able to enter
the educational system at the level which suits him and select the
optional, complementary subjects which interest him. All or most
compulsory disciplines in schools are, however, laid down in terms

of the objectives which the establishment in question pursues, as to both teaching content and general methodological considerations. But this in no way prevents individual possibilities for choice being extended.

Illustrations

1. Many examples exist of institutions encouraging learners to take responsibility for their own education. The Gesamtschulen in the Federal Republic of Germany endeavour to stimulate students' capacities for choosing their own paths and to bring their working methods close both to university studies and modern professional training. Students do not decide on the kind of diploma they want to acquire immediately on entering school. Subject-matter for teaching is divided into three categories: *Studienfächer*, or major choice subjects; *Orientierungsfächer*, or complementary subjects; *Grundfächer*, or basic subjects. The first and second categories form the core of knowledge regarded as necessary for the pupil's adaptation to society, but are, however, subject to choice. Only the third category is compulsory for all and comprises civic and social training, the visual arts or music, physical training and religion. However, a certain freedom of choice is allowed over the amount of work each pupil devotes to each branch.

Pupils are under certain obligations designed to prevent individual choice of subject having a harmful effect on training necessary to the needs of society. First, the core has to comprise the mother tongue, one foreign language and one experimental science; the two latter may be chosen either from categories one or two. Second, the schools correct gaps if necessary by imposing certain subjects on the pupils. For example:
1. Major subjects chosen by pupil: German, English, Latin, French. Complementary subjects imposed by school: mathematics, chemistry.
2. Major subjects chosen: German, mathematics, physics, chemistry. Complementary subjects: English, the second complementary subject left open.
3. Major subjects chosen: German, mathematics, English, biology. Complementary subjects: left to the pupil's free choice, his own first choice being sufficiently balanced.

2. In London, the Prior Weston primary school is an outstanding example of the increased role of the learner and of widespread changes in primary education in the United Kingdom following the recommendations of the Plowden Report in 1966. Child-centred and activity-oriented learning takes place in a classless environment, as to both space and age ability groups. This 'open-plan' provides activity areas for subject study, reading, art and other manual activities and play. A mixture of 5-, 6- and 7-year olds will work on the same mathematics project (e.g. assembling, ordering and analysing the physical measurements and characteristics of the group), with the quicker pupils helping others within the group. Scheduling is flexible and modular-based; pupils may spend one or more days investigating and describing (in writing, mathematical terms or painting) a single selected theme or topic, moving on to another activity when the project is completed. The teaching of reading and writing is based on

221

immediate environmental and individual interests, with emphasis on creative expression rather than copy-book exercises. Self-discipline is encouraged through fostering of consideration of others, co-operative activity and pupil participation in much of the organization of their work. The headmaster and teachers maintain regular contact with parents, who are encouraged to participate in the school's activities and even act as ancillary aids for play supervision, manual training assistance, group reading, etc.

21

Principle

Learner's responsibilities

Any system according educational services to a passive population and any reform which fails to arouse active personal participation among the mass of learners can achieve at best only marginal success.

Recommendation

All learners, whether young or adult, should be able to play a responsible part not only in their own education but in the entire educational enterprise.

Comment

Participation in educational activity not only increases with age, it also differs according to subject. Learners' responsibility is at its greatest for whatever concerns their social, cultural and material interests. It is less for programmes and methods and, in general, has to be more limited for issues such as financing or recruiting of teachers. Pupils should be able to participate separately from, as well as in association with, teachers, parents and others.

Illustration

Participation in educational action is making continual progress. It affects a variety of activities, has strong support and sometimes runs into fierce opposition. Certain forms of participation (inspection, co-management, self-management, etc.) are now practised in primary schools and communities, in secondary and technical colleges, in the framework of certain adult-education institutions and organizations exterior to schools (at the national or provincial level) which handle general problems such as educational programmes, research, teacher-promotion, remuneration, investment, etc.

But the most interesting experiments are to be found in universities, scattered all over the world. While comparatively few examples exist as yet, it is interesting to note the paths being taken by the participation movement, and its extent. For a long while, students were given partial or entire control of the 'social' sector: student hostels, sports activities, sanitary and auxiliary services. Apart from this, they were 'consulted' from time to time on general policy questions or through special committees set up to propose specific reforms. In recent years, student participation has moved into sectors and levels of university structures hitherto regarded as the exclusive domain of a few people deemed to possess the requisite experience or qualifications. More and more, pedagogic methods and study programmes are being brought into the machinery for participation, while the structures of the main management bodies (faculty councils, national or ministerial commissions) are being modified so as to admit student representatives. Students in some countries are beginning to demand representation within the bodies which decide on admissions, examinations, finance and general administration of education, not without a certain success.[1]

Also worth mention is the fact that even in a region such as Asia, which has no experience or special tradition in this field, the organization of student participation in university management is developing, and student influence, whether direct (in the Philippines, India and Indonesia) or indirect (Malaysia, Thailand) is perceptible both at the university and the national level.

Ways and means

Execution of educational strategies depends mainly on: identifying, stimulating and experimenting with innovations; the administration and management of educational systems; the search for means of financing education.

No over-all innovative strategy can result from the mere accumulation of more or less spontaneous partial innovations 'in the field'.

Diagnosis of systems

Drawing up a new strategy necessarily presupposes *an over-all diagnosis of the state of education.*

It is necessary to have as complete a picture as possible of the components and mechanics of the educational system and its relations to other systems connected to it: the economy, the transport system, communications, cultural activities, etc.

From such a diagnosis, we should be able to identify the main areas of imbalance, both internal (low yield, prohibitive costs, etc.) and external (inadequate links to the labour market, social needs, individual hopes, etc.), and to discern existing constraints, whether human, political or financial. Thus we may isolate variables and

Identifying disequilibrium

1. *A Structural View of Student Participation in University Governance: 13 Country Profiles,* Paris, Unesco, 9 June 1970 (doc. ED/CONF.19/4).

distinguish those which we are in a position to change and those which remain impossible or difficult to modify.

This diagnosis will also provide most information required to set up a model reproducing the way education is currently functioning in a given situation. The simplified abstraction thereby obtained is used merely as a bench-mark for probable consequences of changes likely to be made to the existing system.

Choice of options   Identifying options and making decisions then follows a process which, at least in theory, involves the following series of logical operations: simulating foreseeable points of imbalance on a model; cataloguing actual innovations and seeking possible new ones; building a model of the effects of different innovations and identifying appropriate solutions; finally, formulating strategies likely to be adopted at the policy-making level.[1]

Experiment   Whatever may be thought of the theoretical procedure outlined above, a 'test-tube' experiment of this kind must be used before putting innovations into practice (and even more, before applying a system of innovations) if they are to correspond to rational options.

However, if choices are to be as judicious as possible, they must not be based on a limited number of hypotheses selected at random but on the fullest possible range of options. The range of possible innovations must therefore be methodically catalogued.[2]

Research in this respect has yet to yield as great a contribution as might have been expected. Admittedly, in education, it has so far received far more limited resources than in many other areas and some authorities believe a massive increase in credits allocated to pedagogic research would suffice to give innovation a powerful shot in the arm.

1. A recent piece of research into alternative educational strategies in Rwanda, carried out on behalf of the International Commission on the Development of Education, consisted in using the education simulation model to determine, quantify and analyse possible strategies for school and out-of-school education which might be put into effect between now and 1985. Five alternative strategies for education were envisaged and compared. On the basis of this comparison, researchers concluded that: 'The need for educational reform is obvious and although the continuation of the present system represents the least costly alternative, it is at the same time too expensive for what it offers.' This method of simulation and comparison of possible alternatives could be applied and verified to advantage in other countries (cf. Jan Auerhan, *Alternative Educational Strategies (Rwanda)*, Paris, Unesco, 1971, document of the International Commission on the Development of Education, Innovations Series, 18).
2. 'Educational innovations certainly do not come about automatically. They have to be invented, planned, initiated, and implemented in a way that will make educational practices more adequately geared to the changing objectives of instruction and make them more consistent with the changing standards of instruction' (Torsten Husén, *Strategies of Educational Innovation*, p. 5, Paris, Unesco, 1971, document of the International Commission on the Development of Education, Opinions Series, 28).

It is not easy to couple educational and pedagogic research systems to each other. The two can at best be adapted to theoretical university work on learning, or to experiments with certain instruments or methods, but the fundamental problem remains: how may an educational system be made to fit in with pedagogic research when there is a risk that such research may lead in the end to questioning the system in its entirety?

One solution consists in creating experimental districts or sectors in which all variables in a changing situation may come into play at the same time. In other words, the system overcomes the contradiction by coupling a research institute with a particular area and by giving the broadest possible responsibility to the teacher-researcher-administrator team in that area. And it is precisely the 'lag' between the instructor's creative freedom and the cumbersome pedagogic and sociological weight of the system-builders which forms the driving force for renewal, from the researchers' points of view—since they thereby gain an opportunity to ascertain the real problems for research—and from those of the teachers too, since they become able, here, to exercise the creative freedom they should never have lost in the first place.

But an even greater contribution to innovation could be made by organizations established especially to co-ordinate research and experimentation.

Logistic element

Pedagogic institutes and services of the traditional kind lack the capacity to handle such a task. It could, however, be given to organizations composed[1] of a series of 'workshops' (for systems analysis, programme development, alternative programme prototype production, development of educational methods and technologies and for experiments and training), or to scientific institutes[2] grouping and co-ordinating research and practical experiment in various educational fields; or it could also be set in the framework of a system of continual reform.[3]

1. As in Costa Rica, which foresees setting up a centre of this kind.
2. As in the Soviet Academy of Pedagogic Sciences.
3. As in Sweden, which has instituted the principle of 'rolling reform'. Or, further, as in Spain, where one singular feature of educational reform is the permanent evaluation of its application. On the basis of information received in particular from the education inspection services and from institutes of education sciences, the Spanish Government must lodge a report with the Cortès (parliament) at least once a year, on the results of the application of the education law, outlining achievements related to the extension of education and renewal of the school system. Desirable modifications in the working methods of educational reform are determined on the basis of an assessment of these results. The law has accordingly made allowance for the dynamics of expenditure on reform over the entire 1971–81 period, providing for credits to be increased at a rate of approximately 15 per cent from year to year during ten years.

We consider that the introduction of educational innovations should follow closer co-ordination between research and experiment. We recommend setting up national education development centres or other similar organizations to produce a continual series of educational innovations, leading to a 'perpetual reform' of education.

Even in countries where the education system has been largely decentralized, educational reform can no longer be effected through scattered initiatives. There are many reasons for this: governments have become very conscious of their responsibilities in this area, educational problems are a major concern of central administrations and exert a decisive influence on the future of youth, and public opinion is alert to these questions. The central education authority must take part in this, in ways adapted to each particular country, provided of course that it approves of reforms and does not regard innovation as a factor disturbing established systems and its own routine.

Networks for change

The effects of a change initiated by a central administration may spread outwards, like a succession of waves, from one department to another. One slight modification may be responsible for influencing all the networks in an educational system. An attempt to bring about such a modification may set up resistance among administrators, teachers and even among parents, and, if all these reactions combine, may paralyse the system even more. But it may also spark a movement of approval, precipitate latent processes of change, so that when taken together, and complementing each other, the phenomena unleashed in this way may reach the critical threshold required to bring about some fundamental modification and even a transformation throughout the system. Innovation does not automatically trigger a positive chain reaction, any more than an over-all change is achieved by mechanically adding a number of partial changes together. Whence the idea of a network for change, by which we understand the (fortuitous or intended) combination of modifications which are in harmony with each other and which are capable of multiplying their effects or producing them through a kind of echo effect, and thereby engendering some substantial change. This is the type of problem situation which we must be able to define if we are to avoid being over-optimistic, by imagining that some over-all modification can produce over-all changes, or over-pessimistic, by believing that any modification has only a marginal significance in relation to the power of inertia within the system.

Every modern administration must meet two at first sight contradictory requirements: on the one hand, to organize and control its operations as systematically as possible, and on the other, to instil a sense of responsibility at all levels while encouraging spontaneous initiative.

Seemingly contradictory requirements

The first of these concerns may be justified—practical and political considerations aside—by the need to allocate community resources in the most efficient and rational way, to check on how they are used and to define general goals. The second stems from the fact that an enterprise will flourish all the more if the authority under whose jurisdiction it falls can, without violating the harmony of the whole system, decentralize more and, through a flexible, sympathetic and non-interfering approach, encourage initiatives from the field.

These considerations are particularly valid for education, both because of the stake the community has in it (for which the administration is responsible) and because it is one of the characteristically creative realms of human activity.

We may perhaps define the essential concerns desirable in a central educational administration as: having an over-all view of educational activity; harmonizing national political needs with many-sided local and individual initiative; encouraging decentralization of decision-making and application of measures approved; developing participation of those concerned in all stages of educational activity.

Decentralizing the base does not mean subdividing at the top. If decentralization is to be effective, it must spread out from a single centre. In this sense, the custom of maintaining separate government agencies or ministerial departments for general education, higher education and technical education runs counter to educational progress rather than helping it. For this reason *we recommend that one single State authority be given general responsibility for educational activity, or at least for the entire school system.*

Functional reorganization

The reason for the above qualification is that many States are clearly not ready completely to integrate administration of their school system (including higher and technical education) into professional training, radio teaching and cultural education. At a later date, however, most countries will probably proceed to a broad reorganization of this kind.

Certain countries have set up social and economic councils with

227

wide-ranging powers to handle complex problems related to industry, agriculture, transport and investment, etc. And the time will probably come when the over-all concept of 'education' (or of 'human resources') will be given an equally wide application, which could lead to *setting up a government or inter-ministerial education council with or instead of the Ministry of Education.*

Participation

It will probably come to be recognized as legitimate and necessary for those concerned in education to play an ever greater part in developing and applying its policies and in the management of educational institutions.

We recommend decentralization of decision-making, of responsibilities and resources and broad participation of those concerned, at all levels and in all areas, in determining and carrying out educational activity.

There is an infinite variety of modes of participation, co-management and self-management. It is to be hoped that results of comparative studies of these new forms will be made readily available to the international community.

Financing

The question of financing education cannot under any circumstances be defined in terms of 'thresholds to be reached' or 'ceilings not to be exceeded', and less still on the basis of simple extrapolations from the past. For even when the proportion of the GNP or of total State spending allocated to education appears to have reached a critical limit, we may be sure that reforming the educational system, by improving the yield from investments in education, will permit a redefinition of the problem. This may be in relation to budgetary outlays or to the over-all position of the national economy and its resources, for example. Either way, it will become clear that many possibilities remain for developing education.

We recommend aligning financial policy on this threefold objective: increased spending, diversified resources, reduced unit costs.

Increasing expenditure

So far as increasing expenditure is concerned, it is probably true to say that quite a large number of countries are in a position to spend more of their budget on education than they do. In other countries, doing so may depend either on the national revenue increasing more rapidly, or on taking fiscal measures towards greater social equality. In both cases, it would seem advisable for the Ministry of Education and other government agencies directly benefiting from educational programmes (those concerned with industrial, agricultural or social development, for example) to

228

share the financial burden. More often than not, it will be found possible to increase the community's over-all contribution to education as well as the share of educational spending covered by the national revenue.

On the question of diversifying the sources and means of educational financing, local community resources would in many countries seem to be far from having been fully tapped. Moreover, the public does not seem opposed to the idea of paying special taxes for education, so long as they become more directly associated in the way it develops. Nor would they object apparently to subscribing to government loans launched to finance this or that educational project; they also appear to accept the principle of returnable loans for higher education. *Diversifying resources*

Similarly:

While not altering the principle of free primary and secondary education, where this has been established, parents and adult students may voluntarily agree to pay certain fees in certain branches of education.

Nor is there any reason why other direct or indirect means of financing education should be neglected, such as having professional training colleges finance themselves, or private and State enterprises taking over certain technical-training programmes, or awarding contracts to private educational institutions on a non-profit basis.

It is also quite feasible to encourage businesses to take over the organization of professional or general studies, in return for tax exemption; to require social welfare funds to contribute, in particular, to readaptation courses; to float bank loans to help pay for technical equipment; to make tax or customs-free arrangements for products with an educational purpose, such as books, film-projectors, audio-visual equipment, sports articles, etc.

Many methods have been proposed to help achieve the third objective, that of reducing costs without harming results; they include: *Reducing costs*

'Staggering' attendance by using double shifts, matching the age of schooling with the optimal age for learning a given set of skills, and other ways of maximizing the 'productivity' of existing facilities and personnel.[1]

---

1. Reduction of unit costs is, of course, one of the most difficult problems to solve. In some cases, the simple solution of achieving more rational student/teacher ratios is effective, as in Zambia where increasing the ratio at university level from 6:1 to 10:1 meant that from 1968 to 1969 enrolment was increased by 40 per cent, while recurrent costs increased by only 28 per cent, meaning that these costs per student decreased by

Employing cheaper 'media' than formal schooling.

Using radically different pedagogic methods.

Using semi-qualified teachers, with continuing help and 'back stopping', through traditional means (workshops, correspondence courses, etc.) or through broadcasting and television, etc.[1]

Information available on the subject of innovations and experiments of this kind is not yet sufficiently convincing, however, and it would seem preferable, in our view, to keep to the following two methods, as more reliably effective.

First, we should endeavour to reduce the length of studies necessary to acquire a given qualification (without reducing standards), by perfecting teaching methods, speeding the learning process, carefully selecting knowledge to be acquired, and combining study with work, either directly or in successive phases. There is certainly no more effective way of economizing in education than to avoid wasting the pupils' time. We may be sure there are fortunes waiting to be picked up here.[2]

---

almost 10 per cent. In the Ivory Coast, the introduction of television instruction in primary schools, with the accompanying necessary upgrading of teachers' qualifications, increased the unit cost per student from $60 to $80 per year. But the increased efficiency expected from the revamped system aims at reducing the present expenditure (average fifteen school years) per student completing the primary cycle to eight years' expenditure. That is, cost per completed student, now $15 \times \$60$, or $900, will drop to $8 \times \$80$, or $640.

1. One new solution is to distribute education in time and finance it accordingly. If we suppose that each citizen has the right to a certain 'quantity' of education during his lifetime, or if society guarantees him a certain number of years of education, he receives them by drawing 'educational cheques' on 'recurrent education banks'. Each citizen has the right to draw a certain number of modules from his account—throughout his life and whenever he wishes. A module will correspond to a certain amount of knowledge and intellectual and emotional development. Bertrand Schwartz (in *L'Éducation Permanente en l'An 2000*) has taken up this idea, using the terms 'credit-education' or 'credit-training', and proposes four alternative ways of applying it: (a) equal right to education for all at birth, over a certain number of years; (b) equal right for all to continued or later education, whatever the duration of initial studies; for example, the right to three years' study after the end of formal studies; (c) right to education depending on the level of the diploma acquired on leaving school; for example, one year for those failing to reach university entrance level, two years for those leaving at first university level; (d) right to education depending on profession, doctors having, say, the right to four years, engineers to three years, etc.

2. The Soviet Union has carried out experiments on the effects of shortening the time spent on primary-education programmes from four to three years. Tests were made on over 500,000 pupils. The main conclusion was that the new syllabus for three-year primary education is suitable for all normally developed children, whether or not they have received any pre-school training of any kind. The significance of this reform is that, as borne out by experience, pupils can be brought to a more advanced stage of development in a shorter period of time, which provides favourable conditions for their subsequent education.

The suitability of the content of the new primary-school syllabuses is proved by the results obtained with a three-year course under the new syllabuses, as compared with the four-year course under the syllabuses formerly used in many Russian schools. The

230

The second important expedient for reducing costs is to draw on the people's initiative, on voluntary work for building schools, putting up provisional structures, clearing land and other activities assisting education. We should appeal to the sense of responsibility and solidarity among educated sections of the population towards those who have been less-privileged, whether young or old.

Those who wish to do so may perhaps find here the elements of a kind of focal strategy for education, from which any country may borrow what it deems useful, according to its economy, ideology and convenience.[1] The above remarks are, however, only intended as guidelines. The rhythm at which they are applied, in time and space, the hierarchical order of choice and priority and the links

General orientations and particular applications

---

figures (percentages) are as follows (pupils able to do the work on completion of the course): in grade III (with new syllabuses), dictation 95·2, mathematical problems 96·3; arithmetical problems 96·3; in grade IV (with old primary-school syllabuses), dictation 92·5, mathematical problems 79·1, arithmetical problems 93·8.

1. *Explanatory note.* One member of the commission, Mr Petrovsky, having underlined 'the qualities of clarity and balance' in the report, together with 'the feeling of deep respect due to the chairman of the commission for the tact and understanding which enabled him to maintain friendly contact among all members of the commission and encourage the spirit of creative work and mutual good-will', comments, however, as follows:

'Although a series of amendments was inserted into the report following my remarks, the secretariat of the international commission did not see fit to include the general point of view which I expressed in the course of many statements during the commission's meetings, in my detailed comments on various chapters of the report and in the document entitled *Where is Education Heading?*, which I drafted for the commission with Professor A. Markouchevitch. I am referring to the need to adopt a very clearly differentiated approach to questions of educational development in countries with different socio-economic systems, and to the impossibility of relating, by a simple process of extrapolation, the real difficulties and problems inherent in educational systems of countries with a given political and economic structure to countries whose social structure is different.

'I deplore the fact that the report systematically refers to the pedagogic concepts and educational systems characteristic of the capitalist countries, and that its treatment of the very rich experience of educational development in the U.S.S.R. and other socialist countries is manifestly inadequate. To mention only one example: to demonstrate the advantages consequent on an authentic democratization of social and economic life, on the establishment of close ties between education and life and on the planning of education and training for professional people, I proposed, on several occasions and with developing countries in mind, that the report include an analysis of the historic (even if recent) experiment in the development of education in the Soviet Republics in Central Asia, onetime colonies of Tsarist Russia. The result of my efforts was a footnote to the effect that "commission-member Mr A. V. Petrovsky has called attention to the particular interest of educational development in the Soviet Republics of Central Asia which have made astonishing progress in the field of national education in a short space of time"'.

'Can I be satisfied with this brief mention of my point of view, *in lieu* and instead of the scientific analysis of important factors in educational development, which would have been of exceptional interest to developing countries in the preparation of their own educational strategies? Unfortunately, the report contains a number of similar examples.'

between these many variables can only depend on each country's needs and possibilities.

For lack of means a State may be led to impose rigorous, austere discipline on its people, in education as well as in other domains. It may at times impose serious limits on their individual freedom of choice, contrary, in many respects, to the idea of education contained in this report. Yet this is not the essential thing. What is essential, is that constraints and limitations dictated by necessity be conceived not as absolute rules and values but as dialectical means of achieving, sooner or later, the objective conditions which will lead to these means being done away with, that is to say, to the abolition of the constraints and limitations in question.

The kind of balance sought and the order of priorities respected may differ greatly. Some developing countries may put their main effort into primary schools, firmly resolved to complete development of elementary schooling before turning similar attention to the secondary level. Other countries will try to co-ordinate the dual action of getting children into schools and providing literacy programmes for adults. Still others are planning to develop primary and secondary school systems simultaneously. Similar alternatives have emerged among many industrialized nations, although in this case they affect the secondary and higher educational levels. In general, the concern to correct existing disequilibrium will dictate the choice of priorities. Such disequilibrium takes on very different forms in different countries. In one country we may find primary education underdeveloped, secondary education overdeveloped, adult education inadequate and technical education at the required level. In another, primary may be as wished, secondary underdeveloped, workers' training schemes undervalued and higher education overdeveloped. Or school enrolment at primary level may be complete, adult literacy making progress with secondary education for young people and adults going in the wrong direction, higher education underdeveloped and out-of-school education non-existent. In many countries educational strategies in the immediate future should be very largely concerned with correcting lack of balance of this kind.

Yet above and beyond these differences and the choice of this or that over-all educational strategy, the future of education in virtually every country will necessarily be determined in large part by the general direction of development, an idea on which we have constantly drawn.

To conclude in a few words: the indispensable remoulding of education demands that all its elements—theory and practice, structures and methods, management and organization—be completely rethought from one and the same point of view.

Essential elements of reform and change on which concrete work might begin in the 1970s may be summarized as follows.

The concept of education limited in time (to 'school age') and confined in space (to school buildings) must be superseded. School education must be regarded not as the end but as the fundamental component of total educational activity, which includes both institutionalized and out-of-school education. A proportion of educational activity should be de-formalized and replaced by flexible, diversified models. Excessive prolongation of compulsory schooling, which is beyond certain countries' capacities, must be avoided. The extension of continual training will more than compensate for the shorter average duration of initial studies. Briefly, education must be conceived of as an existential continuum as long as life.

'Closed' educational systems should be made 'open'. We must gradually eliminate rigid distinctions between primary, secondary and post-secondary education. Short-cuts and branch-articulations should be introduced into educational channels.

Special attention should be paid to fostering education for pre-school-age children by selecting and cultivating the most positive forms of family and community association in this work. All available means, conventional and unconventional, should be applied to developing basic education.

General education and technical training should be reconciled. Character and intelligence training should be harmonized. Education and work should be closely associated. Technology should be ever-present in the educational process, both as content and as guiding method. Technical education, which is unnecessarily expensive, should be supplemented and in many cases replaced by out-of-school professional training. Training should be so organized as to facilitate reconversion during employment, to lead to optimum professional mobility and to produce the greatest possible yield from the points of view both of the national economy and the trainees themselves. Narrow, premature specialization should be done away with.

There should be more diversified higher-education institutions. Universities should be turned into multi-purpose establishments open to adults and young people, and designed as much for continual training and periodic upgrading as for specialization and scientific research.

Education should be individualized and personalized to the utmost and constitute a preparation for self-learning. The processes of instruction and learning should be accelerated wherever this is in the learner's and the community's joint interest. New techniques for re-producing and communicating educational material, which are eminently suited to most envisaged innovations, should be introduced at a quicker pace, while technology in general should be regarded as a source of new pedagogic methods (where the cost of equipment is not excessive) and as means of making educational activity more democratic.

Educational management should be democratized, and the general public should play a large part in all decisions affecting education.

The above is assuredly not an exhaustive exploration of all details, yet may provide the broad outline for educational action appropriate to emerging needs and possibilities, and oriented towards the future.

CHAPTER 9

Roads to solidarity

Educational development depends essentially on the resources which each national community devotes to it. All countries assume that responsibility. It is of equal interest to all to benefit from international exchanges and co-operation within the world community. Great as the industrialized nations' resources may be, their ambitious educational undertakings would be in danger of remaining at least partly sterile if they were to develop in a vacuum. And even if other nations, too, are making considerable efforts, it remains highly desirable that they receive support and assistance through international co-operation.

Solidarity among all countries

All countries at all development levels should therefore be brought into the common effort towards international solidarity, which at the same time should give special consideration to developing countries.

There is more and more general agreement that the fight against ignorance is as important as the fight against hunger, the success of which requires linking efforts to develop agriculture in countries short of food with a generous redistribution of world food surpluses. Similarly, in education, *efforts in developing countries must be combined with the world potential which could be made available to them.*

Combination of all efforts

The real, specific content of aid is as important as its volume. Effective aid creates the conditions in which it will no longer be necessary by developing the potential which the assisted country requires in order to do without assistance.

Making aid unnecessary

Development should be indigenous. A country may however require stimulation from the outside and external assistance may be a necessary component in development for a more or less lengthy period.

Co-operation in education is currently in the throes of a crisis similar to that running through all international aid. This may be seen from the obstacles aid is facing all over the world: the diminution in the percentage of GNP which some of the world's most developed countries are devoting to it, the dead ends in which many developing countries now find themselves and the broadsides of criticism currently being fired by both giving and receiving nations. The first group attacks wastage and inefficiency, the second complains of attempts to gain political, strategic or commercial advantage, and to impose foreign cultural models, under the cover of external assistance.

None the less, international co-operation is developing and must be developed further, and the financial aspect is only one particular element of the matter. Another essential fact in the contemporary world is the feeling of solidarity. This, in education, affects a large range of activities: intellectual co-operation, the exchange of experience and the common search for new solutions.

Causes and reasons

We recommend developing international co-operation and assistance, both bilateral and multilateral, not only for reasons which the world community has known and generally accepted for the past quarter of a century, but for others which are new and particularly relevant to the current situation in the field of education.

1

*Traditional
forms of
co-operation*

International co-operation in education has assumed three main forms. The oldest one, deeply rooted in history, consists in organizing exchange of information, of books and pupils, between different countries and cultures in order to broaden the field of knowledge and enrich teaching methods. A second, and more recent form, originates essentially in the Unesco Constitution; it aims at promoting peace and international understanding through education. The third form, which is also the newest, consists in aiding education in the interest of economic and social development, by supplying developing countries' educational systems not only with teachers and experts, but with training facilities, pedagogic equipment, school buildings, etc.

However, international co-operation has assumed a new dimension following the need to rethink educational systems, to study the manifold aspects of educational theory and practice, to compare problems and their solutions. This co-operation also exists between developed countries, which draw great benefit from exchanging information and opinions on educational reform and innovation. By developing the theme of international co-operation, exchanges of this kind may lead to elucidating the concepts of education itself and should thereby help to make room for joint research towards new paths.

Enlarging scope

2

There are two major justifications for international aid. The first is that since the expanding need for education is out of all proportion to the resources available for meeting it, many developing countries lack even the means to continue the already intense effort they are making in this direction, without running the risk of entirely exhausting their budgets. Under these circumstances outside financial aid in the form of investments may be extremely valuable, particularly to secondary technical education, post-secondary polytechnical education and higher education.

Aid supplements national resources

The second and probably even more important justification is that international aid may greatly facilitate innovation. Most countries hesitate to venture into new areas for fear of gambling away their already inadequate resources. Others who make up their minds to it can frequently go no further without outside financial help. Just as the Green Revolution owed a great deal to persevering aid from private foundations, aid which is judiciously co-ordinated with innovative movements in the country concerned may make an important contribution to educational change.

Aid promotes innovation

But if international aid is to be really fruitful, those responsible for it must agree to make larger and longer-lasting commitments to programmes covering both investment and innovation.

Co-operation and exchange of experience

If education develops along the lines we have recommended, international co-operation among all countries will become more and more necessary.

1

Intellectual co-operation

Exchange of educational experience is undoubtedly one of the most important branches of such co-operation. Unesco often acts as an intermediary or actively promotes contacts through education ministers' conferences, sessions of the International Bureau of Education, experts' meetings and more or less regular regional or world conferences, and exchanges through other channels. The United Nations and its Specialized Agencies take part in this activity. The experience so acquired is definitely useful to the world community, and the potential benefit of continued meetings of this kind cannot be doubted. We believe, however, that they should be held less often in order to be more carefully prepared, and also that those concerned should pay more attention to the way the decisions taken are followed through in practice.

In addition to more or less institutionalized occasions of this kind, other individuals and associations maintain very many, very useful contacts, such as those between experts, between research institutes engaged in joint scientific projects, between academies of science or pedagogy. These are practical forms of co-operation which must be strongly encouraged.

The dissemination of information on educational innovation and the exchange of experience should become fundamental to international co-operation.

The machinery for exchanging experience is far from functioning perfectly. We have still not managed to develop contacts in a truly international frame of mind, without ideological or political restrictions, shorn of prejudice and reticence. We tend too often to play on the spectacular and political aspects at the expense of necessary depth and 'technicity'. There are more bilateral exchanges on educational and cultural matters between one-time colonies and their former motherlands than between the countries which have

238

recently gained independence. More and more bilateral cultural co-operation agreements are being concluded all over the world, but they aim rather to promote exchanges in the arts and sciences than at the exchange of educational experience and innovation. Unfortunately, very few exchanges of this latter kind take place between countries in different geographical regions, even between those sharing many common features.

We should therefore:

Give increasing importance to particularly significant issues when policy-makers in education hold international meetings.

Organize more meetings among countries with different socio-economic systems.

Increase intra-regional cultural exchanges among countries formerly isolated under colonial régimes.

Encourage conferences grouping representatives of countries which are in different geographical regions but have common characteristics or are following a similar course of development.

Promote as widely as possible the diffusion of information on innovative experiments, and set up machinery enabling government officials and educators directly concerned to study similar experiments in progress elsewhere.

Increase the means at Unesco's disposal for co-operating with Member States in the organization of on-the-spot studies and exchanges of experience among educators.

2

Another form of co-operation concerns opportunities available to teachers for working in other countries. This enriches their training and improves their capacities, whether through keeping up to date on advanced research, work on a specific research project or study of some specialized subject.

Student and teacher mobility

Teachers' mobility is often hampered by juridical or administrative obstacles, as well as by lack of information. Countries whose regulations bar the teaching profession to foreigners should either abolish such restrictions or greatly liberalize them. Career problems (guaranteed employment when repatriated, promotion and pension) are no less important, and various schemes have been devised to help solve them. Certainly, periods of service abroad should be considered an integral part of a teacher's career.

239

Mobility also enables students as well as teachers to broaden their intellectual and cultural horizons and to find their way to the best or most specialized institutions.

The major problems in this respect, language barriers apart, are those of information, curriculum adaptation and diploma equivalence. This last-mentioned problem is surely the thorniest.

Equivalence of diplomas

If we wish to encourage student and teacher mobility, degrees and diplomas awarded by different higher educational establishments must steadily become equivalent to each other.[1] It is essential, however, that equivalence between diplomas does not lead us to deduce that university programmes must be identical or uniform, which would inevitably slow down innovation and hamper the capacity of higher education to adapt itself to local or national conditions.

Given the complexity of this problem, it would appear that diplomas can only be made equivalent to each other in stages and that such an objective should be sought first of all at the regional level, or as an agreement between groups of countries. Meanwhile it would seem appropriate to distinguish between the degree or diploma itself and the right to exercise a profession.

Other important subjects such as curriculum, teaching methods and equipment, pedagogic research and the creation of information centres and data banks accessible to many people are also potentially significant themes for international co-operation.

Programmes for international understanding

Another aspect of international significance requires national action. Students able to travel overseas to become acquainted with other societies remain in the minority, but all students should have the opportunity, through their study programmes, to understand cultures other than their own and so gain some awareness of the unity of mankind, the fundamentally similar conditions and aspirations true of all men. If we are to succeed in promoting such awareness, we must see to it that more and more books are published and translated and organize their distribution and that of other materials adapted to presenting one culture with an authentic picture of the values of another, and so strengthen the feeling of sharing in great universal causes. At present, national curricula in all parts of the world remain, with rare exceptions, dangerously provincial.

1. A regional agreement on recognition of diplomas in Latin America and the Caribbean, drawn up following a Unesco initiative, is expected to be signed in the course of 1973/74. It will then become the first major positive achievement in this field. Other regional agreements are in preparation (for Africa, the Arab States, and for Common Market countries).

240

It would be desirable:

*To increase international mobility among teachers and students, which
implies in particular that governments remove obstacles preventing
foreign nationals from teaching in their countries.*

*To reach formal agreements enabling students and teachers to con-
tinue their activities in foreign countries.*

*To eliminate all racial, religious, political or ideological discrimi-
nation from movement of this kind.*

3

Apart from the tens of thousands of students and teachers who visit
countries other than their own, the numerous technical assistance
experts in developing countries form another large category of
people working for international co-operation and understanding.

*Exchange
of experts*

Teaching and training personnel currently made available to
developing countries total some 80,000 people.

In 1968, Development Assistance Committee (DAC) countries[1]
provided the services of 56,183 individuals (of whom 11,650 were
volunteers) to developing countries: 49,368 teachers,[2] 4,345 administrators and 2,470 advisers.

In the same year, socialist countries sent a total of 21,000 experts
to developing countries.[3]

In 1970, the United Nations Development Programme employed 8,848 experts. Most are from the industrialized countries,
but an increasing number are now coming from the developing
countries: 1,823 or more than one-fifth. India ranks fourth (396
experts) after the United Kingdom, France and the United States,
and Egypt is fifteenth (161 experts).

Giving university graduate and undergraduate students overseas training by means of bilateral and multilateral assistance is
becoming an important element in international co-operation and
also in the flow of qualified people from country to country.

1. OECD's Development Assistance Committee groups: Australia, Austria, Belgium,
   Canada, Denmark, France, Federal Republic of Germany, Italy, Japan, Netherlands,
   Norway, Portugal, Sweden, Switzerland, the United Kingdom, the United States and
   the European Economic Community's Commission.
2. Distributed as follows: primary and secondary education, 36,309 (73·5 per cent); higher education, 5,909 (12·0 per cent); teacher training, 1,161 (2·3 per cent); technical
   and vocational training, 3,739 (7·6 per cent); other, non-specified, 2,250 (4·6 per cent.)
3. OECD, *Resources for the Developing World: the Flow of Financial Resources to Less-
   developed Countries, 1962–1968*, p. 305, Paris, 1970.

In 1968, bilateral aid from the DAC countries financed the training of 41,000 students and 36,000 trainees. Corresponding figures for socialist countries were 15,750 students and 1,600 trainees.[1]

In the U.S.S.R., it is estimated that 30,000 foreign nationals attended specialized secondary and higher educational establishments during the 1970/71 school year.

Meanwhile the United Nations Development Programme granted more than 8,600 scholarships in 1970, 7,120 going to nationals of developing countries (cost: $15·4 million). Major fields were technical, industrial and agricultural training, secondary-level teacher training, training in communications, transport, public administration and development planning.

Working experts and personnel who undergo training in countries other than their own have made a positive contribution to the development of education. This is an important form of international co-operation and must be continued. However, it is not always smooth going in the field of co-operation. Many visiting experts, for example, have difficulty in participating in local professional life. There may be mutual lack of understanding of cultural, anthropological and material conditions, or failure to adapt to the environment. Sometimes, attempts are made to transplant foreign models in mechanical fashion, or to apply directly, in developing situations, the experience of developed countries. And the principle according to which the best kind of assistance is the kind that creates conditions for its own disappearance is often forgotten. Ill-adapted behaviour of this kind has often aroused reticence towards foreign experts among leaders and people in some developing countries.

In a nutshell: experts should be better, fewer, self-displacing, should live closer to their colleagues and to the local populations, and more of them should come from countries where socio-economic conditions are similar to those being visited.

We may add that all too often the forms of co-operation are out of date and the procedures mere routines. Sending experts to developing countries and students from those same countries for training abroad is no longer the most important of all ways of providing assistance. Not, at least, for many countries which have made great progress in training their own professional personnel.

Training abroad This—the problem of nations training their own professionals and executives—should itself be reappraised. Possibilities for overseas training, primarily in neighbouring countries, should be

1. *Diplomatiya i Kadry*, p. 86, Moscow, 1968.

assessed in terms of a national policy towards professional and higher education and a national programme for such training. One fruitful expedient consists in organizing massive training programmes set directly in the framework of development projects financed through foreign investments.[1] This is a useful innovation and could be a particularly profitable solution in many spheres, enabling large-scale training to be adapted to needs and related closely to the environment. In cases where overseas training becomes clearly indispensable, especially for small contingents of specialists in advanced techniques, the scholarship system is not necessarily the most convenient way of paying for it. Despite the fact that it has been the system most preferred until now, other arrangements are possible, including exchanges of research-workers, teachers, students and administrators. Countries may agree on giving paid employment to advanced foreign students, as junior lecturers during their training period, and universities or pedagogic institutes for training and research may pair off with their counterparts in other countries.

In our opinion:
Some kind of 'code of honour' should be devised to govern the behaviour of experts working in foreign countries.
In order to define what the role and position of foreign professional personnel should now be, progress achieved in developing countries must be taken into account. In some cases, this progress is so great that it is time for earlier one-sided assistance to become mutual and for the industrialized nations to benefit from experience acquired elsewhere, with the aid of professional people from the Third World.
Mutual assistance among the developing countries must be increased, especially among countries in the same geographical region.

4.

Despite positive results from intellectual co-operation and from training professional and executive personnel abroad, some results are negative. We have seen research projects designed essentially

Brain drain

1. In 1968, for example, more than 200,000 workers, technicians and specialists were trained in this way in many developing countries, under projects carried out with help from the socialist countries.

TABLE 7. Immigration of scientists and engineers into the United States of America, by last country of residence

'Donors'	1956		1962	
Europe				
European Economic Community				
Belgium		18		18
France		79		47
Federal Republic of Germany		339		277
Italy		72		62
Netherlands		105		113
Total	613		517	
Sweden	144		53	
United Kingdom	433		659	
Others	489		388	
Total		1,679		1,617
Canada		1,003		1,054
Rest of North and South America		718		819
Japan		17		39
Rest of Asia		288		379
Others		121		146
TOTAL		3,826		4,054

Source. *The Brain Drain into the United States of Scientists, Engineers and Physicians*, Washington, D.C., United States Government Printing Office, 1967.

for the profit of the participating country that have ended in a kind of intellectual exploitation. Similarly, education abroad is not always beneficial if it severs the student's ties to his native country, if the training he receives is too far removed from the realities of his country and, above all, if he does not return home once his studies are finished.

The 'brain drain' is doubtless the most serious problem in the field of intellectual co-operation (see Table 7). It has two aspects: emigration of scientists and the failure of students studying abroad to return home. Some industrialized nations are more affected by it than are developing countries. According to an OECD study, three-quarters of the scientists and engineers who emigrate to Canada come from OECD countries; for the United States, the percentage

1963		1964		1965		1966	
24		25		33		37	
89		82		103		112	
353		425		370		346	
53		38		58		107	
72		60		80		71	
	591		630		644		673
	81		90		106		95
	910		1,006		941		1,251
	503		551		540		696
	2,085		2,277		2,231		2,715
	1,157		1,084		1,189		1,105
	858		940		922		843
	81		39		23		75
	1,157		885		456		1,825
	288		176		183		210
	5,626		5,401		5,004		6,773

was 55 per cent in 1967. On the other hand, 33 per cent of foreign scientists living in the United States and 16 per cent of those living in Canada come from developing countries, and immigration to the United States and Canada from these countries is tending to increase faster than that from industrial countries.[1] Within the developing world itself, some countries represent poles of attraction for their neighbours.

These movements sometimes do have positive effects, particularly when they involve high-level researchers unable to find indispensable laboratories in their own countries. Their work is of value to the entire international scientific community, and they might not even be able to begin it at home. The same goes for countries which

1. *The International Movement of Scientists and Engineers*, p. 27, Paris, OECD, March 1970.

lack the means of offering qualified nationals the posts for which they are fitted. Finally, the country may benefit from an inflow of foreign currency sent home by its emigrants. All in all, however, the brain drain runs directly counter to the aims underlying aid for the development of education.

Obvious material causes provide the first explanation of this migration. People are attracted by high salaries, better living and working conditions. Meanwhile unemployment or underemployment at home, the lack of facilities for research and inadequate professional and social satisfaction—not to mention political convictions—all help to encourage or compel intellectuals to leave their homelands.

Whatever may be thought of this interpretation, it is a fact that the brain drain is so disquieting that national authorities, incapable of eliminating its deeply underlying material or cultural causes, are now seeking immediate remedies in the form of administrative measures. While not going so far as to close their national frontiers, they may clamp a quota on emigration, or consider compelling emigrants to repay capital sums invested in their training—which, however, is far from compensating the national community for its real loss.[1] But coercive measures of this kind have only limited effect.

There is more to it than this. The decision to emigrate is very often dictated less by circumstance than by a predisposition formed in early childhood. In many societies, exodus begins at the village. Patterns of life are copied from the towns, the educational system is based on imported school models, and both show scant concern to help the individual integrate into his environment by giving him the feeling that he belongs to a nation and a society. Together with other objectively fruitful values, they inculcate values into schoolchildren which estrange them from their surroundings, feeding intellectual and material ambitions which are becoming harder and harder to realize in a rural setting. Schools thereby push young people out towards the towns, after having helped to turn them away from their own native springs of life, which are most necessary to personality development and to the formation of a sense of national identity. The effect of the educated person's climb to higher

1. It has been calculated, for example, that it costs the United Kingdom £6,000 to train a B.Sc. in engineering sciences. If he emigrates the loss for the British economy (actual value of his professional career) can be estimated at £30,000. On the other hand, his value for the American economy, which he enters, will be about £78,000 (cf. Committee on Manpower Resources for Science and Technology, *The Brain Drain. Report of the Working Group on Migration*, p. 16, London, HMSO, Cmnd 3417, 1967).

social and cultural levels is to turn him into a rootless creature, a potential expatriate, and the path which led him from village to town, from town to capital city, tends in the end to take him overseas.

We believe, none the less, that the heart of the matter lies as much in socio-political and economic factors as in the rootlessness and emigration encouraged by an education which fails to instil the kind of values in people which make them attached to their everyday surroundings. Meanwhile there is no reason why we should not entertain the idea of a certain amount of emigration of trained people finding its own level, one day, as a positive expression of the movement of ideas and the process of universal integration, once that emigration no longer stems from a collective feeling of estrangement and rejection.[1]

We recommend:
Developing authentically national educational systems which enable individuals to achieve an increasingly harmonious and positive integration at all levels into their environment.
Setting up national, regional and international advanced study centres, and providing them with the necessary equipment.
According abundant scholarships or paid vacations allowing scientists to travel for study purposes, to keep themselves up to date on scientific innovation and to make contact with fellow-scientists overseas.
Defining explicit national scientific policies, which scientists themselves should actively help to draft.
Associating scientists with the administration of science, so far as possible, in order to reduce bureaucratic procedure and restrict the part played by administrators.

5

Unesco has played a primordial role in the vast array of international activities designed to foster solidarity among nations, in the exchange of experience and the transfer of knowledge which have

Unesco

1. We should mention here the project to found a 'United Nations University' formed by a network of higher educational institutions. Various groups of experts, including both proponents and opponents of the idea, have debated it, but no decision has yet been reached. The International Centre for Theoretical Physics in Trieste is a convincing example of this kind of undertaking. It makes an effective contribution to scientific research, to the training of scientists from developing countries and also to the international unity of science.

taken place over the past quarter of a century. The range and effect of its work are all the more remarkable in that it has been carried out with relatively modest means in relation to the enormous needs it has to satisfy.

Hardly an aspect of education has not been considered, studied and clarified within the framework of the Organization's activities, and it may reasonably be claimed that without an organization like Unesco, it would have been impossible for a number of fundamental concepts related to theory and practice of education to have spread rapidly through the world. And most probably, without Unesco, many developing countries would have had far more trouble improving their educational systems and, especially, adapting them to meet the powerful emergent social demand for education.

Rather than celebrating the past, however, we should look to Unesco's future. In this respect, it is wise to beware of two contradictory attitudes, both of which are erroneous.

The first involves placing unreasonable hopes in the Organization and expecting it to accomplish tasks which are not in its nature to undertake. Some people want it to be the embodiment of the international outlook, evolving in a world with no other ties but its responsibilities to scientific truth. They consider that its decisions and judgements should testify in all circumstances to the virtues of complete objectivity, impartiality and justice. But this is overlooking reality, since Unesco cannot be considered apart from the complex machinery of world politics.

The other mistaken attitude is to allege that nothing good can come out of an organization too subject to political considerations, that the play of conflicting pressures and the problems of an administration victimized by paralysing constraints condemn it to in-efficiency.

Unesco's work admittedly does not proceed unhampered. Yet the very fact that its activities have political overtones, that when ideas are developed and formulated under Unesco auspices they involve political commitment by the authorities concerned, lends weight to those ideas and facilitates their acceptance.

These considerations appear to us to be fully applicable to Unesco's endeavours for the development of education, especially those devised on the lines of this present report. First, any such action must reflect the societies, the political and economic systems, the physical, social and cultural environments of the countries concerned. Second, as factors of the future and source of new values,

248

these endeavours may be regarded as a vital variable in the human condition.

What then do we want of Unesco, what do we expect of it in the years to come?

International organizations must, each in its own appointed field, handle international problems—of war and peace, of hunger, of racism, colonialism, and environment—in a truly international spirit. It would be appropriate for Unesco to set the example: the renewal of education is in our view now taking on international dimensions and must be considered on a world-wide scale.

We expect Unesco to continue its work for increased intellectual co-operation. No other body is in a position to do better in this domain, particularly in the field of educational reform, where it must stimulate and develop the ferment required for a vast renewal of education.

Unesco must play an energetic part in combating racist and nationalist doctrines and practices throughout its educational activities. It must help education to escape its provincialism and to avoid mere imitation of imported models by making of education something entirely new for the disinherited people of the world.

It must help forge a new conception of international aid, for its Member States and for its own use too. It must drop its usual kind of project and its traditional type of experts' mission which, despite certain useful results, has all too often resulted in discouraging local initiative and transplanting ill-adapted schemes and practices. In particular, a large part of Unesco assistance must focus on studying and experimenting with new educational methods, searching for suitable innovations to replace obsolescent educational practices. To this end, it would be desirable for Unesco to establish an international evaluation system enabling it to carry out in-depth analyses of the results which countries have obtained in education.

Finally, it is only natural for us to hope that the reasons which have guided us throughout this report will also lead Unesco to commit itself in favour of innovation in education, to push its theoretical research and practical activity in that direction—and by this go beyond the limits traditionally imposed on ideas about institutions, methods, programmes, students—so that education may expand to meet the virtually unlimited needs of individuals and societies.

Sources and modes
of assistance

The industrialized nations' financial and technical aid to developing countries firmly supports and orients international co-operation in education.

1

Technical and
financial aid

The largest single element, quantitatively speaking, in the world's outlay on international technical assistance is the aid provided for education and professional training. In 1968, it represented about 40 per cent of all bilateral technical assistance.

Aid[1] received by the developing countries in 1969 was about $8,800 million, with $5,700 million coming from capitalist countries, $1,900 million from the socialist countries[2] and $1,200 million from multilateral organizations.

Official figures indicating total spending year by year on aid to education from all sources have not so far been published. Table 8 has been compiled on the basis of existing data and estimates. The margins are designed to allow for the differing monetary value which may be attributed to aid from socialist countries, and for possible variations in reliability of estimates of private aid.

The over-all amount of this aid in 1968 represented about 10 per cent of all educational expenditure in the developing countries; the percentage varies greatly from one country to another, reaching up to 40 per cent in some French-speaking African countries.

Aid to education, training and research is provided by almost all the United Nations Agencies. It consists of expert services, study grants, training courses, subsidies for national or regional teaching institutions, supplies of equipment and publications.

1. We consider that only gifts or loans at 3 per cent interest or less constitute aid. Some authors consider all loans as well as the direct investment in enterprises as international aid, but these terms would seem to us to be questionable. Such flows of capital are often dictated by business, not assistance, motives. There is no mention of industrialized nations' aiding each other.
2. This figure includes assistance to less-developed socialist countries: Cuba, the Democratic People's Republic of Korea, Mongolia and the Democratic Republic of Viet-Nam; total: $1,150 million (OECD, *Resources for the Developing World: the Flow of Financial Resources to Less-developed Countries 1962–1968*, p. 392, Paris, 1970).

TABLE 8. Aid to education (in million dollars)

Type of aid	1968–69 (per year)	1970–71 (per year) (estimates)
Bilateral aid		
DAC countries	710	760[1]
Socialist countries	150–200	150–200[1]
Multilateral aid	220	400
Private aid	120–170	350–400
TOTAL	1,200–1,300	1,660–1,760

1. Figure reached by extrapolating from figures for aid provided between 1967 and 1968, or by keeping it at the same level.
Source. H. M. Phillips, *International Cooperation in Education*, p. 4, Paris, Unesco, 1971, document of the International Commission on the Development of Education, Opinions Series, 49.

The sums provided by the United Nations Development Programme were allocated over the three-year period 1968–70 as shown in Table 9.

To this sum must be added loans and credits from the International Bank for Reconstruction and Development which totalled $424 million by June 1971; about half of this sum was provided by the Bank's International Development Association (IDA). IDA

Loans for education

TABLE 9. United Nations Development Fund allocations, by sector, 1968–70 (in million dollars)

Sector	1968	1969	1970
Agriculture	53·0	60·3	69·0
Industry	35·6	34·4	40·2
Public-service enterprises	24·4	24·8	31·8
Housing and building	2·8	2·6	3·0
Multi-sectoral projects	14·3	15·4	16·0
Health	9·1	6·6	7·2
Education and science	23·3	19·8	24·0
Social services	2·7	2·0	2·4
Administration	10·4	10·7	12·6
All sectors	175·6	176·5	206·2
Fixed organizational expenses	20·4	25·3	25·5
TOTAL	196·0	201·8	231·7

concludes agreements with countries whose annual *per capita* income is below $300.

By the end of 1971, the Inter-American Development Bank had lent a total of $150·5 million to approximately 600 institutions of higher, technical and vocational education, for buildings, laboratory equipment and libraries; in addition, $6 million went to train higher-level personnel.

The European Economic Community aids eighteen African States, Madagascar and some associated overseas territories. The percentage of capital aid provided through the European Development Fund ($145 million at the end of 1969) is being reduced in favour of study and trainee grants; training is provided more and more in the assisted States themselves (10 per cent in 1963, 44 per cent in 1968).

The increase in aid to education seems less satisfactory if compared to progress in public spending on education in developing countries, which has been faster than that of assistance. The proportion of aid received has accordingly diminished in relation to over-all expenditure. Similarly, the rate of increase in aid to education in developing countries is lower than the rates of growth in GNP in the donor countries. (For example, in 1967–68, industrialized countries' average GNP increased by 9·3 per cent, whereas aid to education from those same countries increased by only 6 per cent.)

Furthermore, multilateral aid remains insufficiently developed. One pre-condition for over-all education reform is that the universal fund of experience and innovation in education be openly available to the international community. Comparatively speaking, bilateral aid opens doors slightly; multilateral aid starts a world-wide circulation of information and experience.[1] It is relatively neutral and open to scrutiny and offers the widest possible opportunity for solutions and comparisons of all kinds and from all sources.

To conclude:

We consider that aid to education can and must be increased.

Due to the specific nature of educational investment, which can only have delayed-action effects, this increase must be achieved in the immediate future, although this does not necessarily imply that it will have to be continually multiplied in succeeding years.

1. Commission member A. V. Petrovsky is of the opinion that one cannot evaluate the advantages of one form of international aid over another in summary statements and that such evaluation requires a concrete historical analysis.

Bilateral aid should not be discouraged, since it performs a useful service and because the countries concerned might possibly refuse to accord it in another form.

Development of multilateral aid is however highly desirable, since it is more in line with the requirements of international solidarity. It should, in any event, be stepped up sufficiently to reach a higher proportion than bilateral aid.

Finally, it is both possible and desirable to co-ordinate the various types of aid to education.

2

Great disparities exist in the geographical distribution of aid to education; in certain respects, they are revealing.

International aid: distribution and conditions

In 1967, 80 per cent of all French aid to education went to Africa, as did more than 50 per cent of all such British assistance. Of total American aid, 38 per cent went to Asia, 31 per cent to Africa and 20 per cent to Latin America. Meanwhile the socialist countries, between 1954 and 1968, distributed their financial aid (not counting aid to other, less-developed socialist countries) as follows: to the Near East and South Asia, 70 per cent; to the Far East, 10 per cent; to Africa, 15 per cent, and to Latin America, 5 per cent.

Africa is the primary recipient of international aid, both in absolute value and *per capita*. About 65 per cent of bilateral aid, 40 per cent of expenditure under the United Nations Development Programme and 50 per cent of World Bank and IDA credits have gone to Africa. Asia comes next in absolute figures, but with its huge population it receives far less *per capita* than the Arab States and Latin America.

Table 10 collates certain statistics for 1968 which give a fairly clear picture of recent trends.

The U.S.S.R. and Eastern European countries gave aid for training in 1967 to 19,400 people (not including people from developing socialist countries); 44 per cent were Asians, 46 per cent Africans and 10 per cent Latin Americans.[1]

Theoretically, aid is provided according to needs voiced by the country requesting it. In reality, when a country lacks qualified personnel to draft its plans, it calls in foreign experts to do so, and

1. *Diplomatiya i Kadry*, p. 86, Moscow, 1968.

TABLE 10. Aid given and received by category, recipient region and donor country, 1968

Category	Recipient regions	Donor countries			
		DAC countries	France	United Kingdom	United States of America
Students	Total	*39,411*	*8,561*	*6,129*	*11,168*
	Africa	14,537	5,478	2,500	3,142
	America	7,150	1,142	813	3,473
	Asia	14,372	1,412	2,383	3,683
Trainees	Total	*31,140*	*6,474*	*4,043*	*5,284*
	Africa	11,523	5,156	1,305	835
	America	7,416	576	1,204	2,303
	Asia	9,214	494	1,057	1,750
Staff[1]	Total	*56,183*	*30,115*	*7,413*	*10,273*
	Africa	42,344	27,015	6,180	3,904
	America	4,552	916	392	1,892
	Asia	6,625	1,698	498	3,304

1. Teachers, administrators, advisers, including volunteers, from DAC countries.
Source. OECD, *Aid to Education in Less Developed Countries*, Paris, 1970.

many projects accordingly contain a large measure of suggestions made by donors.

Furthermore, many developing countries received aid from a variety of sources and often have difficulty in co-ordinating assistance and integrating it into national plans, which can lead to duplication of effort.

There is no truly free aid, which is in the nature of things. Even international aid, in present circumstances, frequently comprises elements which violate the very principle on which it is based. The benefits it should bring in theory are often greatly diminished in practice by excessive estimates of costs and prices, financing charges and supplementary expenses entailed.

Tied aid

It is also worth noting that the real volume of external aid is calculated in monetary terms generally less than appears on paper. The figures printed above, for example, show how much the aid in question cost donor countries. But this is not equivalent to the value of that aid to recipient countries (except in the case of direct transfers, such as scholarships).

Differences are due first of all to the 'tied' nature of some aid, i.e. wherever the receipt of aid is subject to conditions set by the donor country. Tied aid is in many cases the only one enabling developing countries to obtain equipment or technical assistance from donor nations whose currencies are not convertible. Its disadvantage, however, is that expenditure (mainly for the construction of school buildings) returns to companies in the donor nation. These firms make studies, transport equipment and send experts to the building site, which often compels the recipient country to pay prices higher than accepted world rates. In short, tied aid is useful in that it enables countries needing assistance to have more helpers and, all in all, to obtain more substantial aid. But it may also narrow a recipient country's margin for manœuvring.

Sometimes, interest rates for loans are obviously variable. While the People's Republic of China and IDA do not charge interest (IDA takes only a nominal commission of 0·75 per cent), the World Bank put its interest rate up in 1970 from 6·5 per cent to 7 per cent.

Nor, finally, can it be denied that international aid is in general less helpful to the very needy States than to those which, from the point of view both of human resources and economic standards and growth rates, are comparatively privileged.

The poorest countries generally have a limited capacity for absorbing aid and have fewer development projects than those in a more advanced state of growth. On the other hand, if the quantity of international aid which a country receives depends on what it says it needs, then it becomes logical to give aid to the countries which appear to be the most dynamic. The fact remains that this process widens the gap between the most underprivileged nations in the Third World and those which are less so, and the international community cannot remain indifferent to the dangers inherent in this paradoxical course of events.

We suggest that international organizations seriously consider the geographical disparities in international co-operation and assistance. Aid should be more equitably distributed, both bilaterally and multilaterally. This is a political problem as well as one of justice, related to that of decolonization and to the development of truly international relationships between nations.

The practice of tied aid should be gradually dropped, especially in the sense that donor countries should agree to their aid being used in other developing countries (for training in national or regional institutions, for equipment supplied by neighbouring countries, etc.).

This is clearly a development which cannot come about, however, unless the countries concerned make a concerted stand.

We call on all countries and international and regional financial organizations to review their interest rates on loans for education and training. Three solutions seem to us to deserve consideration: (a) the application of differential rates, to the advantage of the least developed countries; (b) interest bonuses conceded by the governments of industrialized nations; (c) greater contributions to the International Development Association.

3

Correlation between aid to education and global development strategy

International co-operation in all its forms is not an independent variable, although it has often been considered as such. To be effective, it must be integrated into national educational policies and reflect national strategies and priorities.

If we accept as true that education is both a product and producer of society and that there is a close correlation between transformations of the socio-economic environment and the structures and means of education, then international co-operation and assistance in the sphere of education must necessarily fall within the general strategy of world development and global aid.

The total amount of public and private funds provided for the developing countries doubled between 1960 and 1970, rising from $7,700 million to $15,600 million (net payments).[1]

The second United Nations Conference on Trade and Development (1968) recommended that the industrialized countries earmark 1 per cent of their GNP for net financial transfers to the developing nations. However, in 1970, their total contribution only amounted to 0·78 per cent of their GNP, which was $4,000 million short of the sum which 1 per cent would have represented. Actually, this average is influenced by the importance of the United States, whose GNP represents half the total GNP of the DAC countries and whose contribution was 0·55 per cent (instead of 1 per cent) of the GNP of the United States. On the other hand, only five countries (Australia, Belgium, France, the Netherlands and the United Kingdom) contributed more than 1 per cent of their GNP in 1970. Denmark, the Federal Republic of Germany and Italy, which reached the 1 per cent objective in 1969, failed to do so in 1970.

1. Gross payments, less repayments on earlier loans (but the interest was not deducted).

Leaving aside total public and private financial transfers and considering only public aid, here too we find that the objective proposed by the United Nations, 0·70 per cent of the GNP in 1975, shows no signs of being reached. The percentage of the DAC countries reached a maximum of 0·54 per cent in 1961. Since then, it has continuously dropped: 0·36 per cent in 1969, 0·34 per cent in 1970.

With regard to the socialist countries, there has also been a lowering of commitment volume. From $1,400 million in 1966 it fell to $724 million in 1968 (not including commitments to the less-developed socialist countries).

As to multilateral organizations, their aid went from $284 million in 1960 to $1,500 million in 1970.

Private contributions have increased considerably; those of the DAC countries rose from $3,150 million in 1960 to $7,604 million in 1970.

For the next few years, we must be prepared for a different trend of expenditure. In so far as it is clear that 'the financing of investment for equipment and investment in education will compete with one another seriously in the State budget',[1] it is evident that, in the resources of international assistance, expenditure on education will clash with the growing needs of expenditure on agriculture, industry, infrastructures, public works, etc.

The only hope of increasing assistance to education is through increasing the over-all sums allocated for world development.[2]

On the whole, the prospects of increased international aid are hardly bright. There is, in fact, a contradiction between assistance given to developing countries and their place in the system of international trade. Although it is not our proper concern, we cannot overlook the fact that developing nations have been severely affected by the unstable world-wide market in raw materials and the collapse of exchange rates. Trade is evolving in a way unfavourable to them and they have to keep transferring an increasing volume of capital to industrialized countries to cover loan repayments and debt service charges. One can only hope that the serious lack of

1. R. Poignant, J. Hallak, Ta Ngoc Châu and C. Tibi, *The Financing of Educational Expenditure, 1970–1980,* Paris, Unesco, 1971, document of the International Commission on the Development of Education, Opinions Series, 15.
2. Commission member A. V. Petrovsky considers that making over 1 per cent of developed countries' gross national product to aid to developing countries is only justified in the case of developed countries which derived enormous profits during the colonial period from exploiting, and which often still do exploit, the developing countries of today. On the other hand, it should not under any circumstances be required of the socialist countries, whose aid to the Third World cannot be regarded as a kind of indemnity tied to some fixed percentage.

solidarity which this situation brings out will not have too harmful an effect on international aid to education.

The only chance of a real increase in aid to education for the developing nations is the hope that economically advanced countries will heed the United Nations call and make a genuine effort, beginning not later than 1975, to make yearly transfers of resources equal to at least 1 per cent of their GNP.

In order to increase gradually the proportion of allocations to education and training in the total volume of aid, it would be necessary to:

Utilize country programming procedures to re-examine the place to be given to education aid in the total volume of transfers of financial resources allocated to development.

Include an educational component in every development project ('package project').

Ensure that governments of developing nations systematically require all foreign investors, public or private, to undertake the training of nationals employed on development projects.

4

New terms for action

If, as we believe, the time has really come for many countries to undertake a general reappraisal of their educational world and the challenges that education must face today and tomorrow; if it is admitted that educational activities should be conceived in a less pedestrian, but more realistic and innovative way; if it is true that piecemeal reform of existing systems will not suffice to build educational systems that meet present requirements, then international activities must also be given a second look.

The fact is that international initiative can no longer be confined to areas in which it has so long chosen to operate, such as qualitative improvements, teacher training, adult-literacy campaigns, etc. It must gradually extend its scope to cover, above all, the search for alternatives to existing institutions, the examination of new pedagogic experiments, joint action for innovation.

Even though the volume of foreign aid may be marginal, this does not mean that it cannot play an important role, provided that it is tailored to meet the most pressing needs.

To change the orientation of aid to education, the world community must spur national authorities to make an inventory of all educational activities carried out in their countries, to fix their goals and identify possible alternatives to reach them.

Educational development centres and other such organizations can be of invaluable help in this respect. As things stand today, the creation of institutions of this sort ought to be given priority in international assistance, without neglecting other needs. In the same way, aid should preferably be directed to 'points of entry' most likely to produce a chain reaction. *The spirit of invention*

With aid channelled largely towards innovation, countries will have to call for new services: participation in the costs of expensive experiments, dispatch of multidisciplinary teams of highly qualified experts who can help work out new alternatives, supply of sophisticated technical equipment, training of specialists in areas such as computer-assisted instruction, advanced documentation techniques, organization of new types of teaching and study centres, modern techniques for measuring behavioural patterns, curriculum design, preparation of teaching aids, etc.

Hand in hand with this reorientation of international aid there should be a radical transformation of the relations between 'givers' and 'receivers', between the foreign 'expert' and his local counterpart. These relations must be replaced by partnership, a working together in search of new ways—sharing not just costs, but the risks of the undertaking, for innovation is not possible without risk in an area as complex and hazardous as education.

The time has come to take a big step forward, not merely on the operational plane, but on the level of ideas and ideals as well.

International co-operation and assistance must become imbued with a spirit of reform, innovation, invention, creation. This is the only way to prevent a future committee, called upon ten years from now to give an account of the Second Development Decade, from repeating, on the subject of education programmes, what a group entrusted with summing up the achievements of the First Decade said, 'that they tried diligently to spread the best of what the pedagogues knew, to develop the old models at a faster rate, but that there was a marked reluctance to challenge the conventional wisdom'.

We hope:
That multilateral and bilateral bodies financing and assisting education will give priority to a new type of project to help countries

make an over-all diagnosis of education, draw up a list of objectives and identify 'points of entry' designed to produce the most effect on systems, content and methods.

That bilateral and multilateral aid will concentrate more on the creation and financing of institutions capable of implementing alternative strategies, and on the establishment of the infrastructure for continuous educational reforms.

That developed countries agree to defray—even under already existing international assistance schemes—some of the operational costs of research and development of new methods and programmes, as well as investment expenditures on costly, modern, educational techniques and technologies originating from industrial societies.

That the developed and developing countries will establish systematic exchanges of data and experience to facilitate the choices to be made and encourage, on all sides, the spirit of creativity so vital in a phase of innovation.

That the international community will finance a larger number of experimental projects calculated to enrich the world store of new experience rather than reproducing stereotyped activities and, as far as possible, replace laboratory experiments by field experiments and pilot projects carried out in exceptional conditions by experimental projects operating in the normal conditions of the country.

That international aid will be designed not to provide consumer goods but to create or develop productive potential; not to deliver prefabricated schools, but to help set up a national construction industry; not to furnish paper, but to assist in establishing a national paper industry, etc.

In short, we hope that international co-operation will concentrate on inventing and spreading innovations; it should move in this direction now, if the search for new solutions is not to be unduly postponed.

5

Political determination, exchanges, resources

Throughout this report we have recommended measures for solving present and future problems in education which on the whole may be regarded as innovations, although some may see them as timid and conservative. We have tried to show that even the richest countries, materially speaking, are not immune from serious problems which they will only be able to overcome through political determination and great imaginative effort. We have not hidden from the fact that adopting such measures, even by countries most determined to break the vicious circle of educational underdevelopment, implies political and socio-economic options of a structural nature, and that their execution will run into great difficulties.

It is obvious that national political considerations will determine whether education undertakes its own renewal in the context of each country's particular conditions and requirements. But the fact remains that for most countries this political will cannot in itself be enough to overcome all present difficulties and solve all problems related to reform or change of their educational structures.

All countries without exception must take advantage of others' experience, must increase contacts and be receptive to everything being done elsewhere. But countries lacking resources and trained professional personnel require appropriate external aid.

In addition to the determination and intrinsic effort of each country—the prime necessity—co-operation and solidarity on a world-wide scale are unquestionably the second condition for success.

Yet, as far as one can see, it appears that facilities for international assistance (whether in bilateral or multilateral co-operation, present-day programmes of existing organs or even the scope of their operations) can never suffice, as things now stand, to help developing countries solve their basic problems, if one agrees that solutions involve not partial running repairs but a profound structural overhaul of their educational systems and extensive use of educational technology.

We all agree that neither the forms of present bilateral and multilateral aid nor the resources available to it—and even the concepts which inspire it—are equal to the educational needs confronting the international community.

Following an examination of this state of affairs, various possible remedies emerged.

Some of us are of the opinion that it is not necessary to create new programmes, centres or special funds in order to introduce innovations—the importance of which we recognize and welcome—into education. Those in question believe that a reasonable balance must be reached between innovation in education and the tried and tested present-day educational models, and this requires proposals aimed at reorganizing and redistributing programmes, centres and

261

existing means in a new way, so that they correspond more closely to educational needs in the years to come.

International Programme for Educational Innovation

Others among us, on the contrary, have devised a method which would appear to deserve attention. It would involve launching an international programme[1] aimed solely at providing scientific, technical and financial aid for States wishing to explore new educational paths and to modernize education, but lacking the resources and organizational machinery necessary to the methodical preparation of innovative strategies, the examination of alternatives and their practical execution. Even countries with plentiful resources could benefit from activities under this programme following appropriate and specific financial arrangements.

This international programme should provide the technical equipment necessary for introducing new educational technologies, for modernizing education, developing programmed instruction, and for installing television in unserved areas (through satellite relays, transmitting stations and provision of a minimum number of receivers in each community). The programme should have no say in the preparation or contents of educational programmes, responsibility for which obviously lies entirely with national authorities and others directly concerned. It would be normal for developing countries to be spared a substantial share of the initial investment costs, on the assumption that afterwards they would, without too much financial strain, bear the costs of running the equipment that has been installed.

In the minds of those of us who advocate it, this international programme for educational innovations would be the mechanism best adapted to meet the new tasks with which the world is faced.

Some of us reviewed the possible sources of financing such a programme. From this examination, it appears it could be funded through resources that international agencies and organisms might place at its disposal, through governmental subsidies which could be created by making budget cuts, and by private contributions.

In the opinion of some members of the commission, however, financing the international programme should be done primarily through channelling into it budget savings equivalent to a fixed percentage of military budgets. It is obvious, of course, that pro-

1. 'International Programme' should be understood to mean here an organism attached to an existing international institution. Its mission would be to mobilize funds from various sources for specific and limited goals, and to assist countries at their request for specific activities engaging both governmental and non-governmental sectors. The World Food Programme is a precedent demonstrating the validity of this type of action.

gressive general disarmament would not only be a vital safeguard for humanity, but would release vast resources for the development of human society. Remote as such a prospect may appear to be, a decision to earmark funds from budgetary economies equal to a minimal part of military expenditures and allocate them to the development of education would certainly be noble evidence of the determination of peoples and their governments to undertake, without waiting for world-wide initiatives, the task of serving man, of freeing him culturally and spiritually and promoting his individual development.

We propose that agencies assisting education, national and international, private and public, review the present state of 'research and development' in education with a view to strengthening the capacities of individual countries to improve their present educational systems and to invent, design and test new educational experiments appropriate to their cultures and resources. We believe that if nations, regional bodies and assisting agencies make the strengthening of these capacities their first order of business over the next ten years, they will enable a number of countries to begin becoming true 'learning societies'.

Some of us propose that a detailed study be undertaken to establish the conditions in which it would be possible to set up an International Programme for Educational Innovations, attached to Unesco and placed under the control of a representative international body—a programme designed to help countries take a decisive step towards a renewal of their education systems.

Appendixes

Composition and
working methods of
the commission

In December 1970, by Resolution 1·131 adopted at its sixteenth session, the General Conference of Unesco authorized the Director-General to establish an International Commission on the Development of Education. The relevant sections of the resolution were:

The Director-General is authorized to prepare and present to Member States the necessary elements for reflection on educational strategies at the international level:

. . . .

(b) by establishing an International Commission on the Development of Education, publishing its report, presenting it with his comments to Member States, the Executive Board, the International Conference on Education and the General Conference, and taking it into consideration in formulating Unesco's future education programmes.

The Director-General appointed the commission in February 1971:

Edgar Faure, former French Prime Minister and former Minister of Education (Chairman of the commission).

Felipe Herrera (Chile), Professor, University of Chile, formerly President of the Inter-American Development Bank and Executive-Director of the International Monetary Fund.

Abdul-Razzak Kaddoura (Syrian Arab Republic), visiting scientist at the Nuclear Physics Laboratory, Oxford University, and member of the Board of Governors of the United Nations International Atomic Energy Agency.

Henri Lopes (People's Republic of the Congo), then Minister of Education and now Minister of Foreign Affairs.

Arthur Vladimirovitch Petrovsky (U.S.S.R.), Secretary of the Psychology and Physiology of Growth Section of the Academy of Pedagogical Sciences.

Majid Rahnema (Iran), formerly Minister of Higher Education and Sciences and Vice-President of the United Nations Economic and Social Council.

Frederick Champion Ward (United States), programme adviser on international education to the Ford Foundation and former Dean at the University of Chicago.

The commission was assisted in its work by a seven-man secretariat of Unesco staff members and outside consultants. The executive secretary was Aser Deleon (Unesco).

The Director-General gave the commission full intellectual autonomy in carrying out its mandate. He suggested general terms of reference (see Appendix 2), but the commission enjoyed complete freedom in establishing the contents of its report and in the organization and execution of its work.

The commission held six executive sessions in Paris during the period March 1971 to April 1972, meeting for a total of thirty days. At its first meeting, the commission agreed to the general terms of reference suggested to it and on methods to carry out its task. Principally, these were: (a) fact-finding missions to all regions of the world for exchange of views with political leaders and round-table discussions with education authorities (see Appendix 3); (b) visits to organizations within the United Nations System, regional institutions and foundations particularly concerned with educational problems (see Appendix 4); (c) attendance at international and regional meetings (see Appendix 4); (d) analysis of documents prepared especially for the commission by specialists on various aspects of education (see Appendix 5); and (e) consultations in executive session with specialists concerning particular educational problems (see Appendix 6).

During its fact-finding missions, carried out by two- and three-member teams, members of the commission had the opportunity to exchange views on educational perspectives with numerous heads of State, with Pope Paul VI, with ministers of education and other members of governments, high educational officials, scientists, researchers, heads of educational institutions, educators, learners, etc.

The commission submitted its report to the Director-General in May 1972.

APPENDIX 2

General terms of reference

1. The commission will draw up a report which the Director-General will submit, with his comments, to Member States, the Executive Board, the International Conference on Education and the General Conference. The purpose of the report will be to assist governments to formulate national strategies for the development of education. It could provide the starting-point for a series of studies and decisions at the national level. It will also serve to guide international co-operation in education, and Unesco's work in particular, during the Second United Nations Development Decade.

2. For the organization of its work the commission will no doubt first wish to establish certain guiding principles. It appears desirable in this connexion: (a) that the term 'education' should be taken in its broadest connotation of a coherent and deliberate action aimed at the transmission of knowledge, the development of aptitudes, and the training and betterment of man in all respects and throughout his life; (b) that quantitative expansion and qualitative improvement should be regarded as two complementary aspects of educational development; (c) that educational development should be studied within the framework of over-all integrated development; (d) that education should be envisaged as both an end in itself and a means of development; (e) that the work of the commission should cover both the developed and the developing countries.

3. On the basis of a critical analysis of the present situation, of the main trends observed during the last decades and of the experience acquired in different countries, the commission will no doubt be called upon to define the new aims to be assigned to education as a result of the rapid changes in knowledge and in societies, the demands of development, the aspirations of the individual, and the overriding need for international understanding and peace. In the light of those aims, it will put forward suggestions regarding the intellectual, human and financial means needed to attain the objectives set at the national level in the planning of the development of national educational systems within the context of economic, social and cultural development. For this the commission will propose criteria and will outline a methodology which governments could use to evolve national strategies suited to the different situations and to the different development objectives.

4. The commission may wish to study the means of ensuring an optimum contribution by education to development in the developing countries, through a typology based on certain major regional or national features.

5. The commission will be required to formulate recommendations for international co-operation viewed from its twofold aspect of intellectual co-operation, on the one hand, and of investments, financial aid and the provision of services and equipment on the other. It will no doubt wish to identify those sectors in which international and regional co-operation can have the greatest multiplying effect, the most desirable forms for that co-operation and the new fields to which it should be applied.

APPENDIX 3

Countries visited by members of the commission

Algeria	German Democratic Republic	Tanzania
Cameroon	Hungary	U.S.S.R.
Chile	Kenya	United Kingdom
Cuba	Lebanon	United States
Arab Republic of Egypt	Mexico	of America
Ethiopia	Peru	Yugoslavia
France	Senegal	Zaire
Federal Republic of Germany	Singapore	
	Sweden	

Visits to international and regional organizations, and meetings

The following organizations were visited by members of the commission:

United Nations
United Nations Development
   Programme (UNDP)
International Labour Office (ILO)
Food and Agriculture Organization
   of the United Nations (FAO)
United Nations Children's Fund
   (UNICEF)
World Health Organization (WHO)
Inter-American Development Bank
   (IDB)

International Bank for Reconstruction
   and Development (IBRD)
Economic Commission for Africa
   (ECA)
Organisation for Economic
   Co-operation and Development
   (OECD)
League of Arab States
Organization of American States
   (OAS)
Organization of African Unity (OAU)

The following meetings were attended by members of the commission:

The International Conference on Education, 33rd Session, Geneva, 15 to 23 September 1971.

Third Regional Conference of Ministers of Education and those Responsible for Economic Planning in Asia, Singapore, 31 May to 7 June 1971.

Final Session of the Symposium on Educational Innovations in Africa—Policies and Administration (organized by ISS/CESO in co-operation with ECA), Addis Ababa, September 1971.

Advisory Panel on Programme Policy on UNDP Activities in the Field of Education and Training, Geneva, 7 December 1971.

Documents prepared for the use of the commission

Almost all of these documents, prepared for the commission and used for its report, have been issued in a mimeographed form and sent to all Member States of Unesco, to international organizations and numerous institutes.

Extracts from these documents will be published as a second volume of the commission's report.

Series A: Situation

1. A Summary Statistical Review of Education in the World	Leo Goldstone
2. Education, Development and Employment	ILO
3. Educational Objectives and Prospects in the Various Regions of the World	José Blat Gimeno
4. The Current Teacher Training Situation	Jiri Kotasek
5. Les Politiques d'Éducation (French only)	René Ochs

Series B: Opinions

1. The Need for a New Strategy of Educational Development	Philip H. Coombs
2. Where is Education Heading?	Carlos Delgado
3. Educational Systems and the New Demands	Henri Janne and M. L. Roggemans
4. Where is Education Heading?	A.I.Markouchevitch and A. V. Petrovsky
5. Education: Present and Future	Mahmoud Messadi
6. Where is Education Heading?	Jean Piaget
7. Ends and Objectives in Education	Christopher M. Labani
8. The Democratization of Secondary Education	Edmund J. King
9. The Need for Physical Education	Rt Hon. Philip Noel-Baker
10. Factors Influencing the Development of Education in the Arab Countries	Abdullah Abdel Dayem (ASCATEP)

44. Methodology of Educational Futurology   W. W. Harman and M. E. Rosenberg
45. Necessary School Reforms, as Seen by an Out-of-school Educator   Marcel Hicter
46. Education from the Point of View of the Young   Thierry Lemaresquier
47. Education: the User's Point of View   Carlos E. Ramos
48. International Cooperation in Education   Iichi Sagara
49. International Cooperation in Education   H. M. Phillips
50. The Generation Gap and International Development   Felipe Herrera
51. Education and Social Change   A. H. Halsey
52. Education for Developing Countries in a World in Transition   D. S. Kothari
53. Conditions Conducive to Educational Innovation   Jean Thomas
54. L'Éducation dans la Perspective des Trente Prochaines Années (French only)   Giovanni Gozzer
55. Méthodes de Révision des Objectifs Éducatifs (French only)   R. Hennion

Series C: Innovations

1. Tendances Actuelles (French only)   S. Lourié and A. Deleon
2. Neurosciences and Education   Robert B. Livingston
3. Television for Preschool Children ('Sesame Street', United States)
4. Innovating Experiments in Education in Cuba   Raúl Ferrer Perez
5. New Educational Technology   Michael Schmidbauer
6. A National Innovation Strategy (Ivory Coast)   Jean-Claude Pauvert
7. New Trends in Adult Education   Henri Janne and M. L. Roggemans
8. Education and the Computer   Claude Saury and Michel Scholl
9. Use of Auxiliaries in Education   Robert M. McClure
10. Primary Education (England and Wales)   Leonard Clark
11. Intensive Educational District Development Projects (India)   S. N. Saraf
12. Integration of Educational Programming and Technical Programming (Iran)   Pierre Furter
13. Educational Reform (People's Republic of China)   Léon Vandermeersch
14. Reform of Primary Education (U.S.S.R.)   Yuri Ivanov
15. Projet d'Éducation Permanente (Alberta, Canada) (French only)
16. Computer Innovations in Education   Andrew R. Molnar

Appendixes

17. The Free Progress Experiment (Pondicherry,   G. Monod-Herzen
    India)   and J. Benezech
18. Alternative Educational Strategies (Rwanda)   Jan Auerhan
19. Rôle des Entreprises dans l'Éducation (United Irène Chedaux
    States) (French only)
20. Innovations dans l'Enseignement Secondaire   Bertrand Schwartz
    (French only)
21. Physical Education, Sport and Open-air Activities René Bazennerye

APPENDIX 6

Outside participants in commission meetings

Third meeting (12–16 July 1971)	James A. Perkins Chairman, International Council of Educational Development (New York)
	Philip H. Coombs Vice-Chairman, International Council of Educational Development (New York)
	Bogdan Suchodolski President, International Association for the Sciences of Education
	Raymond Poignant Director, International Institute for Educational Planning (Paris)
Fourth meeting (4–8 October 1971)	Michel Debeauvais Associate Professor at the Vincennes University Centre (France)
	Sylvain Lourié Director, Division of Educational Planning and Administration (Unesco)
Students	M. Dieme (Senegal) Thomas Forstenzer (United States) Claude Mariage (France)
Representatives of *youth organizations*	Mark Amen World Student Christian Federation
	Michel Jouet Secretary-General World Federation of Democratic Youth

Ahmed Mahi
International Union of Students

Jyoto Shankar Singh
Secretary-General
World Assembly of Youth

Fifth meeting
(6–14 March 1972)

Philippe Blamont
Director, International Centre for
Advanced Technical and Vocational
Training (Turin)

L. Emmerij
Deputy Chief, Employment Planning
and Promotion Department
International Labour Office

H. Quednau
Chief, Human Resources Department
International Labour Office

H. K. F. Hoffmann
Rural Institutions Division
Food and Agriculture Organization
of the United Nations

André Duffaure
Director, National Union of Rural
Family Hostels for Education and
Guidance

Educational statistics

Geographical definitions. If not otherwise indicated, *World total* covers the whole world, including Unesco Member States, non-member States and non-self-governing territories. *Africa* covers the entire African continent, including the Arab States of Africa. *Northern America* includes the United States, Canada, Bermuda, Greenland and St Pierre and Miquelon. *Latin America* covers the South American continent, Central America, Mexico and the Caribbean. *Asia* covers the entire Asian region, including the Arab States of Asia. *Europe and U.S.S.R.* covers all European countries and includes the whole territory of the U.S.S.R. *Oceania* covers Australia, New Zealand and the surrounding islands. The *Arab States* as a separate grouping are always presented in parentheses as they are already included partly under Africa and partly under Asia.

Sources. The source for the population tables (Tables 1 and 2) is the United Nations Statistical Office.

Data on enrolment and teachers (Tables 3 to 10) are based on Unesco Office of Statistics questionnaires which are dispatched annually, and national publications. The great majority of the data are actual figures reported by the individual countries. For a limited number of countries, however, estimates were made by the Unesco Office of Statistics to obtain a regional or a world total.

The tables on adult literacy (Tables 11 and 12) are estimates made by the Unesco Office of Statistics, on the basis of national questionnaires sent to the United Nations Statistical Office.

Data on public expenditure on education (Tables 13 to 15) are based on questionnaire returns by Member States to the Unesco Office of Statistics. The conversion of national currencies into United States dollars was made by the Unesco Office of Statistics. Official exchange rates were used for most of the national totals. Alternative rates, based on rough purchasing power equivalents, were used for the centrally planned economy countries and for several countries in Latin America and Asia for which official rates appeared to yield unrealistic dollar equivalents. The expenditure data thus expressed in United States dollars should therefore be interpreted with great caution.

279

Appendixes

TABLE 1. Population by age group, 1960 and 1968 (in thousands)

Major regions		Total	Age group				
			0–4	5–9	10–14	15–19	20–24
World total	1960	2,981,621	429,002	368,418	317,578	269,301	252,248
	1968	3,491,938	487,015	423,662	385,870	339,590	289,281
Africa	1960	269,577	47,259	37,381	31,817	27,510	23,786
	1968	327,312	58,197	45,958	38,755	33,306	28,569
Northern America	1960	198,675	22,611	20,861	18,661	14,856	12,346
	1968	222,179	21,590	22,843	22,159	20,196	17,357
Latin America	1960	213,422	35,692	29,703	24,907	20,946	12,346
	1968	267,668	44,024	37,351	32,172	27,178	22,665
Asia	1960	1,645,390	259,352	219,646	186,811	160,845	143,768
	1968	1,963,407	299,981	253,653	230,169	200,321	169,861
Europe and U.S.S.R.	1960	638,801	62,176	59,122	53,805	43,880	53,325
	1968	692,764	61,104	61,823	60,736	56,876	49,324
Oceania	1960	15,756	1,912	1,705	1,577	1,264	1,090
	1968	18,608	2,119	2,034	1,879	1,713	1,505
(Arab States)	1960	(93,566)	(16,466)	(13,216)	(11,219)	(9,572)	(8,171)
	1968	(117,271)	(21,365)	(16,929)	(14,140)	(11,967)	(10,142)

TABLE 2. Population by age group, 1960–65 and 1968 (percentage increase)

Major regions		Total	Age group				
			0–4	5–9	10–14	15–19	20–24
World total	1960–65	1·96	1·26	2·02	2·69	3·03	0·92
	1968	2·02	2·17	1·32	2·03	2·73	3·09
Africa	1960–65	2·35	2·57	2·45	2·42	2·34	2·24
	1968	2·59	2·70	2·84	2·58	2·50	2·41
Northern America	1960–65	1·52	0·08	1·77	2·37	4·74	3·97
	1968	1·21	−1·66	0·08	1·80	2·37	4·85
Latin America	1960–65	2·83	2·60	2·99	3·30	3·16	2·76
	1968	2·87	2·70	2·69	3·08	3·48	3·26
Asia	1960–65	2·18	1·22	2·14	2·95	2·71	1·73
	1968	2·32	2·87	1·30	2·13	2·94	2·72
Europe and U.S.S.R.	1960–65	1·12	0·0	0·93	1·94	4·16	−3·86
	1968	0·86	−0·61	0·07	0·83	1·90	4·06
Oceania	1960–65	2·12	1·59	2·45	2·06	4·86	5·65
	1968	2·03	0·81	1·80	2·45	2·03	4·81
(Arab States)	1960–65	(2·74)	(3·33)	(3·01)	(2·80)	(2·71)	(2·53)
	1968	(3·09)	(3·27)	(3·39)	(3·16)	(3·02)	(3·10)

280

TABLE 3. Total enrolment (in thousands) by level of education, 1960 and 1965–68

Major regions		Total Number	Total Percentage increase	First level Number	First level Percentage increase	Second level[1] Number	Second level[1] Percentage increase	Third level Number	Third level Percentage increase
World total[2]	1960	323,587	–	243,487	–	68,926	–	11,174	–
	1965	411,132	4·9	299,337	4·2	93,788	6·4	18,007	10·0
	1966	428,405	4·2	311,700	4·1	96,713	3·1	19,992	11·0
	1967	443,619	3·6	320,814	2·9	101,268	4·7	21,538	7·7
	1968	459,599	3·6	330,832	3·1	105,651	4·5	23,115	7·3
Africa	1960	21,238	–	18,931	–	2,115	–	192	–
	1965	29,861	7·1	25,924	6·5	3,615	11·3	322	10·9
	1966	30,975	3·7	26,748	3·2	3,893	7·7	334	3·7
	1967	32,758	5·8	28,028	4·8	4,373	12·3	358	7·2
	1968	34,421	5·1	29,322	4·6	4,715	7·8	383	7·0
Northern America	1960	48,719	–	28,838	–	16,156	–	3,725	–
	1965	57,370	3·3	32,855	2·6	18,665	2·9	5,850	9·4
	1966	59,187	3·2	33,606	2·3	18,855	1·0	6,726	15·0
	1967	60,269	1·8	33,360	−0·7	19,547	3·7	7,362	9·5
	1968	61,866	2·6	33,201	−0·5	20,674	5·8	7,991	8·5
Latin America	1960	31,425	–	26,973	–	3,885	–	567	–
	1965	42,290	6·1	34,704	5·1	6,694	11·5	892	9·5
	1966	45,099	6·6	36,653	5·6	7,468	11·6	978	9·6
	1967	47,758	5·9	38,288	4·5	8,365	12·0	1,105	13·0
	1968	50,851	6·5	40,751	6·4	8,847	5·8	1,253	13·4
Asia[2]	1960	110,691	–	87,236	–	21,325	–	2,131	–
	1965	148,301	6·0	113,876	5·5	30,703	7·6	3,722	11·8
	1966	157,802	6·4	121,516	6·7	32,105	4·6	4,181	12·3
	1967	164,194	4·1	126,880	4·4	32,724	1·9	4,590	9·8
	1968	171,437	4·4	132,567	4·5	33,962	3·8	4,908	6·9
Europe and U.S.S.R.	1960	108,208	–	79,106	–	24,644	–	4,457	–
	1965	129,343	3·6	89,329	2·5	32,983	6·0	7,031	9·6
	1966	131,237	1·5	90,458	1·3	33,214	0·7	7,565	7·6
	1967	134,400	2·4	91,475	1·1	35,018	5·4	7,907	4·5
	1968	136,615	1·6	92,142	0·7	36,112	3·1	8,361	5·7
Oceania	1960	3,306	–	2,403	–	801	–	102	–
	1965	3,967	3·7	2,649	2·0	1,128	7·1	190	13·2
	1966	4,105	3·5	2,719	2·6	1,178	4·4	208	9·5
	1967	4,240	3·3	2,783	2·4	1,241	5·3	216	3·8
	1968	4,409	4·0	2,849	2·4	1,341	8·1	219	1·4
(Arab States)	1960	(8,585)	(–)	(7,177)	(–)	(1,248)	(–)	(160)	(–)
	1965	(12,613)	(8·0)	(10,034)	(6·9)	(2,290)	(12·9)	(288)	(12·6)
	1966	(13,122)	(4·0)	(10,300)	(2·7)	(2,527)	(10·3)	(295)	(2·1)
	1967	(13,748)	(4·8)	(10,708)	(4·0)	(2,734)	(8·2)	(306)	(3·7)
	1968	(14,396)	(4·7)	(11,016)	(2·9)	(3,041)	(11·2)	(339)	(10·8)

1. General and vocational education and teacher training.
2. Not including the People's Republic of China, the Democratic People's Republic of Korea and the Democratic Republic of Viet-Nam.

281

Appendixes

TABLE 4. Total enrolment by level of education, annual rate of increase for the period 1960–68

Major regions	Total	First level	Second level	Third level
World total[1]	4·5	3·9	5·5	9·5
Africa	6·2	5·6	10·5	9·0
Northern America	3·0	1·8	3·1	10·0
Latin America	6·2	5·3	10·8	10·4
Asia[1]	5·6	5·4	6·0	11·0
Europe and U.S.S.R.	3·0	1·9	4·9	8·2
Oceania	3·7	2·2	6·6	10·0
(Arab States)	(6·6)	(5·5)	(11·8)	(9·8)

1. Not including the People's Republic of China, the Democratic People's Republic of Korea and the Democratic Republic of Viet-Nam.

282

TABLE 5. Enrolment in pre-primary education (public and private), 1961 and 1965–68 (in thousands)

Major regions		Total	Percent-age increase	Public	Percent-age increase	Private	Percent-age increase	Private as percentage of total
				Breakdown of total				
World total[1]	1961	24,671	–	11,847	–	12,824	–	52·0
	1965	30,256	5·2	15,875	7·8	14,381	2·9	47·5
	1966	32,034	5·9	16,899	6·5	15,135	5·2	47·2
	1967	34,004	6·1	17,811	5·4	16,193	7·0	47·6
	1968	35,780	5·2	18,589	4·4	17,191	6·2	48·0
Africa	1961	129	–	32	–	97	–	75·2
	1965	147	3·3	32	–	115	4·4	78·2
	1966	162	10·2	40	25·0	122	6·1	75·3
	1967	171	5·6	42	5·0	129	5·7	75·4
	1968	180	5·3	47	11·9	133	3·1	73·9
Northern America	1961	2,452	–	2,069	–	383	–	15·7
	1965	2,974	4·9	2,465	4·5	509	7·3	17·1
	1966	3,098	4·2	2,546	3·3	552	8·4	17·8
	1967	3,270	5·6	2,688	5·6	582	5·4	17·8
	1968	3,413	4·4	2,809	4·5	604	3·8	17·7
Latin America	1961	996	–	685	–	311	–	31·2
	1965	1,284	6·6	914	7·5	370	4·4	28·8
	1966	1,368	9·6	980	7·2	388	4·9	28·4
	1967	1,429	4·5	1,018	3·9	411	5·9	28·8
	1968	1,613	12·9	1,122	10·2	491	19·5	30·4
Asia[1]	1961	10,149	–	658	–	9,491	–	93·5
	1965	11,184	2·5	871	7·3	10,313	2·1	92·2
	1966	11,816	5·7	940	7·9	10,876	5·5	92·0
	1967	12,773	8·1	1,018	8·3	11,755	8·1	92·0
	1968	13,700	7·3	1,074	5·5	12,626	7·4	92·2
Europe and U.S.S.R.	1961	10,884	–	8,403	–	2,481	–	22·8
	1965	14,584	7·6	11,593	8·4	2,991	4·8	20·5
	1966	15,502	6·3	12,393	6·9	3,109	3·9	20·1
	1967	16,268	4·9	13,045	5·3	3,223	3·7	19·8
	1968	16,773	3·1	13,536	3·8	3,237	0·4	19·3
Oceania	1961	61	–	–	–	61	–	100·0
	1965	83	8·0	0·3	–	83	8·0	99·6
	1966	88	6·0	0·2	–	88	6·0	99·8
	1967	93	5·7	0·4	–	93	5·7	99·6
	1968	101	8·6	0·5	–	100	7·5	99·5
(Arab States)	1961	(183)	–	(31)	–	(152)	–	83·1
	1965	(187)	0·6	(20)	10·4	(166)	2·2	89·3
	1966	(206)	10·2	(22)	10·0	(184)	10·8	89·3
	1967	(219)	6·3	(22)	–	(197)	7·1	90·0
	1968	(230)	5·0	(22)	–	(208)	5·6	90·4

1. Not including the People's Republic of China, the Democratic People's Republic of Korea and the Democratic Republic of Viet-Nam.

Appendixes

TABLE 6. Female enrolment (in thousands) by level of education, 1960 and 1967–68

Major regions		Total		First level		Second level[1]		Third level	
		Number	Percent-age increase	Number	Percent-age increase	Number	Percent-age increase	Number	Percent-age increase
World total[2]	1960	140,200	–	106,443	–	29,985	–	3,772	–
	1967	192,739	3·5	140,744	2·7	43,984	4·8	8,011	9·7
	1968	199,706	3·6	145,077	3·1	45,954	4·5	8,675	8·3
Africa	1960	7,630	–	6,935	–	657	–	39	–
	1967	12,481	7·2	11,007	6·2	1,390	15·6	84	10·5
	1968	13,166	5·5	11,583	5·2	1,491	7·3	92	9·5
Northern America	1960	23,446	–	13,995	–	8,083	–	1,368	–
	1967	28,867	1·9	16,193	−0·7	9,721	3·9	2,953	10·8
	1968	29,598	2·5	16,117	−0·5	10,260	5·5	3,221	9·1
Latin America	1960	15,154	–	13,157	–	1,817	–	180	–
	1967	23,002	5·8	18,635	4·3	4,006	12·5	361	16·5
	1968	24,533	6·7	19,879	6·7	4,242	5·9	412	14·1
Asia[2]	1960	40,908	–	32,974	–	7,437	–	497	–
	1967	61,939	3·7	49,177	4·2	11,473	0·8	1,289	11·6
	1968	64,697	4·5	51,415	4·6	11,893	3·7	1,389	7·8
Europe and U.S.S.R.	1960	51,549	–	38,232	–	11,657	–	1,659	–
	1967	64,564	2·5	44,416	1·0	16,886	5·7	3,262	7·3
	1968	65,702	1·8	44,729	0·7	17,478	3·5	3,495	7·1
Oceania	1960	1,513	–	1,150	–	334	–	29	–
	1967	1,886	2·8	1,316	1·9	508	5·2	62	5·1
	1968	2,011	6·6	1,354	2·9	590	16·1	66	6·5
(Arab States)	1960	(2,765)	(–)	(2,423)	(–)	(313)	(–)	(30)	(–)
	1967	(4,661)	(5·9)	(3,824)	(4·6)	(770)	(12·7)	(67)	(8·1)
	1968	(4,883)	(4·8)	(3,938)	(3·0)	(873)	(13·4)	(72)	(7·5)

1. General and vocational education and teacher training.
2. Not including the People's Republic of China, the Democratic People's Republic of Korea and the Democratic Republic of Viet-Nam.

TABLE 7. Female enrolment by level of education, annual rate of increase for the period 1960–68

Major regions	Total	First level	Second level	Third level
World total	4·5	4·0	5·5	11·0
Africa	7·1	6·6	10·8	11·3
Northern America	2·9	1·8	3·0	11·3
Latin America	6·2	5·3	11·2	10·9
Asia[1]	5·9	5·7	6·1	13·7
Europe and U.S.S.R.	3·1	2·0	5·2	9·8
Oceania	3·6	2·1	7·4	10·8
(Arab States)	(7·4)	(6·3)	(13·7)	(11·6)

1. Not including the People's Republic of China, the Democratic People's Republic of Korea and the Democratic Republic of Viet-Nam.

TABLE 8. Number of teachers (in thousands) by level of education, 1960 and 1967–68

Major regions		Total		First level		Second level[1]		Third level	
		Number	Percent-age increase	Number	Percent-age increase	Number	Percent-age increase	Number	Percent-age increase
World total[2]	1960	12,598	–	8,176	–	3,527	–	894	–
	1967	17,455	3·9	10,403	2·7	5,503	5·4	1,548	7·3
	1968	18,239	4·5	10,769	3·5	5,813	5·6	1,647	6·4
Africa	1960	598	–	480	–	106	–	12	–
	1967	925	6·3	700	4·6	197	13·2	28	6·9
	1968	973	5·2	730	4·3	212	7·6	31	4·5
Northern America	1960	1,932	–	990	–	623	–	319	–
	1967	2,794	4·6	1,254	3·0	1,010	5·5	530	6·9
	1968	2,910	4·2	1,295	3·3	1,061	5·1	554	4·5
Latin America	1960	1,175	–	782	–	330	–	62	–
	1967	1,920	5·3	1,185	2·9	601	9·7	134	8·9
	1968	2,038	6·1	1,257	6·1	634	5·5	147	9·7
Asia[2]	1960	4,007	–	2,868	–	975	–	164	–
	1967	5,469	3·4	3,562	2·9	1,580	3·2	327	10·1
	1968	5,714	4·5	3,708	4·1	1,652	4·6	354	8·3
Europe and U.S.S.R.	1960	4,754	–	2,978	–	1,447	–	328	–
	1967	6,163	3·4	3,603	2·1	2,047	5·2	513	6·0
	1968	6,409	4·0	3,676	2·0	2,180	6·4	553	7·8
Oceania	1960	133	–	78	–	46	–	9	–
	1967	184	0·5	99	–	69	1·5	16	–
	1968	195	6·0	103	4·0	74	7·2	18	12·5
(Arab States)	1960	(269)	(–)	(191)	(–)	(70)	(–)	(8)	(–)
	1967	(453)	(5·8)	(303)	(4·8)	(135)	(8·0)	(15)	(7·1)
	1968	(483)	(6·6)	(324)	(6·9)	(142)	(5·2)	(17)	(13·3)

1. General and vocational education and teacher training.
2. Not including the People's Republic of China, the Democratic People's Republic of Korea and the Democratic Republic of Viet-Nam.

TABLE 9. Number of teachers by level of education, annual rate of increase for the period 1960–68

Major regions	Total	First level	Second level	Third level
World total[1]	4·7	3·5	6·4	7·9
Africa	6·3	5·4	9·1	12·6
Northern America	5·3	3·4	6·9	7·1
Latin America	7·1	6·1	8·5	11·4
Asia[1]	4·5	3·3	6·8	10·1
Europe and U.S.S.R.	3·8	2·7	5·3	6·7
Oceania	4·9	3·5	6·1	9·0
(Arab States)	(7·6)	(6·8)	(9·2)	(9·9)

1. Not including the People's Republic of China, the Democratic People's Republic of Korea and the Democratic Republic of Viet-Nam.

TABLE 10. School enrolment ratios by level of education, 1960/61 and 1967/68 (provisional)

Major regions	1960/61				1967/68			
	Percentage of children of primary school age attending school at any level	Percentage of children of secondary school age attending school at any level	Percentage of children of primary and secondary school age (combined) attending school at any level	Third level enrolment as percentage of population aged 20–24	Percentage of children of primary school age attending school at any level	Percentage of children of secondary school age attending school at any level	Percentage of children of primary and secondary school age (combined) attending school at any level	Third level enrolment as percentage of population aged 20–24
World total[1]	63	52	50	5.9	68	39	56	10.1
Africa	34	12	24	0.8	40	15	28	1.3
Northern America	98	90	94	30.2	98	92	96	44.5
Latin America	60	26	45	3.1	75	35	55	5.0
Asia[1]	50	22	36	2.6	55	30	45	4.7
Europe and U.S.S.R.	96	57	79	8.5	97	65	85	16.7
Oceania	95	50	75	10.1	95	60	80	15.0
(Arab States)	(38)	(16)	(28)	(2.1)	(50)	(25)	(38)	(3.1)

1. Not including the People's Republic of China, the Democratic People's Republic of Korea and the Democratic Republic of Viet-Nam.

TABLE 11. Adult literacy around 1960 and 1970 (in thousands)

Major regions	Around 1960				Around 1970			
	Adult population 15 years old and over	Literate adults	Illiterate adults	Illiteracy (percentage)	Adult population 15 years old and over	Literate adults	Illiterate adults	Illiteracy (percentage)
World total	1,870,000	1,134,000	735,000	39.3	2,287,000	1,504,000	783,000	34.2
Africa	153,000	29,000	124,000	81.0	194,000	51,100	143,000	73.7
Northern America	136,000	133,000	3,300	2.4	161,000	158,000	2,500	1.5
Latin America	123,000	83,100	40,000	32.5	163,000	125,000	38,600	23.6
Asia	982,000	440,000	542,000	55.2	1,237,000	658,000	579,000	46.8
Europe and U.S.S.R.	464,000	439,000	24,500	5.3	521,000	502,000	18,700	3.6
Oceania	10,600	9,400	1,200	11.5	13,000	11,800	1,400	10.3
(Arab States)	(52,700)	(9,900)	(42,700)	(81.1)	(68,300)	(18,400)	(49,900)	(73.0)

TABLE 12. Adult literacy (males and females) around 1960 and 1970 (in thousands)

Major regions	Around 1960				Around 1970			
	Adult population 15 years old and over	Literate adults	Illiterate adults	Illiteracy (percentage)	Adult population 15 years old and over	Literate adults	Illiterate adults	Illiteracy (percentage)
MALES								
World total	916,000	609,000	307,000	33·5	1,127,000	812,000	315,000	28·0
Africa	75,900	20,200	55,800	73·4	96,000	35,100	60,900	63·4
Northern America	66,800	65,600	1,300	1·9	78,000	77,200	850	1·1
Latin America	61,300	44,000	17,400	28·4	81,000	64,900	16,100	19·9
Asia	494,000	270,000	224,000	45·3	624,000	393,000	231,000	37·0
Europe and U.S.S.R.	213,000	205,000	7,700	3·6	243,000	237,000	5,800	2·4
Oceania	5,300	4,800	530	9·9	6,600	6,000	580	8·8
(Arab States)	(26,500)	(7,500)	(19,000)	(71·6)	(34,300)	(13,600)	(20,800)	(60·5)
FEMALES								
World total	953,000	525,000	428,000	44·9	1,160,000	692,000	468,000	40·3
Africa	77,000	8,800	68,200	88·5	97,900	16,000	82,000	83·7
Northern America	69,700	67,700	2,000	2·8	82,800	81,200	1,600	1·9
Latin America	61,800	39,200	22,600	36·6	82,200	59,700	22,500	27·3
Asia	488,000	170,000	318,000	65·1	614,000	266,000	348,000	56·7
Europe and U.S.S.R.	251,000	234,000	16,800	6·7	278,000	265,000	12,900	4·7
Oceania	5,200	4,500	680	13·0	6,500	5,800	780	11·9
(Arab States)	(26,200)	(2,400)	(23,800)	(90·7)	(33,900)	(4,800)	(29,100)	(85·7)

TABLE 13. Public expenditure on education, 1960 and 1965–68
(in million U.S. dollars, in current prices) revised

Major regions	1960	1965	1966	1967	1968
World total[1]	54,350	96,360	106,980	119,090	131,640
Africa	1,110	1,660	1,920	2,170	2,370
Northern America	22,670	39,740	44,050	49,940	56,510
Latin America	1,880	3,230	3,670	4,000	4,430
Asia[1]	3,710	7,380	8,370	9,470	10,660
Europe and U.S.S.R.	24,380	43,280	47,660	52,110	56,220
Oceania	600	1,070	1,310	1,400	1,450
(Arab States)	(700)	(1,020)	(1,100)	(1,210)	(1,340)
Developed countries	49,450	88,190	97,820	108,670	120,290
Developing countries	4,900	8,170	9,160	10,420	11,350

1. Not including the People's Republic of China, the Democratic People's Republic of Korea and the Democratic Republic of Viet-Nam.

TABLE 14. Public expenditure on education 1960–68 (annual increase as percentage; current prices) revised

Major regions	1960–65	1965–66	1966–67	1967–68	1960–68
World total[1]	12·1	11·0	11·3	10·5	11·7
Africa	8·4	15·7	13·0	9·2	10·0
Northern America	11·9	10·8	13·4	13·2	12·1
Latin America	11·4	13·6	9·0	10·8	11·3
Asia[1]	14·7	13·4	13·1	12·6	14·1
Europe and U.S.S.R.	12·2	10·1	9·3	7·9	11·0
Oceania	12·3	22·4	6·9	3·6	11·7
(Arab States)	(7·8)	(7·8)	(10·0)	(10·7)	(8·5)
Developed countries	12·3	10·9	11·1	10·7	11·8
Developing countries	10·8	12·2	13·8	8·9	11·1

1. Not including the People's Republic of China, the Democratic People's Republic of Korea and the Democratic Republic of Viet-Nam.

TABLE 15. Gross national product (GNP), military expenditure and
public expenditure on education and health, 1967 (absolute amounts
in United States dollars[1] and as percentage of GNP)

Major regions	GNP		Military expenditure		Public expenditure on education		Public expenditure on health	
	Million U.S.$	Percent-age	Million U.S.$	Percent-age	Million U.S.$	Percent-age	Million U.S.$	Percent-age
World total[2]	2,395,300	100	172,582	7·2	119,090	5·0	58,735	2·5
Africa	52,000	100	1,727	3·3	2,170	4·2	784	1·5
Northern America	850,900	100	77,301	9·1	49,940	5·9	19,662	2·3
Latin America	110,300	100	2,468	2·2	4,000	3·6	1,927	1·7
Asia[2]	249,600	100	7,150	2·9	9,470	3·8	1,263	0·5
Europe and U.S.S.R.	1,101,500	100	82,676	7·5	52,110	4·7	34,604	3·1
Oceania	31,000	100	1,260	4·1	1,400	4·5	495	1·6
(Arab States)	(25,900)	(100)	(1,854)	(7·2)	(1,210)	(4·7)	(583)	(2·3)
Developed countries	2,102,800	(100)	162,741	7·7	108,670	5·2	54,946	2·6
Developing countries	292,500	(100)	9,841	3·4	10,420	3·6	3,789	1·3

1. For the conversion from national currencies into United States dollars official exchange rates were used for most of the national totals. Alternative rates were used for the socialist countries and for several countries in Latin America and Asia for which official rates appeared to yield unrealistic equivalents. In addition, different conversion factors were used in some cases, for GNP, military expenditure, education expenditure and health expenditure in order to make the respective dollar values more comparable to United States values. The proportions of GNP of the various types of expenditure are consequently not fully comparable.
2. Not including the People's Republic of China, the Democratic People's Republic of Korea and the Democratic Republic of Viet-Nam.
Sources: GNP—estimates based on the relevant United Nations publications; military expenditure—United States Arms Control and Disarmament Agency, *World Military Expenditures 1969*, Washington, D.C.; education expenditure—Unesco questionnaire on educational finance and expenditure; health expenditure—World Health Organization, in *World Military Expenditure 1969*, op.cit.

Public expenditure on education

Note: Figures preceded by an asterisk (*) are estimates.

Country	As percentage of GNP	As percentage of total public expenditure	Country	As percentage of GNP	As percentage of total public expenditure
Afghanistan	...	...	Burma		
Albania	...	...	1967	2.9	18.0
Algeria			1968[1]	...	17.8
1967[1]	4.9[2]	18.7	1969[1]	...	17.6
1968	...	17.6	Burundi[4]		
1969	...	18.8	1967[7]	...	22.6
Argentina			1968	...	25.6
1967[1]	2.0	17.7	1969	...	29.1
1968[1]	2.0	21.0	Byelorussian S.S.R	...	...
1969[1]	2.0	...	Cameroon		
Australia			1967	2.9[2]	11.3
1967	3.7	11.0	1968	3.0[2]	18.6
1968	3.8	11.6	1969	3.4[2]	19.1
1969	4.0	12.0	Canada		
Austria			1967	7.6	21.6
1967	4.6	7.7	1968	7.9	...
1968	4.7	7.6	1969	8.3	...
1969	4.8	7.9	Central African Republic		
Bahrain			1967	*4.0[8]	18.9
1967	...	22.9	1968	*3.3	15.1
1968	...	23.3	1969	...	15.4
1969	...	25.4	Ceylon[4]		
Barbados			1967	4.4	13.0
1968	6.4[3]	21.3	1969	3.6	11.9
Belgium			Chad		
1967[1]	4.7	18.0	1969[4]	2.7	...
1968	5.0	...	Chile		
1969	5.4	20.6	1967[1]	3.5	...
Bolivia[4]			1968[4]	4.9	...
1967	3.5	29.3	1969[4]	4.6	10.6
1968	3.2	26.1	People's Republic of China	...	...
1969	3.1	26.2	Colombia		
Brazil			1967	2.4	23.7
1967	*3.0	13.0	1968[1]	1.5	12.5
1968	3.0	...	1969[1]	1.7	12.7
1969[5]	3.0	15.2	People's Republic of the Congo		
Bulgaria			1967[7]	...	18.2
1967	4.4[6]	...	1968	6.4[2]	21.7
1968	4.5[6]	...	1969	...	24.2
1969	4.7[6]	...			

Country	As percentage of GNP	As percentage of total public expenditure	Country	As percentage of GNP	As percentage of total public expenditure
Costa Rica			1969[4]	2·0	10·7
1967	5·7	35·4	Guatemala[4]		
1968	5·7	34·1	1967	1·9	16·2
1969	6·4	35·0	1968	1·9	16·4
Cuba[1]	...	...	1969	1·9	17·5
Cyprus[9]			Guinea		
1967	2·4	15·5	1969	...	20·8
1968	2·8	16·5	Guyana		
1969	2·5	14·8	1967[4]	4·8	14·9
Czechoslovakia			1968[4]	4·8	14·7
1967	4·6[6]	7·4	1969[4]	4·7	13·1
1968	4·7[6]	8·0	Haiti	...	...
1969	4·5[6]	7·5	Honduras		
Dahomey[4]			1967	2·7	18·6
1967	...	*22·4	1968	2·7	17·8
1968	*4·1	25·0	1969	3·2	19·5
1969	*4·2	*25·8	Hungary		
Denmark			1967	5·0[6]	9·4
1967[10]	6·1	20·6	1968	4·7[6]	7·4
1968[10]	6·4	18·2	1969	4·4[6]	7·3
1969[10]	6·5	17·7	Iceland		
Dominican Republic			1967	4·4	14·4
1967	2·6	14·3	1968	4·6	12·7
1968	2·5	14·0	India	...	...
1969	2·9[2]	16·0	Indonesia	...	...
Ecuador			Iran		
1967[4]	2·8	21·5	1967[1]	2·4	6·2
1968[4]	4·0	21·8	1968	3·3	...
1969[4]	4·0	25·0	1969	...	6·8
Egypt			Iraq		
1967	4·4	15·1	1967	6·3	...
1968	5·0	...	1968	5·5[3]	...
1969	...	21·0	Ireland		
El Salvador[4]			1967	4·3	14·4
1967	2·7	25·4	1968	4·5	11·2
Ethiopia			1969	4·8	10·7
1967[1]	1·1	...	Israel		
Finland			1967	7·0	11·2
1967	6·7	24·8	1968	6·8	10·7
1968	6·4	23·0	Italy		
1969	6·5	23·9	1967	5·2	22·0
France			1968	4·8	19·8
1968[11]	4·4	19·1	1969	4·3	19·2
1969	4·5	22·3	Ivory Coast		
Gabon			1968	6·4	27·7
1969	...	17·7	1969	5·5	22·8
Federal Republic of Germany			Jamaica		
1967	3·6	10·6	1967	3·9	17·2
1968	3·5	10·9	1968	4·7	19·7
1969	3·6	11·2	1969	4·4	18·5
Ghana			Japan		
1967[1]	4·1	...	1967	4·2	20·1
1968	3·9	18·7	1968	4·0	20·8
1969[1]	3·8	20·3	1969	4·0	20·4
Greece			Jordan		
1967	2·3	17·7	1967	3·7	15·0
1968[1]	1·9	11·1	1968	3·5	11·1

Country	As percentage of GNP	As percentage of total public expenditure	Country	As percentage of GNP	As percentage of total public expenditure
Jordan *cont.*			1968	2·5	...
1969	3·3	9·6	1969	...	13·5
Kenya			Monaco	...	
1967	*4·5	...	Mongolia	...	...
1968	4·8	...	Morocco[1]		
Khmer Republic			1967	3·6	16·2
1967	...	21·6	1968	4·0	15·8
1969	...	21·7	1969	4·0	16·5
Republic of Korea			Nepal[4]		
1967[12]	2·4	18·1	1967	0·6[2]	6·5
1968[12]	3·6	21·2	Netherlands		
1969[12]	3·8	21·0	1967	6·9	27·7
Kuwait			1968	6·5	25·1
1967	3·9	*9·5	New Zealand		
1968	4·3	10·1	1967	4·3	11·6
1969	...	11·3	1968	4·3	12·4
Laos			1969	4·4	...
1967[4]	...	10·2	Nicaragua		
1968[4]	...	9·6	1967	2·7	18·1
1969[4]	...	10·7	1968	2·6	19·0
Lebanon			Niger		
1967	2·6	16·5	1967[1]	*1·5[2]	10·4
1968	2·5	16·9	1968[1]	*1·6[2]	11·3
Lesotho			1969	...	15·5
1967[4]	...	21·6	Nigeria	...	...
Liberia			Norway		
1967[1]	2·1[2]	13·8	1967	5·9	18·3
1968[1]	2·0	...	1968	6·1	17·3
Libyan Arab Republic			1969	6·3	16·9
1967	3·6	11·6[13]	Oman	...	...
Luxembourg			Pakistan		
1967	4·9	14·9	1967	1·3	5·5
1968	5·3	15·9	1968	1·4	5·6
1969	5·0	15·2	1969	...	5·2
Madagascar			Panama		
1967	6·8[2]	20·0	1967	4·4	29·9
Malawi			1968	4·8	30·9
1967	4·1	15·9	1969	4·6	34·6
1968	3·9	14·7	Paraguay		
1969	4·1	15·3	1967	1·9	...
Malaysia (West Malaysia only)			1968	2·1	...
1967	6·0	14·6	1969	2·0	...
1968	5·6	15·6	Peru		
1969	5·3	15·6	1967[1]	5·0	23·1
Mali			1968	4·3	26·2
1967	3·6	19·5	1969[1]	4·2	19·4
1968	*4·1	24·2	Philippines[14]		
1969	4·7	24·5	1967[1]	2·8	...
Malta			1968	3·1	...
1967	5·3	17·8	Poland		
1968	5·3	18·6	1967	5·3[6]	...
Mauritania	...	...	1968	5·1[6]	...
Mauritius			1969	5·2[6]	...
1967	3·3	13·6	Qatar	...	...
1968	3·2	10·9	Romania		
1969	3·2	11·7	1967	...	5·8
Mexico			1968	...	5·8
1967	2·5	...	1969	...	6·1

Country	As percentage of GNP	As percentage of total public expenditure	Country	As percentage of GNP	As percentage of total public expenditure
Rwanda			Tunisia		
1967[1]	...	*23·7	1967[1]	5·5	25·9
1968	...	27·3	1968[1]	5·6	25·2
Saudi Arabia			1969	...	15·7
1967	4·9	11·2	Turkey		
1968	4·9	10·8	1967	3·5	20·0
1969	4·3	10·0	1968	3·4	20·2
Senegal			Uganda		
1968	3·9[2]	16·1	1967	2·4[3]	16·3
Sierra Leone			1968	4·3[3]	18·1
1967[4]	2·8	18·8	1969	...	*19·4
1968[4]	2·6	18·0	Ukrainian S.S.R.	...	...
1969[4]	3·0	17·9	U.S.S.R.		
Singapore			1967	7·2[6]	...
1967	4·1[3]	19·3	1968	7·3[6]	...
1968	3·7[3]	16·8	1969	7·3[6]	...
1969[15]	4·5[3]	15·2	United Kingdom		
Somalia			1967	5·6	12·3
1967[1]	...	7·1	United States of America		
Spain			1967	5·6	16·0
1967[4]	1·7	...	1968	5·8	16·6
1968[4]	1·8	*11·7	1969	6·3	...
1969[4]	2·2	...	Upper Volta	...	...
Sudan			Uruguay[1]		
1967	4·9[2]	20·3	1967	2·0	...
Sweden			Venezuela		
1967	7·2	24·6	1967	4·0	18·7
1968	7·9	26·9	1968	4·2	18·4
1969	...	28·0	1969	4·5	20·9
Switzerland			Republic of Viet-Nam[1]		
1967	4·1	19·0	1967	1·1	5·4
1968	4·1	19·3	1968[1]	...	4·2
1969	4·1	19·2	1969[1]	...	4·2
Syrian Arab Republic			Yemen[1]		
1969	4·5	17·1	1967	...	6·8
Tanzania[16]			People's Democratic Republic of Yemen		
1968	3·8[3]	...	1967	3·1	9·7
Thailand[4]			1968	2·5	11·8
1967	3·1	15·5	1969	3·0	...
1968	3·3	15·9	Yugoslavia		
1969	3·4	16·3	1967	4·8[17]	...
Togo			1968	5·0[17]	...
1967	...	16·0	1969	5·1[17]	...
1968	...	16·6	Zaire		
1969	...	20·0	1967	...	20·8
Trinidad and Tobago			1968	...	19·0
1967	3·6	17·3	1969	...	18·7
1968	3·8	16·4	Zambia	...	...

1. Ministry of Education only.
2. As percentage of gross domestic product at market prices.
3. As percentage of gross domestic product at factor cost.
4. Central or federal government only.
5. Not including expenditure of municipalities.
6. As percentage of net material product.
7. Not including foreign aid.
8. As percentage of national income.
9. Expenditure by Office of Greek Education only.
10. Including data for Greenland and Faeroe Islands.
11. Expenditure refers to France and oversea departments together (French Guiana, Guadeloupe, Martinique, Réunion).
12. Expenditure on public education only.
13. Recurring expenditure as percentage of ordinary budget.
14. Not including expenditure on the third level of education.
15. Expenditure over a period of fifteen months.
16. Not including Zanzibar.
17. As percentage of gross material product.

Compulsory education in Member States

The table given below shows the number of years of compulsory school attendance.

However, in many countries where the urgent problem is to provide sufficient schools for all children, the existence of compulsory school laws may be only of academic interest since almost all such regulations exempt a child from attending if there is no suitable school within reasonable distance of his home.

In countries where the duration of compulsory education varies depending on the area or type of school, the different possibilities existing in that country are expressed in a group of figures (e. g. in Canada, depending on the province, compulsory education may be of eight, nine or ten years).

The following symbols are used:

— Magnitude nil or negligible
... Data not available

Duration (years) of compulsory education in Member States

Country	Number of years	Country	Number of years
Afghanistan	6	Central African Republic	8
Albania	8	Ceylon	8
Algeria	8	Chad	6
Argentina	7	Chile	6
Australia	9, 10	People's Republic of China	...
Austria	9	Colombia	5
Bahrain[1]	8	People's Republic of the Congo	10
Barbados	9	Costa Rica	8
Belgium	8	Cuba	6
Bolivia	8	Cyprus	6
Brazil	4	Czechoslovakia	9
Bulgaria	8	Dahomey	—
Burma	—	Denmark	7
Burundi	—	Dominican Republic	6
Byelorussian S.S.R.	8	Ecuador	6
Cameroon	—	Egypt	6
Canada	8–10	El Salvador	7

1. Will be applied in 1973/74

294

Country	Number of years	Country	Number of years
Ethiopia	–	Netherlands	8
Finland	8	New Zealand	9
France	10	Nicaragua	6
Gabon	10	Niger	8
Federal Republic of Germany	12	Nigeria	–
Ghana	10	Norway	9
Greece	6	Oman	...
Guatemala	6	Pakistan	–
Guinea	12	Panama	6
Guyana	8	Paraguay	6
Haiti	6	Peru	6
Honduras	6	Philippines	6
Hungary	10	Poland	8
Iceland	8	Qatar	–
India	5, 7, 8	Romania	10
Indonesia	6	Rwanda	6
Iran	6	Saudi Arabia	–
Iraq	6	Senegal	7
Ireland	8	Sierra Leone	–
Israel	10	Singapore	–
Italy	8	Somalia	–
Ivory Coast	–	Spain	8
Jamaica	9	Sudan	–
Japan	9	Sweden	9
Jordan	9	Switzerland[2]	7, 8, 9
Kenya	–	Syrian Arab Republic	6
Khmer Republic	6	Tanzania	–
Republic of Korea	6	Thailand	7
Kuwait	8	Togo	6
Laos	3	Trinidad and Tobago	7
Lebanon	12	Tunisia	6
Lesotho	–	Turkey	5
Liberia	10	Uganda	–
Libyan Arab Republic	6	Ukrainian S.S.R.	8
Luxembourg	9	U.S.S.R.	8
Madagascar	9	United Kingdom	10
Malawi	–	United States of America	10, 11, 12
Malaysia		Upper Volta	6
Sabah, Sarawak	6	Uruguay	6
West Malaysia	–	Venezuela	6
Mali	9	Republic of Viet-Nam	5
Malta	8	Yemen	–
Mauritania	4	People's Democratic	
Mauritius	–	Republic of Yemen	–
Mexico	6	Yugoslavia	8
Monaco	10	Zaire	8
Mongolia	7	Zambia	–
Morocco	7		
Nepal			
English system	5		
Sanskrit system	–		

2. Age limits and the duration of compulsory education as well as the entrance age and duration for each level and type of education vary from one canton to another.

Literacy in the world today and tomorrow

In the work *Literacy 1967–1969* the Unesco Office of Statistics attempted to update to 1960 the estimate of the world literacy situation that had been made for around 1950. Since that work was published, a few more countries have published the results of their 1960 round of population censuses and the 1970 round of population censuses has begun, although the results of most of these censuses will not be made available for a number of years.

In the meantime the Unesco Office of Statistics has re-estimated the 1960 situation and has made some preliminary estimates for 1970. Table 1 summarizes the situation.

TABLE 1. World adult (15+) population and literacy estimates 1950–70 (revised), in millions

Year	Adult population	Literates	Illiterates	Illiteracy rate
1950	1,579	879	700	44·3
1960	1,869	1,134	735	39·3
1970	2,287	1,504	783	34·2

The percentage of adults, i.e. persons aged 15 and over, who are illiterate has fallen in the two ten-year periods between 1950 and 1960, and 1960 and 1970, from 44·3 per cent to 39·3 per cent and then to 34·2 per cent. This is a considerable drop—5 percentage points in each of the two decades. At the present moment, therefore, one can begin talking in terms of a third of the world's adults being illiterate instead of the old familiar rates of two-fifths in 1960 or nearly a half in 1950. However, because the total adult population has risen by about 700 million in the same period—an increase of some 300 million in the first decade and some 400 in the second—the actual number of adult illiterates has gone on rising. From 700 million adult illiterates in 1950 it rose by 35 million in the first decade and by 48 million in the second—resulting in a figure of 783 million at the present moment. At the same time, however, the number of adult literates in the world has also risen by over 600 million in the two decades—an increase of some 250 million in the first decade and over 350 million in the second.

It is important always to keep sight of this increase in the number of literates when discussing literacy because in the enormous increase in literates lies the evidence of the efforts made by Member States throughout the world in extending primary education and in developing adult literacy programmes. It is interesting, incidentally, to note that the 1970 estimated world figure of 783 million illiterate adults is more favourable than would have resulted had the 1950–60 rate of decrease in the illiteracy rate been maintained. This would have meant a 34·8 per cent illiteracy rate with a total of some 800 million illiterates. In fact the illiteracy rate is estimated to have dropped slightly faster between 1960 and 1970 than was estimated between 1950 and 1960.

TABLE 2. World adult (15+) population and literacy estimates: rates of increase

Period	Adult population: rate of increase		Literates: rate of increase		Illiterates: rate of increase		Decrease in the illiteracy rate	
	Annual	Decennial	Annual	Decennial	Annual	Decennial	Annual	Decennial
1950–60	1·70	18·43	2·58	29·01	0·48	5·00	0·50	5·0
1960–70	2·03	22·36	2·86	32·63	0·63	6·53	0·51	5·1

It can thus be seen that the rate of increase in the number of literates continues to rise and continues to be much greater than the rate of increase in the adult population. However the ever-rising rate of increase of the population still causes the rate of increase in the number of illiterates to rise, although by only a small amount.

It is to be expected that the steady fall in the illiteracy rate will be continued into the seventies. It is not very meaningful at this stage to make estimates for 1980, but the very first thoughts of the Office of Statistics on this subject suggest that the combined effects of the ageing of the population, the increase in primary education and the effects of literacy campaigns will continue to produce even greater progress in the seventies than has been estimated for the sixties.

With an estimated world adult population in 1980 of 2,823 million, it is thought that there will still be 820 million adult illiterates in 1980 with a world adult illiteracy rate of 29 per cent. This would mean, of course, an increase of some 500 million adult literates against an increase of 37 million adult illiterates. Because of population increases, therefore, the absolute number of adult illiterates in 1980 will have risen in the two decades by 48 million and 37 million respectively, despite a total increase of some 870 million adult literates in the period. The effect of the huge increase in the adult population in the seventies of 536 million—as against 418 million in the sixties—will continue to undermine all the efforts made by Member States to eradicate illiteracy.

It might be interesting to look at all these data when presented graphically (see figure overleaf).

The situation can be seen at a glance: population soaring with the number of literates nearly keeping pace, resulting in a small but steady rise in the number of illiterates. The reader can easily imagine the continuation of the lines up to the year 2000 and even the most optimistic of assumptions is not going to drop the number of illiterates below the 650 million mark by the year 2000. On the other hand the illiteracy rate is falling steadily, practically in a

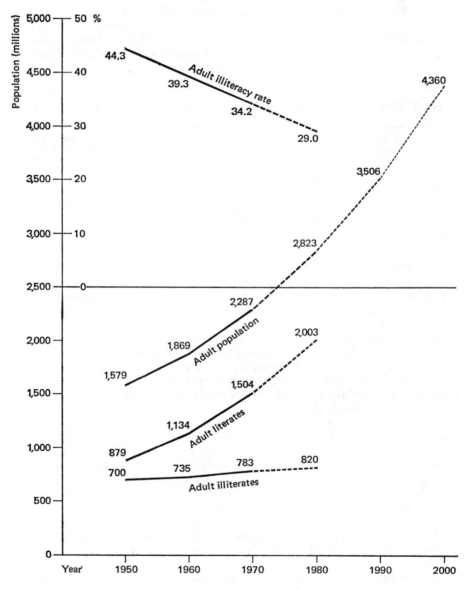

Growth of adult (15 +) population and decrease of illiteracy

straight line, and the most optimistic assumption about the number of illiterates by the year 2000—some 650 million—would mean an adult illiteracy rate of 15 per cent.

It is possible to make only a most speculative estimate about the regional position in 1980. At the present rate of educational progress, and taking into account the ageing of the population, the African adult illiteracy rate should fall from 74 to 67 per cent; the Asian adult illiteracy rate from 47 to 38 per cent; and the Latin American adult illiteracy rate from 24 to 15 per cent. It is to be expected that the rate of progress will be greater in the seventies than the sixties, just as it was somewhat greater in the sixties than the fifties because of the ageing of the population. The over-all estimate of 820 million adult illiterates in 1980, giving an adult illiteracy rate of 29 per cent, has been made on this assumption. However it should be remembered that these estimates in 1980 still mean that both in Africa and in Asia there will be over 25 million extra adult illiterates by 1980.

Index

Abolition of hierarchies among teachers, 218, 219
Abolition of social privileges, 30
Abstract man and concrete man, 156
Academy of Pedagogical Sciences, U.S.S.R., 225
Access to education
  criteria for, 203
  diplomas, 204
  knowledge, 203
  personal aptitudes, 203
Adaptation of education to the learner, 220
Africa, 5, 6, 9, 10, 11, 27, 33, 34, 38, 41, 43, 45, 51, 52, 53, 54, 59, 99, 138, 240, 251, 254
Agricultural development, 30
Agricultural universities, 202
Aid to education, 254 (Table 10)
  analysis of national education systems, 258
  bilateral, 251, 252, 259, 261
  conditions, 255
  developing countries, 256, 257, 258
  difficulties, 255
  distribution, 253
  during economic crisis, 257
  economic development, 260
  international, 257
  renovation, 258, 259, 260, 261
  strategies for over-all development, 256
Algeria, 141
Algorithms, 110
Alienation of the personality, 103
America, 8, 10, 103, 254
'Andragogy', 116
Angelopoulos, Angelos, 97
Angola, 139
Anthropology, 113, 114
Anti-universities, 136
Aptitudes for vocations and examinations, 203, 204
Arab Republic of Egypt. *See* Egypt

Arab States, 27, 33, 34, 38, 39, 43, 45, 52, 53, 54, 240, 253
Asia, 7, 8, 9, 11, 27, 33, 34, 41, 43, 45, 51, 52, 54, 240, 253
Assistance, bilateral, 241
Assistance to education and technical assistance, 257, 258
Atomic bomb, 103
Audio-visual teaching, 63, 111, 114, 212
  and examinations, 204
  languages, 111, 121, 134
  science, 121
Australia, 33, 256
Austria, 73

Bac-ly (Democratic Republic of Viet-Nam) pilot rural school, 139
Bahmanbegui, 137
Bairoch, Paul, 98
Bazin, Robert, 76
Behaviourism, 109
Belgium, 122
Benn, Anthony Wedgwood, 88
Bereday, George Z. F., 16, 161
Bertaux, Pierre, 57
Bezdanov, Stevan, 78
Biancheri, Armand, 64, 145
Bilingualism, development of, 112
Biochemistry, 106, 107
  of memory, 106
Birth rate, increase in, 29
Blonsky, Pavel Petrovich, 139
Bolivia, 19
Boulenger Balleyguier, M., 118n.
Brahman universities, 7
Brain drain, 243, 244
  economic aspects, 275, 276
  educational systems, 246
  migration of intellectuals, 243, 244, 245, 247
  socio-political aspects, 244, 245
  training abroad, 242, 243
Brain research, 105, 106, 107, 108

Index

Brazil, 19, 123, 131, 139
Budgetary options, rationalization of, 128, 129
Burma, 113

Cameroon, 13, 218
Canada, 16, 19, 121, 122, 184, 185, 212
Caribbean, 240
Carlsson, Ingvar, 18
Castel, Robert, 72
Central Africa, 108
Centres
  for advanced studies, 202
  cultural, 188
  documentation, 210
  of excellence, 200, 202
  multidisciplinary, 201
  national, for educational development, 226
  technical-training, 188
Ceylon, 190
Chile, 19
China (People's Republic of), 7, 20
Chomsky, N., 112
Church and education, 8
Cinema documentary films, 37, 121
Classical Greece and Rome, 7
Club of Rome, 97
Coleman, 72
Colleges, 200, 201
Colombia, 94, 95
Colonialism and education, 10, 11, 61
Committee on Manpower Resources for Science and Technology (United Kingdom), 246
Communication satellites, 123
Communications
  technology, 121
  theory, 121
Communities
  educational, 183
  human community and education, 152
  pedagogical, 124
Community, international scientific, 245
Community development, 218
Compartmentalization
  of discipline, 64
  of educational expenditures, 80
  of higher education, 9, 154
Competitive spirit and education, 68, 83
Comprehensive schools, 16
Compulsory education, 36, 189
Computer-assisted instruction, 105, 125, 126, 127
Computers, 105, 125, 126, 127
Confrontation
  educational renovation, 149
  motivations, 103
Congo (People's Republic of), 13
Conscience of the masses, 152
'Conscientization', 139, 144

Consumer society, 103
Coombs, Philip H., 23
Co-operative management, 78, 79, 136, 222, 228
Correspondence teaching, 37, 135, 203, 212
Costa Rica, 19, 225
Counter-culture, 103
Countries
  capitalist, 70, 93
  industrialized. *See* Developed countries
  Socialist, 17, 32, 54, 70, 72, 93, 138, 242, 253, 257
  Western, 54
Courcoul, Bernard, 75
Courses
  agricultural information, 187
  computer-programme, 125
  community-development, 187
  continuation, 194
  evening, 143, 203
Creative imagination, 155
Creativity, 158
  psychological conditions, 148
'Credit-education', 230
'Credit-training', 230
Criminality and urban population, 101
Crozier, 120
Cuba, 13, 20, 140, 219, 250
CUCES, Nancy, France, 120
Cultural centres. *See* Centres, cultural
Cultural development, 74
Cultural revolution, 91, 163
Culture
  and education, 17, 62, 163
  mass, 151
Curriculum, 16, 64, 65, 68, 180
Cybernetics, 102, 105, 106, 115, 143, 144
'Cynerbopoid', 153
Czechoslovakia, 19, 125, 216

Data banks, 210
Daumard, Pierre, 41
Decentralization, 80
  of decision-making, 227
Decolonization and international co-operation, 255
Decolonization of education, 31
Decompartmentalization of institution-alized educational systems, 184
Decroly, O., 139
Deformalization of education, 186
Deformalization of traditional structures, 187
Delinquency and urban over-population, 101
Delphi method, 129
Demand for education, 14, 23, 24, 26, 28, 31, 32, 33, 34, 35, 48, 161, 184, 191
  and economy, 98, 99
  increase in, 24, 31, 32, 35, 40

302

irreversibility of, 35
and need for education, 14, 26, 30, 31,
  32, 34, 35, 162
regional distribution, 32
Democracy, 101, 102
Democratization of education, 10, 19, 22,
  54, 70, 74, 75, 78, 79, 90, 104, 161,
  162, 202, 205
Democratization of higher education,
  202, 205
Demographic explosion and school
  enrolment, 38
Demographic growth, 27, 28, 36, 40, 92,
  100
economic growth, disequilibrium, 93
Denmark, 216
'De-schooling' of society, 20
Devaluation, 41
Developed countries, 27, 30, 33, 34, 37,
  39, 49, 50, 55, 59, 68, 70, 81, 82,
  91–4, 96, 98, 100, 115, 122, 131,
  182, 198, 201, 202, 232, 235, 236,
  237, 243, 244, 248, 251, 257, 260,
  261, 262
Developing countries, 25, 27, 30, 32, 34,
  36, 39, 49, 50, 52, 55, 59, 68, 81,
  82, 90, 91, 92, 93, 94, 96, 98, 100,
  101, 108, 115, 116, 122, 131, 132,
  137, 164, 182, 190, 198, 201, 202,
  232, 235, 236, 237, 243, 244, 248,
  254, 255, 257, 258, 260, 261, 262
development of education, 248, 249, 291
See also Third World
Development
of education, and developing countries.
  See Developing countries, development of education
of educational innovation, 181
of the masses, 40
of the personality, and education, 14,
  18, 39, 58, 60, 68, 69, 75, 81, 139,
  141, 143, 145, 149, 155, 184, 191,
  217, 234
quotients, 118
of workers, 37, 199
Development Assistance Committee
  (DAC), 241, 256
Development Decade. See United Nations
  Development Decade
Dialectical thought, 147
Dialogue, 75, 80
Dieuzeide, Henri, 155
Diplomas, 7, 59, 75, 76, 77, 190, 204, 240
Disaffection of youth, 103
in educational policy, 149
Disalienation of society, 15 n.
Discrimination
racial, 54, 70, 71, 74
social, 71
Diversification in post-secondary edu-
  cation, 17, 200, 201

Doctrines, idealistic, voluntarist and
  determinist, 56
Dresden Data-processing Institute, 125
Dumazedier, Joffre, 102
Durkheim, 30

Early Bird, 123
Eastern Europe, 253
Ecology, 143, 150
in education, 150
Economic underdevelopment
and educational inequality, 60
and illiteracy, 141
Economics in education, 11, 14, 15, 18,
  26, 27, 28, 30, 48, 56, 60, 61, 68,
  69, 78, 81, 98, 99, 136, 143, 171,
  174, 175, 199, 231, 237
Ecuador, 14
Education
adaptation to environment, 196
adult: 17, 45, 74, 83, 120, 135, 143,
  150, 185, 189, 205, 206, 207, 212,
  217; development of the personality,
  205; training for society, 215
aims, 23, 54, 81, 83, 104, 132, 133,
  139, 145, 146, 148, 158, 160, 161,
  197, 233
'appropriate rhythm', 194, 196
artistic, 67
authoritarian, 7, 58, 64, 69, 81, 119,
  135, 182
basic: 18, 183, 184, 187, 194, 233; for
  adults, 183
Buddhist, 7
community, 77, 185
competitive spirit, 63, 83
continuing. See Education, lifelong
current situation, 12–22
de-institutionalizing, 20, 186
demographic evaluation, 82
development of the personality, 14, 18,
  39, 58, 60, 68, 69, 75, 81, 139, 141,
  143, 145, 155, 184, 191, 205, 217,
  234
discontinued, 190
discrimination in. See Democratization
  of education
diversification, 186, 233
economic, 152, 195
educational strategies, 206
employment possibilities, 69, 125
equal access to, 71, 72; and family
  environment and resources, 72; and
  inequality of opportunity, 71, 72, 79
equal opportunity, 14, 59, 70, 71, 74,
  75, 79, 83
evaluation of the human species, 4, 5
experimental psychology and, 109
family, 4, 15, 57
formal, 185, 187, 189, 194, 217
functional, 206

303

Index

Education (*cont.*)
  and future society, 13, 15, 23, 30, 40, 234
  global, 48, 194, 205
  at home, 184
  'incidental', 5
  individual voluntary, 122
  initial, 117, 183, 185, 199, 201, 202, 203
  institutionalized, 14, 20, 36, 44, 113, 120, 121, 255
  integrated, 179, 185, 194
  interdisciplinary research in, 113
  international, 152
  international peace, 236
  international understanding, 236
  job mobility, 82, 104
  liberation of the individual, 56, 144
  lifelong, 5, 8, 48, 69, 74, 77, 78, 79, 83, 104, 117, 119, 126, 142, 143, 152, 158, 161, 163, 182, 183, 184, 185, 187, 188, 189, 198, 203, 230, 233
  loosening of State control, 18, 19, 20
  manual, 68
  mediaeval, 8
  modern society, 22, 23, 24, 142
  mutual, 18, 119, 120, 121, 219
  natural, 137
  non-formal, 5, 188, 189, 190, 194, 217
  non-institutionalized, 190
  objectives, 52, 60, 83, 104, 145
  open, 15
  operational research, 128, 129
  oral, 6
  out-of-school, 4, 5, 6, 17, 20, 21, 26, 37, 41, 44, 48, 52, 71, 136, 138, 152, 160, 162, 163, 179, 182, 184, 186, 187, 198, 206, 209, 213, 215, 217, 233
  personalized, 17, 75, 234
  physical, 68, 156
  politics, 10, 15, 25, 31, 57, 78, 150, 151
  polytechnic, 196
  polyvalent, 16, 67, 180
  popular, 11, 20, 183
  post-basic, 184
  post-school, 17, 189
  post-secondary, 184, 200, 202, 233
  pre-school: 17, 180, 184, 192, 233; and cultural policy, 191; and educational policy, 191; and educational strategies, 191; and mass media, 191
  products and needs of society, 13, 14
  professional development, 163
  recurrent, 190, 197, 230; and repeating, 74, 119, 189, 190, 194, 202
  right to, 10, 50, 71, 183
  scholastic, 216
  scholastic success of children and adult education, 205, 206
  self-perpetuating function of, 57

  sexual, 156
  simulation models, 224
  social liberation, 11, 56, 144
  and society, 13, 14, 18, 19, 20, 23, 30, 40, 55–84, 98, 105, 115, 137, 138, 144, 145, 146, 147, 153, 160, 161, 162, 163, 171, 174, 175, 176, 177, 208
  socio-economic development, 12, 13, 15, 18, 61, 69, 82, 98, 99, 236
  struggle against drug abuse, 156
  third-age, 180
  traditional, 6, 7, 8, 69, 187
  training in human relations, 156
  training for social life, 57, 150, 221
  vocational training, 184, 196, 197, 221
  world educational needs, 261
  youth, 5, 74, 83, 143, 216
Education policies, national, 261
  and individual initiatives, 227
  and international co-operation, 256
  and local initiatives, 227
  See also Educational policy
Education systems external and internal pressure, 87
Educational activity
  adult, 150
  decentralization and need to break down bureaucratic aspects of, 80
Educational administration, 15, 19, 223, 233
Educational cells, 136, 183
'Educational cheques', 230
Educational conservatism, 22, 56, 57, 103
Educational contents, 15, 61, 69, 240
Educational cycles, 200
Educational development centres, 258
Educational expenditure, 12, 25, 26, 40, 42, 44, 45, 46, 47, 50, 54, 78, 82, 214, 215, 223, 228, 229
  and economy, 46, 48
  and educational policy, 46
  reduction of, 47, 229, 231
  reorganization of, 48
  research on educational systems, 228
  scientific research, 115
Educational financing (diversification), 228, 229
Educational immobility, 57, 64
Educational institutions, diversification of, 186
Educational materials, 127, 211, 212
Educational methods, choice of, 186, 189, 206, 220, 233
Educational models, 10, 14, 15, 60, 105, 224, 233, 261
Educational needs, 24, 25, 26, 27, 28, 34, 35, 141, 142, 200, 201, 231
  and educational demands, 14, 26, 27, 28, 30, 31, 32, 33, 34, 35

305

Industrial development
  depletion of natural resources, 96
  destruction of animal species, 100
  destruction of nature, 99, 100
  environment, 99, 100, 101
  mental concentration, 100
  nervous fatigue, 100
  vocational illness, 100
Inequality of geographical distribution of
    education, 24, 51, 52, 61, 70, 71,
    72
Inequality of opportunity, 72, 73, 81
Inflation, 41
Information banks, 136, 210
Information and communications media,
    40, 52, 61, 62, 63, 90, 101, 121, 125,
    136, 186, 210
Information theory, 114
  application in pedagogical research, 115
Innovations
  educational, 19, 174, 175, 176, 181,
    223, 237, 262
  pedagogical, 122, 123, 134, 184, 185
In-service teacher training, 217
'Instituted combinations', 120
Institutionalized school curricula, 185
Institutionalized schooling and non-
    institutionalized education, 190
Integration of educational means, 63
Intellectual co-operation, 236, 237, 238,
    243, 244, 249, 261, 263
  brain drain, 243–4
Intelligence Quotient (IQ), 118
Intelsat, 123
Inter-American Development Bank, 96,
    251
Intercultural Documentation Centre
    (CIDOC), Cuernavaca, Mexico, 20
Interdependent educational networks, 183
Interdisciplinary research in education,
    143
Interest rates, 255
  diversification, 256
Intermediate technologies, 131, 132, 133,
    211
Internalization of educational strategy,
    177–8
International assistance, 261
  bilateral, 236
  multilateral, 236, 241
International Bank for Reconstruction and
    Development, 251
International Bureau of Education, 195,
    238
International Centre for Theoretical
    Physics, Trieste, Italy, 247
International Commission on the Develop-
    ment of Education, 5, 17, 20, 30, 48,
    57, 224
International Conference on Education,
    Geneva, 1971, 73

International Conference on the World
    Crisis in Education, Williamsburg,
    Va, 22
International co-operation, 202, 235, 236,
    238, 239, 241, 242, 243, 244, 248,
    250, 256, 260
  bilateral, 236, 241, 319
  crisis in, 236
  decolonization, 255
  intellectual exploitation, 244
  multilateral, 236
  national education strategies, 256
  pedagogical research, 237
  tradition, 236
International Development Association,
    256
International experts, 242, 243
  behaviour of, 242, 243
International financial assistance
  to developing countries, 237
  and educational innovation, 237
International Labour Office, 94
International Programme for Educational
    Innovation, 262
International scientific solidarity, 247
International solidarity, 49, 54, 235, 236
  and economy in developing countries,
    96, 97, 98, 99
  in education, 54
International technical assistance, 250,
    251
Internationalization of educational
    content, 240
Iran, 19, 137, 141, 208
Islam, 8
Italy, 73, 196, 256
Ivory Coast, 121

Janne, Henri, 74, 119, 160n.
Japan, 13, 19, 33, 73, 96, 113, 122, 124,
    125, 135, 199, 201, 202, 233
Job retraining, 18, 28, 120, 134, 197,
    199, 201, 202, 233

Kapitsa, P. L., 155
Kenya, 194
Kiev Institute of Technology, 125
Kinany, A. K., 8
Kindergartens, 192
Kirpal, Prem, 31
Knowledge, multiplication of, 40, 87, 88
Korea (Democratic People's Republic of),
    27, 36, 41, 250
Korovlev, P., 142

Labani, C. M., 76
Laboratories
  language, 134, 210
  mathematics, 130
  technical training, 210
Labour legislation in education, 190

307

Index

Landa, L., 130
Landau, Erika, 156
Lapassade, Georges, 158
Laroche, J. L., 130
Latin America, 7, 10, 33, 39, 41, 43, 44, 52, 53, 54, 71, 96, 124, 192, 240
Learning
    alternate period, 194
    full-time, 186, 194
    the learning society, 160, 162, 164, 182, 263
    mother tongue, 112
    part-time, 184, 186, 194
    to read, birth of the school, 6
    and society, 184
    verbal, 129
Leisure and post-industrialized societies, 102
Lemaresquier, Thierry, 75
Lengrand, Paul, 22
Lenin, V. I., 155
Lê Thành Khôi, 12
Lewin, Kurt, 120
Lewis, Anthony, 160
Liberal arts, 7
Liberia, 113, 218
Libraries, 136, 138, 210
    national, 37
    public, 37, 138
    school, 37, 138
    specialized, 37
    university, 37
Life expectancy, lengthened, 28
Lifelong education. See Education, lifelong
Linguistics, 112
Literacy, 13, 17, 20, 25, 26, 27, 31, 39, 40, 63, 71, 122, 133, 140, 141, 185, 258
    adult: 17, 38, 40, 62, 207, 332; and educational development, 39, 40, 208; and society, 208
    development of the personality, 40, 141
    functional, 141, 207, 208
    mass-literacy campaigns, 208
    political, 40
    programmes: 39, 71; and diversification of, 208
    study and environment, 208
    traditional, 207
    vocational training, 208
    world literacy programme, 141
Lizop, Edouard, 160 n.
London University Institute of Education, 58
Lourié, Sylvain, 48
Lukacs, G., 120
Lvov Institute of Technology, 125

Macaulay, Lord, 10
Maccoby, Michael, 113
McHale, John, 88
McMurrin, S. N., 145

Maheu, René, 63, 160 n.
Malaysia, 223
Mali, 141
Malnutrition, 107, 108
    family environment, 107, 108
    mental development, 107, 108
    physical development, 108, 109
    premature ageing, 108
    production, 108
    racial group, 107, 108
    social environment, 107, 108
Man of the future, 153
Management
    automated, 125
    co-operative, 130
    in education: need to break down bureaucratic aspects and for decentralization, 80
Management Training Programme (MTP), 199
Man–machine systems, 127, 143
Mardjane, M., 61
Markouchevitch, A. I., 30
Marx, Karl, 65
Mass education and radio, 212
Mass media
    pre-school education, 191
    information media, 140
Mastery of man
    over himself, 154
    over reality, 148, 154
Mastić, M., 72
'Mathetics', 130, 161
'Mayflower' School (Nigeria), 139
Mead, Margaret, 13
Means of transport, 89, 90
Mediaeval Europe, 8
Mediaeval universities, 8, 9
Medicine and education, 131
'Megalopolis', 100
Memory, 107
Merton, 120
Mexico, 19, 20, 113
Middle East, 199
Minorities, 64, 113
Minsk Institute of Technology, 123
Mobility
    between educational levels, 233
    horizontal, between teaching establishments, 74
    international: students', 239, 240; teachers', 239, 240, 241
    of students, and diversification of choice, 189
    university students', 25
    vertical, in teaching establishments, 74
    vocational, 67, 83, 104, 233
Modern educational systems in the teaching profession, 219
Modern society
    in education, 22, 23, 24, 143

308

man and contradictions in, 154
and the teaching profession, 215
Moline, Roger, 16
Molnya, 123
Mongolia, 250
Montessori, Maria, 139
Motivations, individual, in functional
   literacy, 141, 174
Moumouni, Abdou, 6
Multi-media systems, 130, 135, 211
'Multi-universities', 17
Museums, 37
Mutations
   scientific and technical, 30
   socio-economic, 30
Mutual aid
   between developing countries, 243
   international, 258

National educational expenditure, 42, 44,
      45, 47, 48, 49, 50–1
   choice of educational priorities, 46–9
   gross national product, 42, 51
   total budget, 42, 47
National revenue and demography, 93–4,
      94–5
National scientific policy, 247
Near East, 253
Neill, A. S., 139
Netherlands, 19
Networks of change, 226
Neurophysiology, 106
New values, quest for, 149
New Zealand, 35
Niger, 218
Nigeria: 'Mayflower' School, 139
Noise, psychophysiological disturbances,
      100
Non-institutionalized school curricula, 185
North Africa, 99
North America, 33, 43, 45, 52, 245
Norway, 73
Nurseries, 192
Nursery school, 191, 192, 219
Nyerere, Julius, 5, 10

Oceania, 43, 45
Ontario Institute for Studies in Education,
      210
Open University (United Kingdom), 135
Operational research, 112, 128, 129, 130
Options, choice of, 186, 201, 202, 206,
      220, 224, 233
Oral expression, 61
Organisation for Economic Co-operation
      and Development (OECD), 30, 54,
      44, 241, 250
Organizations, multilateral, 257
Oury, F., 120
Over-all development strategy, 30, 98,
      99

Over-all education process, 163
Over-all planning, 171, 172

Package projects, 258
Paid study tours abroad, 247
Paideia, 5n., 162
Parkway Program, 202
Participation
   communities and pre-school education,
      191, 192, 233
   educational strategies, 177
   of family, in pre-school education, 233
   financial: of communities, in adult
      education, 206; of communities, in
      education, 194, 230; of enterprises,
      in education, 199; of families, in
      education, 194, 229; of State in adult
      education, 206; of State in education,
      194; of students in education, 229
   international life, 152, 153
   of parents, in educational activity, 78,
      218, 219
   of scientists, in administration of
      science, 247
   self-management and co-operative
      management, 78, 79, 102, 105, 119,
      144, 151, 159, 183, 206, 222, 224,
      227, 251
   of society, in educational activities, 161,
      162, 198
   of students: in educational action, 17,
      19, 74, 78, 79, 119, 135, 136, 161,
      219; in university government, 17,
      222, 223
   of total population, 30, 78, 132, 133,
      140, 218
   of workers in educational activity, 219
   of youth, in organization of school life,
      219
Peace, 152
Pearson Commission, 93
Pedagogical experimentation, 224, 260,
      263
Pedagogical industry, 131, 132
Pedagogical methods, 116–44
Pedagogical research, 114, 115, 125, 224,
      237, 240, 249
   organizations, 225
Pedagogy
   cybernetic, 115, 116
   and ecology, 175
   institutional, 120
   modern and traditional, 116
   non-directive, 121
   selective, 126
   and technology, 132, 196
People's universities, 37
Per capita income, 93
Perkins, James, 17
Persia, 7
Personalization of educational action, 156

Index

Peru, 19
Petersen, P., 139
Petrovsky, A. V., 18, 30, 252, 257
Peuchot, Maurice, 126
Philippines, 19, 223
Phillips, H. M., 250
Philosophy of education, 5, 76, 185
Physical Science Study Committee
　(United States), 65
Piaget, Jean, 110, 118
Plowden Commission, 72
Poignant, R., 257
Poland, 203, 216
Politics in education, 10, 11, 25, 31, 32,
　78, 136, 137
Pollution, 64, 65, 99, 100, 101
Polytechnic education and manual
　activities, 196
Pope Paul VI, 152
Population
　increase of active, 94
　increase of school, 27, 35
　school, 11, 35, 125
Population census, 24
Post-secondary education, 200–1
Prebisch, R. Y., 96
Pre-colonial Africa, 5
Pre-history, 4
Press, 37, 53
Primary education, 11, 13, 16, 32, 34, 35,
　36, 37, 38, 50, 51, 52, 53, 73,
　193, 222, 232
　for all, 53, 194
　full-time, 195
　integrated, 194
　part-time, 195
　televised, 214, 215
Printing, 6, 9, 61
Private education, 15, 25, 41
Professional institutes of technology, 201
Professional training, 29, 201, 242, 258
　abroad, 242, 243, 244–5
　economic needs, 242, 243
　environment, 242–3
Programme Evaluation and Review
　Technique (PERT), 129
Programmed instruction, 105, 109, 115,
　128, 210
　examinations, 204
Psychoanalysis, 112, 118
Psycholinguistics, 112
Psychology, 108–11, 117, 118, 127
Psychopedagogical phases, 117
Psychopedagogy, 110, 118, 116–18, 150
Psychophysiological disturbances, 100
Psychophysiology, 118, 191
Public educational expenditure in devel-
　oping countries, 251, 252

Quantitative imbalance between supply
　and demand for labour, 68

Racial discrimination. *See* Discrimination,
　racial
Radio and mass education, 53, 122, 212
'Recurrent education banks', 230
Reform
　role of central administration, 226
　continuous, of education systems, 225
　of educational structures, 19, 22–3
　of social structures, 30, 59, 183
　of teacher training, 218, 219
Regional conferences of ministers of
　education, 53, 238
Relativity, 147
Religion and education, 7, 8, 9
Renovation of education, 12, 19, 61, 79,
　105, 115, 128, 149, 162, 164, 233,
　249, 262
Reorganization
　of central administration, 226, 227
　of education, 77, 184, 261
　of the teaching profession, 215
Repetition in schools, 14, 43
'Research and development' in education,
　263
Revolution
　industrial, 10, 11, 28
　intellectual, 126
　scientific and technical, 11, 40, 87, 88,
　89, 90, 91, 92, 93, 96, 105
Revolutions, Socialist, 11
Ribonucleic acid (RNA) and memory, 107
Richta, Radovan, 160 n.
Rites and taboos, 6
Rituals and education, 138
Rogers, Carl, 121
Rolling reform, 225
Roszak, T., 103
Ruillen, Lewis, 59
Rural exodus, 90, 246, 247
Rwanda, 19

Saury, C., 117
Scandinavia, 16
'Scenarios', 129
Scholarships, 73
　foreign, 243, 247
Scholastic profile, 125
Scholastic success, 16
　in cultural heritage, 72
　educational technology, 210–11
　family environment, 72, 205
Scholl, M., 117
School
　integration into the community, 138
　of life, 4, 5
　for parents, 138, 191
　pilot rural school, Bac-ly, Democratic
　Republic of Viet-Nam, 139
　polyvalent cultural centre, 134
　and society, 137, 143
　transport, 125